PELICAN BOOKS

PROGRESS FOR A SMALL PLANET

Barbara Ward was born in 1914 and took a degree in Politics, Philosophy and Economics at Somerville College, Oxford (1935). She has worked as a university lecturer and for the *Economist*; and was a Governor of Sadler's Wells and the Old Vic (1944–53), as well as a Governor of the BBC (1946–50). She has been awarded honorary doctorates by, among others, Fordham, Columbia and Harvard Universities and Smith and Kenyon Colleges. Her publications include *The West at Bay* (1948), *Policy for the West* (1951), *India and the West* (1959), *Spaceship Earth* (1966), *The Lopsided World* (1968), *Only One Earth* (1972, with René Dubos) and *The Home of Man* (1976). Barbara Ward was Schweitzer Professor of International Economic Development at Columbia University from 1968 to 1973. Since 1973 she has been President of the International Institute for Environment and Development. She was made Dame Commander Order of the British Empire in 1974.

Progress
for a Small Planet

Barbara Ward

PENGUIN BOOKS

Penguin Books Ltd, Harmondsworth, Middlesex, England
Penguin Books, 625 Madison Avenue, New York, New York 10022, U.S.A.
Penguin Books Australia Ltd, Ringwood, Victoria, Australia
Penguin Books Canada Ltd, 2801 John Street, Markham, Ontario, Canada L3R 1B4
Penguin Books (N.Z.) Ltd, 182–190 Wairau Road, Auckland 10, New Zealand

—

First published in the U.S.A. by W. W. Norton 1979
First published in Great Britain in Pelican Books 1979
Published simultaneously by Maurice Temple Smith Limited

—

—

Made and printed in Great Britain by
Richard Clay (The Chaucer Press) Ltd
Bungay, Suffolk

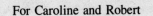

For Caroline and Robert

CONTENTS

Photographs appear following pages 98 and 212.

FOREWORD

IT GIVES ME pleasure to write a foreword to Barbara Ward's latest book, *Progress for a Small Planet*. We owe her a great debt for focussing our attention on the key issues of major international conferences. Her *Home of Man* contributed to a broader understanding at the United Nations Conference on Human Settlements—Habitat. *Only One Earth*, which she wrote with René Dubos, was a basic text and inspiration to the United Nations Conference on the Human Environment. Her *Spaceship Earth*, in 1966, was a truly seminal work. In the present book, she links together all these themes in one work which addresses itself to the question "What is development? How can it be sustained? What technology is needed?" In recent years national governments and the international community have been engaged in a simultaneous and fundamental reappraisal of environment, development, and the use which might best be made of scientific and technological capabilities. Old definitions and values are being considered. Old strategies are being re-examined. Old priorities are being reordered.

It is being realized that environment and development are inseparable, since development goals are only achievable through a certain environmental quality. It is further being realized that technology, far from determining the development process, should be determined by it and by its goals. Similarly, technology should not impose on the environment, but should be in harmony with the environmental setting. It is for this reason that we in the United Nations Environment Programme have emphasized the concept of eco-development, and stressed the importance of selecting those appropriate technologies which can make possible the meeting of human needs within the constraints of a sustainable environmental resource base.

It is pertinent, then, that Barbara Ward's book seeks to address the question of how sustainable development may best be achieved. In doing so, the author discusses the many and complex interrelations between energy provision, materials and food supply, and the process of urbanization, within the contexts of national and international policy formulation and the world economic order. The result is a unique book which is both stimulating and controversial, one which will generate consensus in some questions and constructive criticism in others. Whilst the views expressed are, of course, those of the author and do not necessarily reflect UNEP's or my own, I have no doubt that *Progress for a Small Planet* will have a profound and beneficial impact on all those grappling with the problem of how to ensure and to advance the sustainable development of mankind and of human society.

Mostafa K. Tolba
Executive Director, United Nations Environment Programme

AUTHOR'S NOTE

ANY BOOK which attempts to take into account the major threats to the integrity of our planetary environment must involve a really daunting amount of research, travel, consultation, correspondence, checking of information, and correlation of statistics. The resources of the International Institute for Environment and Development alone would have been quite inadequate to cover such a task. It was therefore a special stroke of good fortune for the Institute that both the United Nations Environment Programme and the World Bank were ready to contribute most generously to the project, and the first thanks of the Institute, of the author, and of her fellow workers are naturally due to both of these deeply concerned and profoundly helpful world institutions.

The scale of the work has been such that it is simply not possible to name individually all those to whom gratitude is due. But mention must be made of Dr. Michael Royston's original and indispensable studies of conserving technologies, of David Satterthwaite's insight and diligence in overseeing the general research effort, of Christina Kimes and Michael Allaby for invaluable information and advice, of Juliet Brightmore and John Austin for securing the photographs, of the readiness of colleagues at the IIED—David Runnalls, Richard Sandbrook, Gerald Leach, Brian Johnson, Jon Tinker—to add their critical reading of the manuscript to all their other labors, of Irene Hunter for her continuous support and unfailing readiness to struggle with the author's far from exemplary calligraphy. The author is also grateful for all the comments she received from the UNEP staff and for the kindness and skill displayed by Baron de Rosen, director of the Industry Program, in arranging for them to review the material.

Three last points: First, most statistics in the text are drawn from the World Bank, government sources, or the United Nations; metric units have generally been used, save for terms such as "gallons" and "miles per gallon," which have been retained because of the English-speaking world's general unfamiliarity with the metric equivalents; and a full list of sources for the statistics can be obtained from the IIED, 10 Percy Street, London WIP ODR.

Second, all the royalties from this book are pledged to supporting the work of international environmental education.

Last of all, it must be stressed that judgments, criticisms—and errors—are the author's own.

Barbara Ward

Progress
for a Small Planet

PROLOGUE

WE ARE living in what is, by all odds, the most tumultuous type of historical epoch. Ever since the invention of the city some six or seven thousand years ago and the quick advance of urban societies into the habit of empire building, the periods of collapse between imperial systems have been, without exception, the times of greatest violence, uncertainty, and confusion—and yet of potential creativeness. At the apex of society, citizens have waited, with apprehension or ambition, to discern the next center of power—after Sumer and Akkad, Nineveh, after Nineveh, Babylon, after Babylon, Thebes, after Thebes, Alexandrian Greece, after Greece, Rome. A similar sequence of competing rising and collapsing imperialisms can be discerned in every continent. Even the Chinese endured half a millennium of "civil" war before the Chin dynasty re-established unified government, and then Mongol conquerors and Manchu dynasts were still to follow. It may be that the Buddha's concept of life as a "melancholy wheel" has its basis not so much in the revolving constellations and returning harvests as in the deadly repetition of imperial rise, conquest, decline, and fall.

These changes of authority naturally brought with them changes in the order of ideas. City gods became universal deities. Rites and sacrifices and those who offered them changed function and significance. Customary laws were modified or remade, or under the more demonic conquerors, temporarily wiped out. At a deeper level, the world's great ethical traditions—whether Hindu or Taoist, Confucian, Zoroastrian, Buddhist, Jewish, Greek, or Christian—have their roots in a practical and deadly experience of the consequences of unlimited power, violence, and greed. These rages of the human spirit were seen at their most vile in the wake of imperialism's outer conquests and inner decay. The excited hooligan cries of spectators watching beasts eviscerate slaves in the circus amphitheater at Hippo were louder, we are told, than the cries of defenders attempting to repulse invaders at the city gates. From such experiences, it was not too great a step, even in practical terms, to believe that Lao-tzu's three treasures—"frugality, compassion, the desire not to be foremost in everything"—might work better or at least could not conceivably work worse. The grounding of ethics in desperate and tragic historical experience is part of the record of the "melancholy wheel."

But in all previous endings of empire, at least two elements of continuity were not much disturbed. One was the level of population. After the increases made possible by settled farming and intensified by irrigation, human numbers in general did not change rapidly. In Roman times, after four thousand years of cities and empires, there were still only about 250 million people on this earth. The numbers would grow, largely in the East, to 500 million by the sixteenth century. Imperialism did of course affect population figures and pressures. The capturing of slaves was one of the earliest purposes of conquest. But this only points to a pervasive lack of manpower and the determination to rob the next kingdom's reserves.

Manpower is the clue to the second element of continuity—the maintenance of the underlying agricultural systems largely invented and elaborated in Neolithic times and soon providing the basic needs—and the soldiers—of the new urban imperial systems. Wars—imperial, national, civil—interrupted but barely changed this basic work, although they did hasten collapse in areas using irrigation. The peasant or serf or tenant or worker in some communal system labored on. As the poet put it:

> They heard the legions thunder by
> And plunged in sleep again.

Substitute "work" for "sleep" and you have the millennial activity from which all conquerors, aristocrats, urban officials, and national bureaucracies drew their existence. And here the systems of, say, Anatolia or Szechwan would have been virtually unchanged from the beginning of the first conquests on to the last round—the fateful round of European conquest from which we are the first generation to emerge.

It is not to be supposed that history is being canceled for us. The same disruptions can be discerned—uncertainty of power at the apex, changes in ideologies and concepts, the sense of confusion, the search for a changed vision of the good life. But to these are added a number of new elements which bring wholly new dimensions of uncertainty to what is, by all historical tradition, an uncertain age. The first and best known is the sudden, vertiginous climb in population—from half a billion* in the sixteenth century to one billion by 1820, to two billion by 1930, to three billion by 1960, to four billion by 1976, and with the practical certainty of a further two billion to be added by the century's end. But this change, startling and sudden though it certainly is both in historic time and in human consciousness, may be less fateful than two others which, with as radical a break, cut off our own day from all earlier phases of imperial transition.

This is the first time in history that the ending of one imperial system has been attended not by an uneasy expectation of a successor, but by the passionate proclamation of the principle that imperialism itself is impermissible. No one argued whether Alexander of Macedon had the *right* to conquer the Persians, or the Romans to destroy Carthage, or even the Athenians to wipe out Melos. The victims did not enjoy it, but "woe to the defeated" was the accepted norm. The proposition that strength justified its own measures was only questioned by prophets and sages. In the so-called law of nations, power justified itself and conquest expressed it. But today the acceptance of national self-determination—however grudging on the part of the European conquerors, however distrustful on the part of the formerly colonized—has led, in a quarter of a century, to the formal ending of *political* imperialism. Everywhere the curtain has fallen, save in pockets of southern Africa or in the former czarist empire, and there the possibility is still open that the Soviet Union may develop by way of a common ideology the unity which the two other "superstates" have secured—China over two thousand years in large measure through cultural and racial uniformity, the United States in the last two hundred years by conquest and settlement in mainly open lands, by vast mixed migrations, and by increasingly open government.

While the old political dominion was being dismantled after 1945, a number of planetary political, social, and economic institutions were established within a United Nations system, designed to express the new independence of nations, yet their recognition of a measure of interdependence. However, within a very short time this interdependence

* Throughout the book, "billion" is understood to denote "thousand million."

began to be felt increasingly as an unacceptable colonial hang-over, since its basis was the continued and very high measure of dependence by the ex-colonial lands—the "South,"* as they came to be called—on the "North," the old imperialists, the world's white minority of European descent. At the end of the Second World War, about a third of the world's peoples in this North controlled more than three-quarters of the world's wealth and trade, over 90 percent of its services, and a nearly total monopoly of its trained minds for scientific and technological research. The last quarter decade has seen an increasing awareness that political dominion can end and economic dependence remain, and this too is unacceptable. The whole drive to establish a "new international economic order" is the extension into the daily life and daily bread of society of the same principles of self-determination which, politically, have largely secured acceptance. The fight for an end to all types of economic "imperialism" is beginning to engage much of the same kind of fierce dedication that went into the earlier political struggles.

Nor should we limit this new instinct of emancipation to the world's apex, where governments dispute the unresolved dilemmas of combining self-determination and interdependence. The drive for emancipation and participation, for basic human rights and responsibilities, spreads steadily throughout society—from the housewife in Arizona to the untouchable in an Indian village. No matter what legions thunder by, fewer and fewer people are now asleep. The turmoil is as wide as the planet. And it includes at the base as at the level of intergovernmental negotiation the claim not only to political rights but to social and physical rights as well—to be fed, to be employed, to be freed from disease and back-breaking labor, to enter the new world of education and planetary communication.

These claims bring us to the third revolutionary change. This is total economic transformation. Britain, then Europe and northeastern America, invented and developed the industrial revolution, which by powering human work with energy first from coal, then from oil, natural gas, and hydroelectricity, increased by fantastic amounts the possible scale of output and the productivity—the "more for less"—with

* The terms "Third World," "developing countries," and "South" are used interchangeably to denote those nations lacking a predominantly industrial and service-sector economy and with per capita GNP generally below $1,500. These nations are the home of three-quarters of the world's peoples. Virtually all of them have more than a third of their labor force in agriculture, while in many of them, more than two-thirds of the population live and work on the land.

which it could be achieved. The new machine goods not only wiped out local artisans—one thinks of Europe's starving weavers. It also ended the Orient's predominance in manufacture. Muslins no longer came from Muslim Bengal, calico from Calcutta. Manchester, then Massachusetts and Lille and Roubaix, took their place, and with the coming of the machines and the machines to make the machines, the entire balance of power swung in the nineteenth century to the new industrial manufacturers. The colonial or semicolonial areas became the sites of new mines and plantations opened up by the North to serve its growing need for the raw materials of expanding industrialism and in the whole non-Western world, only Japan, by a unique act first of exclusion and then of imitation, avoided almost total dependence on Northern systems of markets, services, financing, and investment.

True, as industrialism developed, all was not well *within* Northern societies. Early manufacturing, based on memories of feudalism and a perverse overvaluation of property rights, had disfranchised the mass of workers back to conditions which were little better than the slave-worked mines and galleys of earlier imperialisms. Only slowly did increasing education, the beginnings of trade union organization and collective bargaining, start to redress a balance as uneven *within* industrial society as it was in the world at large. Narrow domestic markets, new industrialized entrants—above all, Germany—competition for overseas supplies, culminated in two devastating wars. The fundamental attacks upon the system made first by Marx and later by Lenin were all basically concerned with this total lack of balance. Marx believed that the low purchasing power of the masses would not keep pace with the productivity of the machines, and the consequence would be increasing crises and finally the collapse of the system. Lenin prophesied that competition for inadequate markets and colonial supplies would bring disaster through imperialist struggle. Both missed the significance of growing working class organization and bargaining power. Neither could have foreseen Lord Keynes.

In the immediate aftermath of the Second World War, it seemed as though some of the contradictions foreseen by the critics of industrialized society were being overcome. A steady increase in internal demand, based upon the government's virtual guarantee of full employment, would end all those crises and slumps of "overproduction" (which were in Marx's view due to underconsumption). And the now increasingly emancipated ex-colonial South would industrialize, modernize, and expand by "stages of growth" comparable to those achieved in the North. The new wealth would, again as in the older industrialized world, "trickle down" to the mass of the people until all, North and South, rich and poor together, would hasten forward to the felicity of the high-consumption economy. By the early seventies, however, new perceptions began to appear, containing contradictions possibly as irrevocable as Marx had thought his to be. In one decade, the vision of sustained Northern growth mediated through world trade and investment—and a little aid—into sustained world growth began to look uncomfortably like a mirage. A new upheaval was under way, and it is in the middle of it that we live today.

A first problem among the new uncertainties is the sheer availability of resources to power and produce continued world growth. This is partly an absolute problem. The most recent estimates suggest that the peak of world oil production will be reached in the 1980s or 1990s, with the peak for natural gas early in the next century. Thereafter, decline will set in. As we shall see in later chapters, there are serious constraints on the use both of coal and of uranium as replacements for oil and natural gas. Exploitable reserves for both are finite. Since industrial nations use, per capita, fifteen times more coal, oil, gas, and uranium than the Third World, any advance by the poor nations toward fully industrialized standards could add enormously to the demands on severely constrained and finite fuel reserves.

This fact points to the second uncertainty about supplies. When we turn to minerals, there is obviously a built-in difficulty in estimating their length of continuance. They are not destroyed and can be recycled. Provided higher prices are paid, low-grade ores become usable. New technologies also enable lower-grade ores to be exploited. As a result, improved mining technology and rising world market prices for any mineral resource can enlarge usable reserves. But energy is the final constraint. At some point, the energy costs of exploiting very poor ores becomes too high for their use to remain economic.

There is also a more immediate obstacle to the availability of basic minerals. The Third World possesses very few of them. If one adds up the mineral resources of North America, the Soviet Union (which has, for instance, more than half of the world's coal reserves), Australia, and South Africa, they have the bulk of the world's reserves of chromium, coal, vanadium, uranium, molybdenum, potash, and the platinum group; more than half the manganese, iron ore, zinc, silver, and lead;

and more than a third of the natural gas, copper, and bauxite. These five areas dominate world trade in many of these resources. True, this degree of concentration reflects in part the relative lack of surveying and exploration in the Third World. But even according to the most optimistic estimates for the scale of still-to-be discovered reserves, the imbalance would only be lessened. The virtually unique exception of the Arab states, with high oil reserves and tiny populations, at present rather clouds the general perception of the Third World's profound disadvantage. But if the drive for greater equality between North and South is accepted—as it must be—as one of the dominant political passions of our day, it is clear that no traditional methods of growth, trade, and "trickledown" can redress so vast an imbalance in basic mineral resources.

The third critical area of potential shortage may be emerging in both North and South. This is the loss of land for productive agriculture. The chief areas of danger lie in the arid lands and along the denuded hillsides of the Third World which are exposed, with the steady rise of population, to increased risks of overgrazing, overcultivation, the clearing of tree cover, and a resulting erosion of their fragile soils. Nor should one underestimate the risk, in irrigated areas, of increasing salinity and waterlogging. According to estimates made by the United Nations Environment Programme, 300 million hectares* of land may be lost to soil erosion between 1975 and 2000. In addition, another 300 million hectares may pass from agricultural to urban use. (Often the best land is thus absorbed, since the market centers for productive farming regions are the natural nuclei of new or expanding cities.) Here, the North too faces a depletion of its rural resources. Between 1960 and 1970 some of the most heavily populated and urbanized countries lost sizable percentages of agricultural land—the Netherlands 4.3 percent, for instance, Japan 7.5 percent, Belgium as much as 12 percent. All in all, the lost 600 million hectares would represent half the world's present cultivated land. This is not a firm estimate, since against it must be set plans for opening up and irrigating new land. But by definition these areas—in Africa, in Latin America—tend to have difficult terrains, less fertile soils, and uncertain rainfall. Otherwise they would have long since come under the plow.

It is probably at about this point in any discussion of material limits

* One hectare equals 2.47 acres, i.e., roughly 2½ acres.

that outraged and contemptuous protests begin to be made by critics who see in the whole idea of obstacles to growth a failure of nerve. How can we doubt, they argue, that for every difficulty human ingenuity, science and technology, will find a workable answer? All fears about declining fuel supplies are offset by the immediate prospect of the fast breeder nuclear reactor, which actually produces more fuel than it uses. There is virtually no mineral for which very low grade ores or substitutes cannot be found, provided energy is available. In any case, the chemical industry can invent compounds never known in nature and many of them will be more versatile and usable than your common or garden ores. And microbiologists can engineer bacteria to eat oil spills, to leach needed minerals from the lowest-grade ores, or even to become miniature pharmaceutical factories producing, for example, insulin to aid the world's many diabetics. Nor need land shortages be feared. Entirely artificial food systems based upon sophisticated greenhouses—hydroponics—and single-cell protein production need no arable land at all.

As for the relative poverty of the South, the argument continues, science knows no boundaries. New hybrids, the development of grains which, like legumes, can fix their own nitrogen, and more effective agricultural chemicals will met the rising demand for food. Fusion power will supply all the needed energy. In the interval between the universal use of science and technology and the present lopsidedness, the North will increasingly concentrate on the highest technologies, on research, computerization, and automation; the South will supply the shoes and the textiles, and little by little we shall discover that growth and "trickledown" are not the mirage of a twenty-five year boom but simply the steady unfolding in the whole of the planet of that human progress through science which seemed as obvious to Karl Marx as to Adam Smith.

And then, once again, such is our intellectual confusion, the debate swings as fiercely to the other side. The bones of a human hand fused within the glass which melted when the plutonium bomb exploded over Nagasaki can be taken as the symbol of a wholly new distrust in the beneficence of science and the certainty of progress. Mankind's new knowledge of evolution has shown that organic life could not develop until the planet's surface was shielded from the sun's radiation—by the filling up of the oceans, then by the ozone layer formed from the increasingly oxygen-rich atmosphere. Such minute life forms as phytoplankton played a vital role in building up the concentration of atmospheric oxygen. The massive release of potentially lethal radiation inside the protective shield of this atmosphere could be the most fateful and dangerous of all human interventions in the biosphere.

One must add to this the fact that one of the by-products of nuclear power—plutonium—can with little difficulty be used to make a nuclear bomb. It is also one of the most lethal cancer-causing agents. It remains dangerous for hundreds of thousands of years, and since man only invented it in the last four decades, with billennia needed for nature to evolve any biological system for neutralizing its effects, such a system has somewhat naturally failed to appear. What beneficence, the critics argue, can follow from such deadly risks? And to the risk of weapons proliferation must be added another political risk—the stocking-faced terrorist with the mini plutonium bomb.

Nor are the risks only nuclear. At the planetary level, the by-products of fossil-fuel consumption and chemical industrial processes may be altering dangerously the world's climatic balance and, with such simple domestic tools as aerosol sprays, attacking the atmosphere's thin ozone layer which is the chief filter and protection against cancer-dealing solar radiation. At a more local level, the critics point out that the careless by-products of decades of industrialization can produce rivers like the Rhine, where soon no amount of treatment may be enough to guarantee safe drinking water, or communities like Niagara Falls in the United States, where toxic industrial chemicals casually buried turn up again to threaten the whole community's natural integrity and health.

Nor do human beings escape direct contamination. Citing recent disasters at chemical works such as those at Seveso in Italy, critics deny the beneficence of chemistry's powers of infinite substitutability and claim that man-made compounds are being released, without adequate examination, into the atmosphere, there to make cancer a pandemic killer in fully industrialized societies. Genetic engineering, too, brings with it risks, such as an inadvertent release of a dangerous mutant strain, or the unforeseen consequences of overambitious experiment. And if these are the dangers produced by the modernization of what is now only one-quarter of mankind's population, what consequences would follow in a world of high consumption and high technology serving at least six billion people?

Even the social processes which accompany the scientific and technological revolution no longer carry the old gleam of emancipation. Vast cities surrounded by indistinguishable surburban belts are said to blunt the sensibilities and weaken that native capacity for culture and amusement which is innate in peasant societies and for which television may be a very inadequate substitute. The increasing use of automation and computerization in developed societies may be at one and the same time increasing the monotony and impersonality of work and doing away with needed employment. The motorcar, the biggest love of the modern citizen, also kills 160,000 people a year in Europe and North America and maims three to four million more.

In the developing countries, high technology introduced into industry or agriculture while labor is the only unlimited resource lies at the root of one of the greatest and most disturbing upheavals of the postwar world—the vast, internal migrations which empty country people into metropolises, their populations racing to the ten-million mark, where 40 percent and more of the inhabitants are underemployed and huddled in squatter settlements of unexampled indignity and squalor.

Can any imperial interregnum ever have confronted so vast an array of contradictions? No power on earth can still the general demand for social betterment and a nearer approach to economic balance. Yet the means at mankind's disposal for producing the vast increase in material goods required to underpin the contentment of six billion earthlings may be so potentially destructive that the system could be handing out plumbing, cars, and breakfast foods with one hand and cancer of the lungs with the other. Industrial systems may spread while the ozone layer is depleted, technology be shared and the icecaps begin to melt. Is the planet thus set upon an absolutely unavoidable collision course—between rising numbers, rising claims, and rising pollution and shrinking natural resources and unacceptably dangerous alternatives? Compared with these fundamental issues of human destiny, how local, how transient appear all earlier historical crises. It is not the question of Rome's survival or Nineveh's or Chang'an's. It is the human race itself that must resolve the dilemmas or conceivably follow the dinosaurs—at a much speedier pace—"the way to dusty death."

Yet it is surely possible that neither side in the agonized debates has all the truth. The hope of a postimperialist society in which sharing, common policies, and mutual support come to influence the habitual relations of governments is not wholly vain. If the powerful had never been ready to compromise, modern industrial society would not have achieved even its modest measure of social democracy and civil peace. What can be achieved over a whole continent is not inconceivable within an even wider structure—for instance, the North–South dialogue on the form of a fully uncolonial world. Nor are all the technological and scientific means of achieving a better balance either potentially lethal or socially deadening. The range of modern science has spread to an ever intenser understanding of the small and the fragile as well as to the appropriation of the searing processes of the sun itself. Above all, the constant underlying tug of the world's ethical perceptions has not ceased through four centuries of sometimes arrogant rationalism and often naïve faith in automatic progress. What else is the rejection of imperialism *in principle* than a realization that no nation has the right to be "foremost in everything"? What are the North's modest steps toward development assistance but an acceptance, however inadequate and fluctuating, of the need for "compassion"? What is the whole realization that humanity befouls its airs and waters, spews out cancer-producing chemicals, and puts the biosphere at risk but a reflection of an urge, even if it is still only a very faintly articulated urge, for "frugality"—in other words, for conservation, for more sparing styles of living, for that thrift which can yet make the new planetary society survive and thrive? In this "morning's war" between hope and destruction, between insight and despair, the forces are not all on the side of night. Already new insights and new possibilities, unknown to any earlier phase of imperialism's rise and fall, can be perceived. It is their examination, in the most realistic and practical manner possible, that the following chapters will attempt.

Two preliminary words are necessary about the arrangement and content of the discussion. Given the fact that over 90 percent of the world's industry and a not much smaller proportion of fossil fuels are consumed in the industrialized North of our planet, given, too, that the endowment of resources, levels of skill, cultural advantages and disadvantages, varies so very greatly between developed and developing peoples, their prospects and policies will be treated separately. The fact that developed nations are treated first implies no judgment of value. They simply have done more in the technological and scientific field, including the commission of many more mistakes. It is therefore logical to consider first where mankind may be tending, then to consider whether the road is safe, and at that point to take up the condition of nations that have not yet made the changes or incurred the damages and could conceivably find a better route.

The second point concerns the content of the discussion. In virtually every chapter, a central conclusion is that if mankind is to survive in safety and dignity, some fundamental changes in direction are required. There are two ways of persuading people to undertake the often unwelcome task. The first is by direct exhortation. The second is by showing working examples of how changes—even very *great* changes—can be brought about. The chapters to come are largely based on this second method.

And the last confusion of our troubled age is that here, too, the balance between opposite convictions is as evident as on most other issues. On the one hand, there has been, as we shall see, little short of a revolution in people's thinking about resources and environment, about risks and priorities, in the last ten years. Yet the new period of questioning follows three decades of the most lavish material advance ever known in human history. For twenty-five years after the Second World War, with oil at less than two dollars a barrel, material standards of living rose at unprecedented rates, yesterday's luxuries became today's necessities, cars multiplied by their tens of millions, tourists by millions more. And this surge of consumption followed the rationing and hardship of a five-year war and the long dismal decade of the Great Depression. It is inconceivable that such social and material changes accomplished at such vertiginous speed, should not leave the human psyche in some bewilderment. No society in history before our own has ever even thought that perpetually rising living standards were conceivable, let along a basic right. Indeed, perhaps half the world's peoples still have no larger material ambition than assured survival. Is the vision of affluence now to be snatched from those who have briefly enjoyed it and from the rest who hear of it for the first time? It is hard to imagine a more formidable obstacle to the acceptance—once again at breathtaking historical speed—of less ambitious visions or less self-centered concerns.

Part One: New Directions for the Industrial Order

1 ENERGY: HOW BIG IS THE GAP?

IF CHANGES in the basic conditions of life occur at such speed and on such a scale, we can expect equal confusion and controversy in the reasons given for their emergence. But perhaps one or two general propositions are broad enough to ensure a measure of agreement. Clearly the fundamental cause of our century's upheavals is the steady, continued, yet as steadily unpredictable working out of the world's technological and scientific revolution. But within this broad context, three separate transformations seem to deserve especial emphasis. The first is the furiously accelerating growth—uninterrupted until 1973—in the use of nonrenewable energy resources, together with the underlying assumption that this, more than any other factor, has explained the postwar fact of unprecedentedly rapid and world-wide economic growth.

The second is the conjunction of two violent and related changes. One is the very great increase in the discards from all sections of developed world economies—industry, the production and selling of food, cities, households. The other is an equal increase in the kinds of wastes not known to nature but manufactured by chemistry's new ability to manipulate and transform the table of elements and their compounds.

The third, the broadest and the most difficult to define, is the social context of the whole experiment, in part derived from history, in part induced by its own inner achievements (and contradictions), in part indeed the fruit of chances, contacts, errors, life, death, the mutability of human affairs. Yet in ways that are at once all-pervasive and almost impossible to define, this context determines much of the rest. With two hundred years of hindsight, our social condition is perhaps not the one we would have chosen for humanity's plunge into the age of scientific mastery. As the old farmer remarked when asked the way to a distant town, "If I wanted to get there, sir, I would not start from here." But we are too far along the road to avoid its risks and errors. The hopeful and human task is to know enough about them not to follow all over again the old alleys and false turns.

We can begin with the role of energy. In this century, we have virtually identified the whole successful functioning of the economic system with a steady increase in our consumption of energy.* As the economy grows, more energy helps to fabricate more goods and services, of all kinds, for more people. High demand is maintained. Employment is expanded. Countries not yet modernized—mainly in the Southern parts of the planet—are to go through suitable "stages of growth," pulled upward in the wake of Northern prosperity. It is this sense of intimate interdependence between prosperity and energy use that has, since the 1973 oil crisis, led to the emergence of the concept of an "energy gap" as a center of controversy.

Its meaning is quite simple. As fossil fuels become unavailable or exhausted, will the prosperity they make possible vanish too? What "gap" must be filled with new energy sources in the next three decades to offset the declining availability of oil and then of natural gas? Now, as history shows, there *is* a very real sense in which this identification of economic growth, modernization, and higher energy use has a large basis of fact. Once the wobbles for slumps and recoveries are evened out, production and energy use are in fact seen to have risen together. In the eighteenth century, coal first supplied the steam power which permitted the concentration of cottage workers in large factories. In the late nineteenth century, oil and natural gas, cleaner and more convenient, began to eat into coal's share as the main primary fuel. All of these, with hydropower added, can be used to generate superconvenient electricity, which with a flick of a switch can do the work of a thousand men with shovels. Since the Second World War, the fission of uranium 235 has entered the list of electricity producers, and even if its share in the

---

* In strictly scientific terms, energy cannot be consumed or conserved. It is indestructible. But useful and "high-quality" forms such as fossil fuels or electricity are, in effect, "consumed" when they are used, since their energy then becomes dispersed in the form of low-grade heat—warm air or water—and cannot be used again to cook the dinner or power the car's engine.

world energy supply is no more than a few percent, its supporters see it as the "natural" replacer of oil, just as oil replaced coal in many uses.

So, virtually until the 1970s, the rising tide of energy was felt to be the motor power of a world advancing toward general prosperity, and in all estimates of future use the tendency was simply to extrapolate past percentages of growth in fuel consumption (even when, as in Japan in the sixties, they were as high as 12 percent a year). High energy, high technology, high employment and consumption, appeared inextricably linked by over a century of solid practical experience. Few seem to have noticed some odd discrepancies—for instance, that the United States used twice as much energy per capita as wealthy West Germany and even wealthier—and chillier—Sweden. Under the flood of oil at under two dollars a barrel, such divergences made no impact. The dream went on of riches without end, powered by limitless energy.

This mood has inevitably affected governments and institutions. With few, though increasing, exceptions, rising trends in energy use continue to be equated with higher living standards. Extrapolations from past consumption—even from the quite exceptional explosion of energy use in the 1950s and 1960s—have been used as the basis in planning for future fuel imports or for electric power derived from "orderly" investment in steadily mounting numbers of ever larger power stations. When power companies charged their customers lower rates the more electricity they used, and based expansion plans on this induced demand, their rationalization was that higher flows would increase technical efficiencies and lower unit costs. The true reason, since genuine economies of scale were exhausted in the sixties, was the fundamental growth euphoria of the whole economy, shared by companies and clients alike.

Now in the seventies, there has come a check to the earlier confidence. It began in the political form of the Arab oil embargo But in fact its roots go deeper than any diplomatic maneuvers. The supply of oil and natural gas—the great boosters of the postwar growth bonanza—will become constrained well before the year 2000. The oil-exporting nations, aware that their sole resource base is being rapidly depleted, may soon restrict production below the level needed to meet still rising world demand. Natural-gas reserves may last longer. But gas is difficult and expensive to transport across oceans, and constraints on its supply will appear in the industrial nations as indigenous reserves run out. Meanwhile, to give only one instance of depletion, the United States has already consumed about half of its own oil, once one of the largest reserves in the world. In 1970, Canada's energy minister was predicting sufficient indigenous reserves to guarantee a 923-year supply of oil and a 392-year supply of natural gas. The latest official Canadian figures, which take into account the cost and difficulty of exploiting new indigenous reserves, now talk of only a 10- to 20-years guaranteed supply of oil and natural gas. And this decline is occurring before most of mankind has even approached the outer fringe of the ''high-energy economy.'' The kind of scenario which assumes the world moving upward toward American standards of energy consumption could exhaust reserves in a few decades. It would also send fuel prices through the roof, since we should not forget that the basic fuels of the modernized economy have been bone-cheap—through the degrading exploitation of labor in the coal-steam age, through the rock-bottom price of oil during the fantastic growth decades of the fifties and sixties.

When in 1973 the Arab oil embargo was imposed, its introduction was sudden and political. Yet it did, like Dr. Johnson's prospect of hanging in a fortnight, begin ''wonderfully to concentrate'' the developed nations' minds. The Arabs, in a sense, did them the service of jolting them into a perception of fuel stringency twenty years before natural decline in oil production would have started to set in—in which case, it would have probably occurred too late for anything but panic protective measures.

In short, the bonanza is over. The oil shortages that came from the refusal by Iran's new regime to gear oil production to suit Western demand have reinforced new perceptions of constraints on fuel supplies and rising costs. Ideas tend toward stark confrontation. The enthusiasts are confident of a nuclear future to replace vanishing fossil fuels, to maintain expanding energy demand and thus comfortably fill the ''energy gap.'' The ''doomsayers'' prophesy planetary nuclear destruction. But we must start the debate with a paradox—that in its present form the controversy is largely irrelevant for the rich nations. Virtually everyone involved has unconsciously assumed that energy consumption must go on rising year after year to keep up living standards and fuel economic growth. But for advanced Western nations, this assumption is no longer true. Indeed, the nations with the highest per capita energy consumption could over the next few decades reduce their fuel consumption while actually improving living standards and achieving genuine economic growth.

To give only the most obvious example, a factory can install insulation to cut down its space-heating bills and new equipment to improve the energy efficiency of its production process. It then recoups this investment through lower fuel bills and thus lowers fuel consumption, maintains production, and cuts costs. Take a simple cautionary tale from the cement industry. The most modern European cement kilns consume less than half the fuel of the average United States cement kiln to make a barrel of cement. With fuel prices climbing and with fuel purchases representing as much as 20 percent of the total operating costs of some cement plants, one can hardly expect America's managers to overlook this discrepancy. With new plants, they should be able to show large decreases in energy consumption while production is actually increasing.*

A similar tale emerges from the construction industry. Only recently has this industry—and the clients for whom it builds—started to take into account the cost over time of heating and lighting a new building. Highly insulated walls and ceilings, double-glazed windows, and other energy-saving measures can halve the amount of fuel needed to keep the building comfortable and well lit. The range of energy-conserving measures ignored when oil was only two dollars a barrel radically changes when oil is sixteen dollars a barrel and there is still no cheaper fuel to turn to. And a few governments are beginning to give various incentives to encourage citizens and enterprises to conserve fuels and to turn to indigenous energy sources to relieve the pressure on their balance of payments caused by huge oil-import bills. For example, the Dutch government extends generous grants to householders installing insulation, while the United States and West Germany give grants or tax rebates to households purchasing solar equipment. This whole area of energy conservation, alternative energy sources, and "income energies" will be examined in greater detail in later chapters. Here the point is to underline how they can slow down the growth in demand for conventional fuels over the next three decades and thus make nonsense of much recent controversy over the "energy gap."

Certain profounder trends in developed societies also suggest that the need for energy will be most unlikely to go on growing explosively.

---

*This point about improved capital equipment is, of course, not new. The amount of energy needed to produce a ton of pig iron has fallen from eight to under one ton of coal equivalent since 1800, simply because equipment has with experience and experiment become more efficient.

A whole range of social pressures making for stable levels of energy use will begin to exercise a more and more dominant effect. This is partly a result of the issues already mentioned—the fuel economies already achieved in many modern industrial processes. But the whole industrial sector is becoming inherently less energy-intensive in the goods it produces. The energy cost of "advanced" consumer goods such as color televisions, stereo systems—or even home computers—is minimal compared to their value. And they are simply one example of a profound shift in the economy's patterns of work, activity, occupation, and energy use. In terms of value produced, iron and steel demand around thirty times more fuel than do services such as tourism, entertainments, office work. But these are the "growth sectors." In the new giant bureaucratic structures of many public and private activities a new "quaternary" sector can be defined. More and more of the world's business is conducted through computer print-outs, satellite communication systems, information retrieval and databanks. Jobs within this sector are among the least energy-intensive of all occupations. The consequence is that as heavy industry—and indeed most types of goods production—continue to decline as a proportion of the national economy, the amount of fuel needed to carry on the nation's enterprises can reach the celebrated state of "zero-growth."

This trend within the productive sector is matched by another in developed society at large. Populations are becoming stable. Their growth in the past has been a major factor in the explosive expansion of fuel demand. Although energy use for each person in the United States has only doubled in the last seventy-five years, the sheer multiplication of persons has led to a sixfold expansion in the use of energy.

The household is a major energy consumer both directly through demand for heating and power and indirectly since the number of automobiles is related to the number of households. In future, the trend will change toward stability. It will be masked for a time by the entry of the postwar "baby-boom" children into the housing market and the rise in the number of people living on their own. Thereafter, housing demand will also become steady. For the United Kingdom, one long-range forecast* which takes into account stable population, smaller households, and a rational degree of fuel conservation suggests that by 2025, the number of households will have increased by a fifth while

* Gerald Leach et al., *A Low Energy Strategy for the United Kingdom* (Science Reviews, U.K., 1979).

their total energy consumption will have fallen by the same fraction. And this despite the fact that houses would become larger and better heated.

Similar calculations can be made for the likely demand for automobiles in the future. "Cataclysmic" growth is nearly over when most households already have a car. The combined effects of all these long-term trends—in types of employment, in population, in the formation of households and the buying of cars—add up to one certainty. Extrapolating the past thirty years' energy trends into the future and then postulating "energy gaps" is quite simply a fruitless and time-wasting exercise. Plans based upon them—for extra fuel consumption, for a higher production of electricity and the building of more power stations—will lead to an embarrassing overcapacity. For Britain, primary energy consumption in 1977 was the same as in 1970, even though the economy had grown by 10 percent in those seven years. Growth in electricity demand has been far slower than had been expected in the early 1960s and early 1970s. The result is evident overcapacity in the electricity grid and in the electricity-equipment industry. It also entails a drastic need to revise expansion plans.

Since 1973, governments have in fact begun to scale down their projections for future fuel use. There *is* a certain cautious acknowledgment that conservation can reduce energy demand and completely change the calculus of potential energy gaps. But projections still greatly underestimate the technical range and potential use of fully conserving strategies. They are simply not seen as a cheap and effective method of increasing energy supply. It is a strange aberration. If an intensive housing-insulation program lowers the nation's demand for oil, gas, and electricity by 10 percent, this is equivalent to increasing supplies by the same amount. And since the whole process of increasing supplies—especially indigenous energy supplies for countries with no oil—is exceedingly expensive, the range of conservation measures that are cost-effective compared with increasing supply costs is vast. But we must allow for the sheer weight of accepted ideas and interests and the immense effort needed to change them. No company—public or private—increases its turnover by reducing the need for its output. The same inertia accounts for the fact that most governments do not yet make any very considerable efforts to consider the role of full-scale conservation, together with alternative and renewable sources of energy, in making their own predictions. They tend to be still caught in the "tradi-

tional wisdom'' of energy gaps and economic growth and to look for the
answers in more supply, not in more conserving use. In short, they conform to traditional practice and concentrate not on saving but on increasing the output of the more familiar alternatives—above all, coal
and nuclear power.

However, in a longer perspective, there *is* a "gap" between the
kinds of energy-gobbling habits and installations of the recent past, the
steady growth of energy demand in a still developing world, and the
possibly distant (but not entirely postponable) decline in conventional
fuel supplies. A sane energy policy certainly does not consist in being
stampeded into premature decisions by pressures which do not and need
not exist. Equally, a long-term strategy cannot neglect the evolving
facts of use, decline, and possible exhaustion in present fuel supplies.

2 THE NUCLEAR OPTION

THE ALMOST hypnotic attraction that nuclear energy exercises over many minds is twofold. One is its extravagant availability. The other is the incredible scientific and technical triumph of discovering the ways in which this abundance can be controlled and used. Thus it both provides apparent security against all shortages and energy gaps and at the same time triumphantly reaffirms the dream of mastering nature for human purposes—"for the use and betterment of man's estate." Just because the first uses of this vast energy source were to blast two cities into hideous patterns of destruction, a certain desire to redeem the knowledge, to prove that it can be constructively used, that it is not simply fit for destruction, undoubtedly influences—however subconsciously—the creators and users of nuclear power.

Let us take the issue of incredible abundance. The use of nuclear power is possible because of our new understanding of the atoms that make up all matter. It is the forces that bind together the constituent parts of the atom's nucleus which, when ruptured, release an overwhelming flood of energy. The central sustaining flow of energy for our solar system comes from the nuclear bonds which hold atomic nuclei together in the sun's core. The sun is a gigantic fusion reactor in which hydrogen nuclei fuse into helium. The loss of mass is released as the energy that irradiates the solar system.*

Only two-billionths of this energy is intercepted by the earth. Yet it is enough to provide the entire globe's basic "space heating." Without

---

* As Einstein suggested, mass and energy are interconvertible: e (energy) $= m$ (mass) $\times c^2$ (speed of light squared). Since c is 30,000,000,000 centimeters per second, mass can be considered a very concentrated form of energy. The energy in one gram of mass is sufficient to keep a 1-kilowatt electric fire on for nearly three thousand years. In nuclear fission or fusion, there is a considerable "loss" of mass as it is converted into energy—thus explaining the enormous power of both.

the sun, all life on the planet would simply freeze to death. Trees and plants capture one-fiftieth of 1 percent of this radiation. Yet it is enough to ripen every harvest. The sun also powers the planet's cycle of water purification and desalination, which provides the rains that give us the fresh water on which land-based life depends. In a very real sense, we already live in a nuclear-powered economy—fired by a reactor that is a safe 93 million miles away.

But there is another route to tapping the power of the nuclear bonds. The heaviest naturally occurring element, uranium,* contains a small proportion of uranium 235. Under certain conditions, one of uranium 235's nuclei can split ("fission") and in so doing release neutrons that can then split another nucleus that in turn releases neutrons that split another nucleus, in a self-sustaining chain reaction that can build up to a catastrophic release of energy, as was proved when the fission bomb was dropped on Hiroshima.

Uranium 235 makes up only 0.7 percent of naturally occurring uranium—the more stable uranium 238 making up the rest. Thus "weapons-grade" uranium is made by enormously increasing the concentration of uranium 235. But there exists another element that can be used to make nuclear bombs—plutonium 239. The more stable uranium 238 nucleus can absorb a neutron, but instead of splitting, it quickly changes (after two intermediate stages) into plutonium 239. Plutonium's effectiveness was demonstrated when a plutonium bomb virtually obliterated Nagasaki.

If we take "fissile" elements—uranium 235, plutonium 239—on the one hand and the sun on the other, we can see that there are two possible sources of nuclear power: fission, where large nuclei split, and fusion, where at vast temperatures small nuclei fuse. The power of fusion has also been used for weapons—the hydrogen bomb detonated in 1953 used a fission bomb to start a fusion reaction, greatly increasing the destructive capabilities of the nuclear weapon. The problem in making anything more useful than bombs out of this enormous reserve of energy is clearly to keep fusion or the chain reaction of fission going along steadily, carefully controlled, emitting usable streams of energy in the form of heat which, like coal, can fire the boilers to produce the steam which generates the power in the stations that man has built.

*Numbers attached to elements like uranium and plutonium indicate the numbers of protons and neutrons in the nucleus. Uranium 238, the more stable form of naturally occurring uranium, has three more neutrons in its nucleus than uranium 235.

In fission reactors, a variety of means are used to keep the chain reaction under control. The uranium fuel rods in the reactor core have far lower concentrations of the fissile uranium 235 than does weapons-grade uranium. Control rods pushed in and out of the reactor core control the number of uranium 235 nuclei that fission—and thus control the rate of the chain reaction. A variety of what we might call first-generation fission reactors have now been steadily at work for more than a decade. Their actual accident rate has been low—no small achievement for a new and intensely powerful and complex technology. It is entirely understandable to see in the whole process a tremendous breakthrough of human intelligence, having the capability of producing the flows of energy modern society appears to require. But, of course, the nuclear issue has its own special reservations simply because nuclear power is like no other energy ever used by humanity in the biosphere. As we all know, its use has been called a Faustian bargain. But in view of the power of the sun's radiance, the power of the fission and fusion bombs, and the potentially lethal effects of the radiation emitted by the nuclear reactions, the nuclear fuels, and the nuclear wastes, the possibility of utilizing these processes on earth could bring an even more ominous myth into play—Prometheus stealing heaven's fire and chained forever to a bare rock.

Precautions taken in all nuclear power stations have to prevent the risk of excessive heating—which could lead to a "meltdown" and a possible release of deadly radioactive material. They also have to safeguard the staff and the public from the various kinds of radiation emitted by fuels, wastes, and the reaction itself. High doses of this radiation can kill any living organism's cells outright. Lower doses can prevent a cell dividing or damage the genetic material. Or they can induce cancers in any body tissue. The problem is therefore to isolate all potentially dangerous radiation from organic life. A nuclear reaction functioning normally releases comparatively little radiation to the atmosphere. But if the vessel containing the reactor core is breached by a meltdown, the radioactive material released could contaminate thousands of square miles and all the people living within this area. The Mitre Report, *Nuclear Power: Issues and Choices,* listed the possible consequences of an "extremely serious accident" in the United States light-water reactor as a contaminated area of 3,200 square miles, an economic loss of $14 billion, 3,300 immediate deaths, over 250,000 deaths over the next thirty years from radiation-induced diseases, and genetic defects in some 30,000 people over 150 years. The actual number of people affected by such an accident would obviously depend on such factors as population density around the reactor and how the wind dispersed the released radioactive material. But these figures give an idea of the possible extent of disaster. Statistically, the probability of such an accident occurring may be very small. It is the sheer scale of its effects that makes it different in kind to any other sort of accident unleashed by human intervention.

The other equally serious safety issue is the problem of the waste products. Some by-products of the nuclear reaction "poison" the uranium fuel over time. As a result, the fuel rods have to be removed and fresh ones put in their place. But clearly, the intensely radioactive rods cannot simply be dumped. They contain some unused uranium 235, which, if extracted, could be put back in fresh fuel rods into the reactor. They also contain the various fission products—the new nuclei formed when the uranium 235 nuclei split. These include strontium 90 and caesium 137, both of which have to be isolated from all organic life for hundreds of years until they finally decay, lose their radioactivity, and thus become safe.

There are even more dangerous by-products. During the fission reaction, some of the uranium 238 in the fuel rods is converted into plutonium and into other elements from the same chemical family—the so-called actinides. Many of these are extremely radio-toxic. And some have to be isolated from organic life not for hundreds but for hundreds of thousands of years. Plutonium itself is so carcinogenic that the minutest particle, if inhaled, can cause cancer. Some of the actinides are even more radio-toxic than plutonium. As nuclear programs expand, the years needed for secure waste disposal will extend further and further into a future ever more loaded with steadily increasing volumes of dangerous wastes. Some fission products of today will decay to safe levels only toward the end of the twenty-fifth century, a period which, taking us backward, would predate Columbus's discovery of the Americas. Some actinides will be safe only toward the five thousandth century, which, again going backward, might even predate *homo sapiens*. Meanwhile, no one is yet certain that the various methods proposed for containing these high-level wastes—vitrifying them in glass blocks, incorporating them into synthetic rock—and then storing them in "stable" rock formations deep underground will actually give the needed protection. As yet, no safe waste-disposal technique has been perfected that can guarantee the needed thousands of years of absolute security.

In addition to the high-level wastes there is a whole host of less lethal ones such as discarded fuel-rod cladding, filters, and the like which also have to be safely and securely stored. There is also a wide range of low-level radioactive materials which are discharged into the environment—a variety of gases routinely discharged from reactors and their supporting industrial plants, contaminated clothing and equipment, liquid wastes from cooling ponds, and so on. The worries with these are less spectacular. But low-level wastes can find their way back to human beings through an incredibly diverse and interconnected series of environmental pathways—not only fish that eat marine organisms that are contaminated with radioactive liquid effluents but also radioactive sediment from liquid wastes which may return to land over time. No one denies the efforts that are being made to produce safe fission power. But we can hardly fail to recall the aphorism, To point out all one's efforts to solve a problem is not the same as finding the solution.

These uncertainties make perplexing and even alarming a reliable balance sheet of the benefits and costs of nuclear reactors and supporting installations in present use. Like Everest, they are there. They are producing electricity and thus taking the strain off other sources of energy. Accidents in Western Europe and North America have not been catastrophic. When in 1975 a single candle set fire to the cables near the reactor core at Browns Ferry, a large nuclear power station in Alabama, and caused all "fail-safe" systems to fail, other means were found to avoid a meltdown and to close down the reactor. (The accident is reported to have cost $100 million, but no one was injured.) There have been several worrying instances of well above average levels of cancer among those working in nuclear installations—for example at Hanford and at the nuclear-submarine yards in the United States. Some nuclear engineers there have resigned over the issue of safety—especially the strength of the vessel surrounding the reactor core. There was a near brush with catastrophe at Harrisburg, Pennsylvania, in 1979 when a series of mechanical failures and human error nearly caused a meltdown. Radioactive steam and gas escaped. Pregnant women and young children within five miles of the power station were advised to leave the area. Evacuation plans for 165,000 residents had been prepared before the reactor was finally shut down. Even so, radiation levels within the containment dome are reported to be so high that sections of it must remain sealed for at least a year. The Russians appear to have had a nuclear accident when an explosion among nuclear wastes two decades ago polluted a vast area—and all the people living there—with radioactive material.

Meanwhile, the amount of electricity generated by nuclear reactors has been rising and proponents can argue that compared with the accident rate for, say, Savery's steam engine, these early stages of a new technology—apart from the Soviet accident—give reason on the whole for optimism and for pressing forward with a program which lessens dependence on imported oil. But one should note in passing that for most nations, dependence on imported oil will only be replaced by dependence on imported nuclear technology and fuel, since these are monopolized by a handful of nations.

Even so, these arguments for relative "independence" and for "reducing oil consumption" are a powerful counter to yet another of nuclear energy's drawbacks—its rising costs. Nuclear processes—mining and refining the ore, enriching it, fabricating and using the fuel rods, storing the wastes—begin to look as though it will cost $2,500 to $3,000 to deliver an extra kilowatt to the consumer. In other words, it can cost $300 to install the nuclear capacity to power one 100-watt light bulb. We should remember, too, that nuclear reactors will have to be dismantled after twenty to thirty years of operation, and this will demand the disposal of thousands of tons of highly radioactive material, which in turn will cost millions of dollars. At such prices, nuclear power begins to look commercially very unattractive. In fact, in 1976 Westinghouse Corporation reported losses of up to a billion dollars, General Electric of $500 million. General Atomic, a subsidiary of Gulf Oil, withdrew from the nuclear business altogether in 1975. Only foreign sales saved the large German supplier Kraftwerk Union from going the same way. But even its future remains uncertain now that its two major foreign customers, Brazil and Iran, have cut back their ambitious expansion plans because of costs or crisis. In fact, the suspicion has arisen that in buying nuclear power stations at this stage, the Third World may be buying what the industrialized world is showing less and less inclination to order itself.

Admittedly, cost has not been the only problem. A long Western slump has slowed down the growth of electricity demand. And earlier projections for the rapid expansion of nuclear power overlooked the fact that nuclear-generated electricity cannot yet compete with other energy sources for the two major energy demands of an industrial economy— space heating and power for road and air transport. It is generally too expensive for space heating. And electric vehicles are many years from making a significant contribution to transport. Yet these two categories make up some two-thirds of an industrial nation's total energy demand.

One should also add that a profound and growing public mistrust of nuclear power, and angry interventions to stop construction at sites proposed for particular reactors, also explain why few reactors have been ordered in the last four or five years. It is significant that in West Germany in June 1978, the Green Front, a new ecological political grouping, took some 17 percent of the vote in the Hamburg election on basically an antinuclear stand. A few months later, on a wider scale, the Austrian people in a special national referendum voted against the com- missioning of the nation's first nuclear power station. The margin was small, with 50.5 percent of the voters opposing the commissioning. But they did so against the fervent advice of a popular chancellor.

These difficulties of expense, of wastes, of possible malfunction, and of public mistrust are enough to slow down the more optimistic conclusions about nuclear energy's long-term contribution to electricity generation. But the present commercial nuclear power stations are also using a wasting resource. Fissile uranium, like fossil fuels, has finite re- serves. True, what is not worth recovering at twenty-five dollars a kilo- gram may look very attractive at fifty. Lower-grade ores can then be exploited. But nuclear programs based on present commercial plants cannot be the basis of a massive—and long-term—energy strategy, since the fuel they use will simply run out.

However, there exists another type of fission reactor—at present only in experimental forms—which promises to expand some sixtyfold the energy obtainable from uranium. It can also make a nation with a major nuclear industry independent of imported uranium. This alterna- tive is the fast breeder reactor. The fast breeder can use as fuel the pluto- nium extracted from the wastes of conventional reactors. We have al- ready noted that fissile uranium is found only in low concentrations in naturally occurring uranium. The rest is the more stable uranium 238. The fast breeder can actually convert this uranium 238 into plutonium fuel while generating electricity—and at the end of the day there is more nuclear fuel than at the start. The fast breeder can thus use the far more abundant uranium 238 as a fuel, after converting it into plutonium.

But in the same measure, the potential risks are almost beyond computation. The margins of safety for the nuclear experiment which wear thin enough for the present generation of nuclear power stations break down with fast-breeder programs. The reactor core contains far more fissile material than in conventional reactors—and there exists an undeniable possibility of the core rearranging itself to give a nuclear explosion. If this is not contained by the reactor's shielding, the far more potent brew in the reactor core, with the higher concentration of fissile material and of the especially lethal and long-lasting actinides, could cause ten to one hundred times the damage of a comparable release from a conventional reactor.

Moreover, since the fast breeder's operation depends upon the widespread use of plutonium, it must increase the risk of plutonium diversion to the making of nuclear bombs. A fast-breeder program demands reprocessing plants to separate out the needed plutonium. Once a nation can separate plutonium from its nuclear-reactor wastes, it can easily move on to bomb fabrication. A lump of plutonium the size of an orange is enough to make a bomb. In fact, an American student was able to design a crude but effective plutonium bomb using only standard and easily available reference texts.

It is for this reason that the United States is not constructing such reprocessing plants—in an attempt, through its example, to deter weapons proliferation. Britain and France have taken no such precaution. Their reprocessing plants will separate plutonium from the nuclear wastes they reprocess as part of an international commercial operation. Both claim that such reprocessing makes it much safer to deal with high-level wastes from existing reactors. The plutonium ceases to be a waste and becomes a potential fuel for fast breeders. But neither nation has seriously considered alternative methods of waste processing to ensure safe disposal methods that do *not* involve separating plutonium from other discards, and the reason is their intention to move on to the fast-breeder phase.

This commitment completely changes the scale—and danger—of the use of nuclear power. Quite apart from the special dangers of the supercharged reactor and of weapons proliferation, with the vastly expanded fuel base, the global program could involve sixty times the reactors, tens of thousands of tons of plutonium, and a vast increase in the toxic wastes which must still be disposed of. Incredibly, an official estimate made in 1976 by the U.K. Atomic Energy Authority forecast the commissioning of at least three large conventional and one very large fast breeder reactor every year in overcrowded Britain after 1990—with three or more fast breeders commissioned every year after 2010. And all this before any serious expert has suggested a certain program for waste disposal.

Those who support the fast-breeder program argue that no military thefts have yet occurred. They also point out that the bulk of the plutonium will be safely inside the reactor core and that for transportation between reactors, reprocessing plants, and fuel-fabrication plants, the material can be carried in eighty-ton containers which even the most determined hijacker could not pick up. Various ways of minimizing the weapons-proliferation danger have been suggested—for example, keeping the volume of plutonium in circulation to a minimum and using new reprocessing technologies that leave the separated plutonium in too impure a state for easy bomb fabrication. But any country acquiring basic plutonium-handling reprocessing technology can (with minor modifications) produce weapons-grade plutonium. And the eighty-ton container to transport the plutonium is no security against the ultimate and almost certain risk—the inside job. Among the white-coated PhD.'s working in the nuclear industry, who can be certain that no educated terrorist, rejecting what the Baader-Meinhof group term the "criminality of affluence," may not be prepared to procure the needed plutonium with the "idealistic" motive of blowing up what is perceived as a rotten society? This contemptuous and hate-driven rejection of contemporary civilization is at the root of much of Europe's young Baader-Meinhof type of terrorism in recent years. It can hardly be said that social improvement is now so evident that the disgust and the violence will conveniently fade away.

Nor are the young and the alienated alone to be feared. A kilogram of heroin sells for $150,000 on the black market—what will be the going rate for an orange's worth of plutonium? And short of outright criminality, there is already evidence of inside connivance. When two hundred tons of uranium on route from Antwerp to Genoa disappeared without trace in 1968, the whole business was hushed up with the apparent co-operation of one or two high officials in Euratom—the European Atomic Control Agency. We could expect no better outcome from the future in which the number of fast breeder reactors would be constantly on the increase. Security arrangements would have to become so strict and widespread as to threaten civil liberties and even then, they would not deter the Baader-Meinhof spirit. There is only one conclusion. The plutonium path is too dangerous for mankind to follow.

This conclusion does not invalidate the possibility that some nations—especially those lacking fossil-fuel reserves—may make use of fission as a temporary means of bridging the gap between the depletion of oil and natural-gas supplies and the expansion of safe, renewable energy sources. Clearly they must demonstrate first that they can safely store all the wastes arising from such a program—and demonstrate that such storage is more than the present range of stop-gap measures. There is sufficient reasonably priced uranium to fuel modest nuclear programs for at least fifty years. New uranium discoveries and new extraction and enrichment technologies can enlarge the resource base. In addition, there may be alternative methods of making the planet's supply of nuclear fuel go further. One possibility now being investigated is the use of the "thorium cycle," where naturally occurring thorium is converted into another fissile form of uranium—uranium 233. This may be one way of extending the amount of usable energy obtainable from fission without the separation and "liberation" of plutonium and without the need for intrinsically more dangerous reactor designs.

We are left with one further long-term nuclear option—the possibility of fusion power. Fusion as a process appears to create far fewer noxious wastes, has virtually unlimited fuel in the oceans' deuterium, and produces no weapons-grade material. Further research is clearly in order. But despite recent breakthroughs in fusion research, even the most optimistic forecasts do not see fusion making a significant contribution to our energy needs until well into the next century. Even then, the sheer size of the commercial plants suggests a high degree of centralization and hence a certain built-in vulnerability. Like present commercial nuclear-reactor designs, perhaps they should be used—*if* there are no alternatives—since a world without energy is arguably as dangerous to life as any risks from either of these. But in fact the whole nuclear debate turns on a different point—that there *are* other strategies for energy, which do not involve such dauntingly dangerous alternatives, and that with their use and with more conserving ways of living, humanity can have not only energy but safety too. These options must now be examined.

3 ENERGY ALTERNATIVES

BEFORE WE LOOK at the various alternatives to nuclear power, there is one fact—almost an unconscious fact—of bureaucratic and academic inertia, or rather momentum, which must be recognized. When vast sums of money, powerful institutions, and governmental departments become committed to a course of action, it is incredibly difficult for them to change course. Like Leviathan, they require enormous sea room for any change in direction, and sometimes, perhaps again like Leviathan, they do not appear to be creatures susceptible to a very lively change of ideas.

Energy research has been, for the last thirty years, almost wholly dominated by the nuclear option. The reasons have been suggested—a desire to "redeem" the bomb for peaceful purposes, institutional inertia, the existence of large organizations and teams of experts committed to the nuclear experiment and anxious to make more of it. And this inertia has, paradoxically enough, been increased by the throw-away world price for crude oil in the fifties and sixties. Few agencies had any interest in alternatives or in conservation or in cost effectiveness while oil and natural gas appeared to be pouring from an endless cornucopia. Private interest assumed a continued bonanza. Most research was conducted by public money and was, as it were, locked into the nuclear option since that was where, in the war, the bulk of research money had been expended and where it might now be turned to more acceptable use. The figures tell the tale. In 1971, 90 percent of the public money for energy research and development in the United States went to nuclear energy. By contrast, energy conservation received around 1 percent, solar energy none at all. France, West Germany, Japan, and the United Kingdom also had energy-research budgets dominated by the nuclear option. By the mid-seventies, nuclear-research budgets were exceeding $150 million a year in each of these nations. In the United States, the figure exceeded a billion dollars a year. And up to 1974, resources for any alternatives were comparatively very minor. In fact, in Britain and Western Europe, many promising lines of research in coal technology were simply dropped in the 1950s, as bone-cheap oil and gas surged in.

Nor was the international scene any different. The *only* agencies concerned with energy—the International Atomic Energy Agency and Euratom—were, as their names suggest, concerned wholly with nuclear issues. And yet, as a final perversity, we have to accept the fact that in spite of all the research, all the dedication, all the fixation of purpose, no nation in the world gets more than a few percent of its energy supplies from nuclear power. In 1976, the United Kingdom's nuclear power stations supplied less than 2 percent of the energy delivered to the consumer—and this in return for thousands of millions of pounds invested in the program, thirteen functioning nuclear power stations, the enrichment and reprocessing plants, and all the nuclear-research institutions.

But the fixation on nuclear research, the overwhelming preponderance of nuclear interest, does not, of course, mean that there are no alternative fuels or strategies. It simply means that until recently, officials and institutions and committed scientists have not been thinking about them or clamoring to have them open to wider research and better funding. But the first point to be made absolutely clear is that mankind does not face a stark choice between abundant energy and shrinking supplies in a matter of decades. The time spans for reflection and choice are much longer and can be used in far more varied ways as oil and gas begin to phase themselves out.

As we have seen, there is fairly general agreement that constraints on both oil and natural-gas supplies will occur within the next two decades. By the year 2000, new discoveries are not expected to more than equal 1977 consumption. The increasing pressure on supplies will tend to limit the consumption of oil more and more to its most valuable uses—as a feedstock for the chemical industries and in transport. But on what scale and how fast oil and gas resources will diminish can hardly be fixed, since—to give only three obvious examples—a breakthrough in the generation and use of hydrogen as a fuel, a spreading use of alcohol fuels derived from plants, or even a widespread increase in electric vehicles, would very considerably prolong the use of oil for other purposes. However, there is no basic quarrel with the contention that a profligate humanity will probably have run through much of its millennial reserves of oil and gas in less than a century. For the twenty-first century, other fuels will be required.

Two alternative sources of oil itself—tar sands and oil shale—may well exist in very considerable quantities. But tar sands are relatively inaccessible and costs are still uncertain. Oil shale must contain a certain percentage of an essential ingredient—kerogen. Most reserves appear to have too low a level, and even where, as in the Rocky Mountains, large high-grade reserves exist, the technical problems of extracting them at a competitive price and without unacceptable environmental disruption have yet to be resolved. Neither of these sources will contribute significantly to world fuel supplies until *in situ* methods for extracting the oil are fully developed.

It follows that for the next century, one of the most interesting and cost-effective sources of fuel will quite simply be good old-fashioned coal. There is of course one proviso—that a much greater technical and social effort be mounted for the safety and well-being of the world's coal miners. But if this is undertaken, there can be no doubt about the possible scale of use. The most recent estimates—those made for the World Energy Conference in 1977—put the world's coal reserves at over 600 billion tons, all but 70 billion in the Northern Hemisphere. Even assuming a tripling of present annual output (about 2,230 million tons in 1975) a century of assured supply lies ahead for the industrialized nations, and a wide range of new technologies begin to make coal look a much more attractive primary fuel than in the days of pea-soup fogs.

The introduction of fluidized-bed combustors allows coal of all grades—with the addition, where suitable, of municipal trash—to be burnt on a bed of inert ash or sand through which air is blown up at such speed that the mixture of burning fuel and ash is transformed into a "fluid" bed. Temperatures can be controlled and chemicals added to prevent slag or clinker being formed in pipes and boilers, and the process largely eliminates the enormous amounts of sulphur and nitrogen oxides that used to be produced.

These new combustion beds have the convenience of coming in various sizes. To understand the importance of this, we must look briefly at the process of electricity generation. The heat produced by burning the fuel—or by the nuclear reaction—in a power station is used to raise steam which then powers the turbines which generate the electricity. About a third of the heat is transformed into electricity. The rest is usually dispersed as waste heat in cooling towers or dumped as hot water into nearby rivers or the sea. There are further losses in transmitting and distributing the electricity to the consumer. To get one unit of energy from the power station's furnace to the home as electricity means up to three units of waste heat along the way.

The simple solution is to put your power station next to a factory or in an urban area. The waste heat can then be piped to heat nearby buildings or used for process heat in factories. A company might even have its own power station providing both heat and electricity—the so-called cogeneration unit. But large power stations are usually too remote from factories and urban areas and produce too much waste heat for it to be easily usable. Nuclear power stations tend to be sited in remote country areas where there are large volumes of water for cooling and few citizens to object to their construction or be contaminated in the event of a serious accident. But coal-burning fludized-bed combustors can be safely used at the core of industrial or urban areas within combined heat and power, or cogeneration, units. What was formerly regarded as waste heat is now used for process heat or district heating, enormously increasing the efficiency with which the fuel is used. Alternatively, the combustors can be used simply as boilers for process heat or district heating.

Britain's National Coal Board is already operating an experimental pressurized fluidized-bed combustor, built onto the end of a power station at Grimthorpe in Yorkshire, which can raise 85 megawatts of heat.* An unpressurized version has been developed by a British firm, Babcock and Wilcox, and has interested American buyers sufficiently for the Ohio State Energy and Resource Development Authority to order four such boilers for its own experimental use. Large pressurized fluidized beds that burn coal for electricity generation are being developed in Britain and in the United States.

Fluidized-bed combustors are also beginning to be manufactured to burn coal on a domestic scale, to take the place of oil-fired furnaces; coal deliveries to these small units may soon be simplified by the provision of convenient powdered coal, with delivery systems geared to

---

*Although "watts" and "megawatts" are units usually associated with electricity, they are units of power and thus can be used to state the power of any energy source.

removing the spent ash. In the public sphere, coal-fired fluidized-bed combustors may also be used to power both trains and ships.

Fluidized-bed technology is playing a central role in some promising experiments in Britain that could lead to commercial "coalplexes." The basic idea is to use suitable coal as a feedstock in refineries designed to extract the various useful components from coal, just as oil refineries today produce a wide variety of products from crude oil. Both petroleum and feedstock for the chemical industry can be derived from coal, and various different techniques for extracting valuable liquids and gases from coal have now reached the pilot-plant stage in Britain as part of a £120-million research and development program for coal announced in May 1978. The West Germans, too, have announced a long-term investment program to revitalize their flagging coal industry, since coal is the nation's only abundant fossil-fuel resource.

Technology is further advanced in another possible and useful transformation of coal—into substitute natural gas (SNG). There is of course nothing new in the basic aim. In fact, the first United States company to set up a coal-into-gas business began in Baltimore as early as 1816. "Town gas," as it came to be called, was made all over the industrialized world by heating coal in airtight retorts, releasing its gases, and using the 70 percent of the material remaining as coking or heating fuel. The mixture of released gases formed a usable domestic fuel. In fact it had only one severe drawback—the inclusion of carbon monoxide, a poison which made gas ovens a favorite resort for suicide. The absence of this poison from natural gas, and its higher calorific value, meant that the discovery of natural gas closed down municipal gasworks everywhere. But with the prospective constraints on natural-gas supplies, new techniques are being developed to produce coal-derived gas that is virtually identical to natural gas. Britain has an operating pilot plant and is working with the United States on the design and development of a complete demonstration plant for Ohio. The West Germans are building a pilot plant in Dorsten. If the economics prove feasible, such coal-transformers could provide a substitute natural gas for use in the nation's pipelines as supplies of natural gas begin to run out in the twenty-first century. And for nations with coal, manufacturing SNG may be cheaper than importing natural gas from the Middle East. Another possible coal-gasification option is the production of a gas with lower calorific value than SNG which can be used to generate electricity in a combined cycle generator with an over-all efficiency of 45 percent or more, far higher than that achieved by nuclear and conventional coal-fired power stations.

However, none of these new possibilities means coal is anything more than a temporary and provisional answer to the planet's energy problems. Its supplies, though vast, are finite. The more accessible coal desposits are in only a few countries—the Soviet Union, North America, and China have over 90 percent of the known world reserves. Nations lacking large coal reserves, such as Japan and Italy, cannot be sure that well-supplied nations with exportable reserves will be ready to meet their needs. Coal also offers almost no answer to shortages in most Third World Nations—a point to which we will return.

There are also grave environmental problems. Unless scrupulous regulation is observed, strip mining can turn whole countrysides into landscapes as desolate as those of the moon. But the largest question mark hanging over a steady increase in coal burning—or indeed fossil-fuel use of any kind—is the global environmental risk of so increasing the amount of carbon dioxide in the atmosphere that catastrophic changes in climate might be precipitated. There is no certainty here. A further complication is the effect of other pollutants in the atmosphere, and there is uncertainty about the contribution deforestation may make to increasing the atmospheric concentration of carbon dioxide. We must return to the critical issues of reafforestation and climatic imbalance on a later page. Here it is only necessary to point to these risks in relation to increased use of coal. They call for steady monitoring. They over-whelmingly reinforce the case for drastic policies of energy conservation. But they do not make coal the necessary villain of a drama in which violent climatic change ends the human experiment.

No doubt, when social historians look back on our day, they will be astonished at our almost obsessive concern with sufficient supplies of energy. Our planet is, after all, one vast system of energy. The sun's rays that fall just on the roads of North America contain more energy than all the fossil fuel used each year in the whole world. The winds that rage and whisper round the planet are a vast energy reserve caused by the uneven solar heating of blazing tropics and arctic poles. The World Meteorological Organization (WMO) estimates that if placed on the earth's most steadily windy sites, windmills totaling 20 million mega-watts of electric generating capacity might produce electricity at a commercial price. (At present, the world's total electric generating capacity is under 2 million megawatts.) In the Southern continents, less than 6 percent of the power that could be produced by large hydroelectric schemes has been developed, and this figure leaves out the multitude of small hydro sites, so numerous that once developed, they could exceed an electrical output of many thousand megawatts.

Nor should we forget the energy locked up in plants and wastes. Indeed, in some developing lands, 90 percent of the energy is derived from wood, often with disastrous risks of deforestation. At the other end of the scale of sophistication, the U.S. Naval Undersea Center at San Diego has an ocean-farm project cultivating Californian kelp. The hope is that the solar energy captured by the plant on an ocean farm of, say, 470 square miles could theoretically be converted into as much natural gas as is consumed in America at present. All in all, the fear of running out of energy must be said to have a social, not a rational base. Modern citizens have become so accustomed to fossil fuels and so transfixed by the necessity of building vast electricity systems that they simply do not see that their whole life is surrounded by a multiplicity and variety of energy reserves which not only exceed all present sources but have a further advantage: they are not exhausted by use. A ton of oil burnt is a ton lost. A ton of kelp will be growing again next year. Even more reliably, the sun will rise and release an annual 1.5 quadrillion megawatt hours of solar energy to the planet's outer atmosphere. There can be no running out of such resources.

But can they be harnessed? A tornado is a fine exhibit of energy unleashed but is hardly a useful one. The fundamental question with all the renewable sources of energy is how to develop the technologies for using and storing them, and to do so at reasonable cost. Admittedly, this issue of "reasonable cost" begs a number of questions. It fails to take into consideration the huge and now discounted investment in nuclear-weapons research upon which fission power is based. It neglects a whole range of environmental and social costs—from strip mining coal to radioactive-waste disposal. And over a twenty-five-year period, the whole energy picture was totally distorted by the fact that oil and natural gas, both wasting resources, fell in price while their scarcity was actually increasing.

The truth is that all of us, consumers, technicians, engineers, scientists, have a tendency to see what we are used to seeing, and a twenty-five-year energy "binge" based on fossil fuels has conditioned us to looking for a very narrow range of solutions. Perhaps the first need of all is for citizens in developed societies to open the eyes of their imagination and conceive of energy patterns which will come in new shapes, forms, and sizes. If they do, they will find it already clear that the technologies *are* available, *will* become cheaper, and *could* even lead to a more humane and civilized mode of existence.

We can begin with the most abundant of all sources—solar energy. The first point is that at least one-third of most developed nations' energy budgets is required for temperatures of well under 100 degrees centigrade—in other words, for hot water and space heating. Sunlight can provide useful heat for both of these needs at exactly the right temperature—and there are no distribution costs, since the sun can fall on each building. We should also remember that the sun already does much of our space heating without any cost or equipment at all. Picture the problem if every house, store, and factory had to begin heating itself from a temperature of minus 240 degrees centigrade.*

But for particular uses and locations, the diffuseness and irregularity of the sun's radiance have to be overcome. Much can be done by the almost forgotten arts of good siting and good design, so that, for instance, a southern orientation is combined with overhanging roofs which allow the low winter sun to shine through windows and exclude the excessive heat from the higher summer sun. Thick walls of masonry are also heat traps in winter and exclude unwanted heat in summer. The traditional architecture of the Middle East, besides being beautiful, has a singular technical appropriateness for dealing with high daytime temperatures and chilly nights.

But the sun traps can be more specific. Instead of just relying on generally well constructed buildings, one can add a "thermal storage wall." A thick block of masonry is placed behind a "window" of glass and traps the solar heat coming through. A simple series of vents circulates the heat round the house, and when the weather changes, the vents are reversed to expel the hot air and cool the house down. In 1961, a whole school was built in Wallasey, in Britain, on this principle, with a glazed south wall and thick concrete walls and floors to store the heat captured from the sun. Internal heat, given off by lights and people, is also circulated; the whole school is insulated; and from the day of its inauguration, it has used no other fuels at all—and this without any com-

*This is an estimate for the earth's temperature if there were no sun. Other factors, such as geothermal energy—the heat flowing from the earth's core—also contribute, although they appear minimal beside the massive inflow from the sun.

plaints about chilblains or little pinched red noses. Yet Wallasey is hardly in the sunbelt.

Other kinds of solar collection units can be smaller and more easily added to places that are already built. The simplest form is a "flat-plate collector"—a glass-covered panel which allows the sunlight to pass through the glass and be trapped as heat inside what is basically a boxlike apparatus whose collecting powers have been much enhanced by the use of new materials. This heat is then passed on to the house's hot-water system, or can supplement its space heating.

Literally millions of these solar collectors have been sold in Japan, Australia, Israel, and the United States. In fact, in northern Australia they are a mandatory part of house construction, and at the other end of the globe, solar panels in Long Island have shown that they can provide 75 percent of a house's hot water and pay for themselves in saved fuel costs in not much more than five years. The Tennessee Valley Authority is installing solar collectors on a thousand Memphis houses. Householders pay for their collectors over twenty years through a fixed monthly charge of thirteen dollars added to the electric bill. But the solar collectors provide three-quarters of an average family's hot water, so the reduction in electricity consumption is expected to more than offset the extra monthly charge. And the TVA stands to gain as much. The more solar collectors it installs, the fewer new power stations it has to build. If successful, the scheme will be extended to a hundred thousand houses.

In the near future the cost of these solar panels will be significantly reduced. Many of them are made almost by hand by small firms. Once the market is large enough, the big manufacturers will begin much larger production runs and turn out these units at very much lower cost. The big manufacturers are also conducting research into concentrating solar collectors so that higher temperatures can be reached. These would greatly widen the solar collectors' possible range of use.

Possibly the most interesting and promising of all solar devices is the photovoltaic cell, a spin-off from space exploration, which directly turns the sun's radiance into electricity which can then be used for all manner of domestic and commercial purposes. Such cells, incorporated into the roof, could give homes and factories in hot climates virtually their own independent energy source and still leave over heat for space and water heating—one reason why some prophets see the tropics as likely to become as thoroughly transformed by solar power as was the chilly north by coal and steam. A major breakthrough is needed in the price of photovoltaic cells, but this appears to be on the way, as production costs are falling dramatically year by year and may soon be near the "competitive" price of $500 per peak kilowatt: in 1958, unit costs per peak kilowatt were $200,000; in 1977 they were $10,000; by the early eighties they should reach $500 and by the late eighties even fall as low as $50–$150.

Another possibility that is arousing increasing interest is that of using solar power as an integral part of new or existing generating systems, so that traditional fuels—coal, oil, gas—can be saved and reserved simply for peak periods (or for cloudy days). Two forms look promising. One is a "power tower." A boiler is fitted into a tower, and computer-guided reflectors follow the sun round the sky focusing the beams on the boiler, which then produces steam for driving the turbines. A two-hundred-foot tower with 5,500 mirrors focusing on it is now operating in Albuquerque and this will serve as a testbed for a 10-megawatt solar power tower in California, which by 1981 will become the first solar power station in the United States to deliver electricity to the grid.

This kind of linkage is clearly interesting other power companies. The French have already used a small prototype tower to feed electricity into the grid as part of their solar-research program. The EEC has agreed to build a 1-megawatt tower in Sicily to study the possibilities of expansion. Experimental power towers are also being built in Spain and Japan.

The other area of research is "solar farms." Parabolic reflectors, spread over a wide land area, concentrate sunlight onto pipes containing salts or gases. As they heat up—to as much as 600 degrees centigrade—their energy is transferred to storage tanks, and it can be drawn on when needed to produce steam for electricity generation. The limitation on both the solar farm and the power tower is that they require large sites and are perhaps most suitable for desert areas, where they are not too likely to be next door to busy consumer centers. (On the other hand, they may well require no more distant and isolated sites than those thought safe for nuclear power stations, given citizens' growing unwillingness to have nuclear power plants too near their own particular neighborhoods.) On this point of land requirements, we should note that the small-scale solar collectors which fit on rooftops and walls do not compete for land with agriculture, urban development, or recreation, since they are placed in areas already in use.

When we turn to wind power, once again the problem lies with the technologies for effectively using the inexhaustible cost-free but diffused wind power round our planet. Techniques can vary from the simplicity of the fleets of windmills in central Crete, where over ten thousand of them pump up the farmers' irrigation water by catching the wind in triangles of white sailcloth, all the way to the completely new and complex concept which now interests the U.S. Department of Energy. The inventor, James Yen, has designed a circular tower and uses the wind to induce a mini-tornado inside. Then the difference in pressure between the outside air and the inner turbulence drives a turbine. This kind of tower could clearly operate on a quite small and dispersed scale or, like solar towers, be used to supplement grid systems.

Conventional wind turbines are also being thought of for windier sites, and a great variety of new techniques—from traditional propeller types to contrivances that look like vast eggbeaters turned upside down—are beginning to leave the researchers' drawing boards. One such upside-down eggbeater—a so-called Darreius rotor—is already feeding electricity into the grid in Canada. Since the larger the scale, the greater the capture of energy, it seems likely that the WMO picture of a wind-driven world, although much exaggerated, could have some elements of reality by 2025. Scandinavian governments in particular are assessing wind turbines' role in future energy supplies. A Danish college at Tvind has built the world's largest wind turbine to cut down its enormous fuel bills—and is now virtually self-sufficient in both heat and electricity, exporting surplus electricity to the regional grid. The county of Elsinore in Denmark is seriously investigating the possibility of building a bank of wind turbines along Zealand's north coast to supply all the county's electricity. The United States has three 200-kilowatt wind turbines feeding electricity into various grids, and one ten times this size is being constructed in North Carolina. Sweden, Britain, and West Germany are also constructing large experimental wind turbines.

When we turn to falling water as a source of energy—for hydroelectricity—the big reserves are in the developing world, since the industrialized nations have used up most of their best sites, and there is a limiting factor here—in both developed and developing lands. The reservoirs of big dams cannot be permitted to flood irreplaceable natural ecosystems or invaluable farmland. Where larger new water-power resources may be available in the industrialized nations is on the coast. There are a number of sites such as the river Severn in Britain or the Bay of Fundy in North America where the rise and fall of tides is on a sufficient scale to justify the kind of system the French have been operating at La Rance, where reversible-blade turbines allow power to be generated both when the tide ebbs and when it flows. The Russians, too, have an operating tidal power station—although at pilot-project level—and are now looking at several sites at which viable tidal power stations may be possible.

Quite new experiments are being considered for use in areas where the seas are normally stormy. It is suggested that the waves' power can be used to generate electricity, and several research groups in Britain, Sweden, and Japan are experimenting with different ways of tapping this source. There is a particularly promising project in Mauritius. Yet another proposal is to use the difference in temperature between deep and surface water as a power generator. In the tropics, the sun-warmed surface water is ten or more degrees centigrade warmer than water 1,000 to 15,000 feet below it. By the early 1980s, a 25-megawatt prototype should be operating off the Florida coast, with the possibility of a commercial demonstration plant by 1985.

All these renewable energy sources—sun, wind, waves, tides—can be used as substitutes for fossil fuels and contribute to the production of electricity. But they can only produce power intermittently—the wind, for certain, "bloweth where [and when] it listeth"—and this may well not be at a time of peak load or urgent domestic demand. During sunless, windless, waveless winter days in, say, northwestern Europe, all the renewable-energy technologies will not be producing very much. Yet consumer demand for energy will be very high. Oil—as gasoline or as a heating fuel—and natural gas are easily and cheaply stored. Fuel can be drawn from the store when its heat or its power is required. But you cannot simply turn on the sun or the wind. So methods of storing their energy must be found if they are to meet a sizable part of an industrial nation's energy ends.

A good deal of research is therefore being concentrated on methods of economical storage of energy for heat or power. Large volumes of water or rocks are normally proposed as heat stores—although special salt solutions are likely to be far more compact and easy to install, once the technology is fully developed and mass produced. Another promising approach is the use of reversible chemical reactions that give off or absorb heat, depending on the direction in which the reaction is going. As spare heat—say, from a solar panel—is fed into the vessel containing the chemicals, the reaction goes one way, absorbing the heat. The reaction can then be reversed when the heat is needed.

Storage, however, is a problem with all grid systems, coal-based, oil-based, nuclear, which supply electricity. That we may be surprised by this fact simply reflects the degree to which we have become accustomed to the idea of having a very large number of generating stations which come on stream only at times of peak load—over the breakfast eggs or Sunday lunch or when the advertisement break in a highly popular television series sends half the population to the kitchen for a cup of coffee. These "surges" are only containable today within a system of continuous and expensive *over*capacity. The trick is to get types of storage that are cheap enough to take its place. Otherwise it will have to be maintained (at high expense) for the dank, still days when wind and sun power will be insufficient for peak use. A variety of ways are being explored. Surplus electricity can be used to compress air, charge up a large flywheel, or pump water up to a high reservoir. In each case, the "energy store" can be drawn on when needed as we now draw on our extra generating capacity. Another possibility is to generate hydrogen from water, store it, and then use it when needed to fuel a conventional power plant or generate electricity directly in a fuel call. Then, at the consumer end, the surges can be minimized by encouraging small domestic energy stores. For example, a greatly reduced electricity tariff for off-peak hours can encourage the use of hot water tanks that heat up "off peak" and then supply the house's hot water needs for the whole day. Such tanks would, incidentally, have to be larger than conventional ones and, of course, well insulated.

There remain two further sources of energy income—geothermal fields and organic materials. Both of these are far less intermittent sources of energy than the sun or wind. Geothermal energy comes from the heat flowing from the earth's interior, and geothermal plants are generating electricity or providing space heating in several countries, including Iceland, Italy, Japan, Mexico, New Zealand, and the United States. However, the number of geothermal fields that are hot enough to generate electricity efficiently is limited. And the fields which provide no more than the heat needed for space heating are often at some distance from urban areas that could use them. It does not look as though geothermal energy has more than a regional contribution to make.

Organic material is itself an energy store—or it can be converted into a liquid or gaseous fuel for convenient storage. We will look at possible ways of using organic wastes in developed lands in a later chapter. The chief opportunities for "biomass conversion" on an important scale are in the wet tropics, and discussion of them, too, belongs in a later chapter. But there are opportunities for increasing energy crops in fully developed lands. Some experts, for instance, maintain that if, on a sustained-yield basis, the Swedes converted their forests from pulp and paper making to the provision of fuel, they would not need to export paper in order to secure imported oil. Self-sufficiency in energy would be secured—and the world's flagging wastepaper industry would receive a tremendous boost. One need not think only of trees. A fair amount of good agricultural land could be used more intensively. For instance, it has been estimated that planting winter rye in the American plains would produce an energy crop before the spring maize sowing. Inevitably, the perennial farming risk—of taking out more than is put in and in effect mining the soil—has to be watched. But good husbandry is in all cases the precondition of successful farming. Fuel crops are today omitted from the annual cycle not because they are deleterious, but simply because with rock-bottom oil prices they have not been worthwhile. Now, with rising prices and shrinking reserves, all the new possibilities—sun, wind, water, plants—can begin to enter the public imagination, and there are at last signs that the mood is changing. The range of new experiment is not negligible and there is evidence of growing momentum. For instance, the U.S. Department of Energy's solar budget for 1979 is between $400 million and $500 million. The Swedish government will be funding over three years a major program of research into biomass conversion, wind power, and solar power The French spent some $32 million on solar energy in 1978. Apparently, they see solar technology as a major potential industry with excellent export prospects. The Japanese government has a billion-dollar research program, Operation Sunshine, to develop energy-income technologies that could lessen their extreme dependence on imported fuels. As all these technologies begin to take hold, the effects may go much further than the provision of energy. They may well imply profound and beneficent changes in the whole developed way of life; give choice, variety, and safe options to the central process of energy use; and begin to dig mankind out of the nuclear rut.

4 SAVING FUEL

IN THEORY, at least, a lasting and beneficent shift to safe and renewable forms of energy can be made more credible and secure by the sheer wastefulness of our present use. So wide is the margin for almost painless saving that one might think it obvious that the route of conservation would be easily, even gratefully, followed. But it is not so. After the energy bonanza of the fifties and sixties, most citizens in developed lands tend to take it for granted that more and more "energy slaves," doing everything from cooking instant dinners to running customers down to the supermarket to bringing the National Philharmonic Orchestra in stereo into the family living room, are entirely indispensable. Older axioms have faded. The essential link in word and meaning between "thrifty" and "thrive" is no longer made. While President Carter declared the effort to use less energy to be "the moral equivalent of war," American citizens pushed gasoline demand in the summer of 1977 to its highest level in four years and crude-oil imports to an all-time record. And it took eighteen months of dispute before a weakened version of the president's national energy plan was passed by Congress.

The nature of the most vocal opposition—that of oil, electric, and automobile companies—has been strong enough to give the ordinary citizen the alibi that tolerance, indeed support, for high and wasteful fuel consumption is simply a reflection of powerful "vested interests." Provided it is understood that these "interests" include state-owned corporations like Britain's Central Electricity Generating Board or Italy's ENEL or France's Électricité de France, one can accept an element of truth in the criticism. There certainly can be no doubt about the power. Almost without exception, oil, electric, and automobile companies are among the largest businesses, public or private, in North America and Western Europe.

None of these companies wants high fuel prices to discourage steadily expanding consumer demand. This explains the American oil companies' total opposition to such measures as taxes on oil and the electric utilities' opposition to any move to end the lowering of rates for increased use. Improving technology, increasing economies of scale, and rock-bottom fuel prices did, in the past, allow the utilities to keep electricity prices fairly stable and thus justify such practices. But as we have already noted, the scope for further economies of scale is now limited and larger markets will not necessarily mean lower unit costs. If declining block rates are still common, the practice is often expressly designed to dissuade larger commercial and industrial concerns from installing such fuel-conserving technologies as cogeneration equipment. Enthusiasm for rapidly expanding nuclear programs is partly based on hopes of lowered costs—although these have been somewhat dampened by the escalating costs of new nuclear power stations. But it is also based on visions of the "all-electric" economy which would give electric companies a vista of ever-expanding use and, it must be admitted, something very close to monopoly control over the whole economy.

Yet to pile all the blame on the vested interests leaves out the finally responsible "interest"—the citizens themselves. They cannot be held responsible for the waste inherent in most forms of electricity generation and transmission—although they should at least know about it. But they *can* be blamed for the mixture of indifference and ignorance with which the possibilities of energy conservation tend to be met. And just as long as there is insufficient citizen pressure, the chances of governments responding with well thought-out and practical energy-conserving programs remains slight indeed. It is exceptional to find decisions such as that reached by the West German Social Democratic party in November 1977 to postpone further nuclear expansion, giving priority to coal-fired power stations until the full scale of the risks—and possibilities—of storing the nuclear wastes are better understood and mastered. This germ of an "energy strategy" in the program of a major political party was inserted there precisely by citizen insistence and concern.

Provided this type of commitment can be maintained and expanded in developed societies, a very wide range of actions and policies may be employed to reduce energy consumption without in any real way cutting down citizens' convenience or service. On the contrary, in many instances, the same benefits turn out to be available at lower cost. The difference in per capita energy use between various countries with comparable living standards is *prima facie* evidence that this saving is not only practicable but even painless. It is no more uncomfortable to live in Stockholm than in Minneapolis. And more detailed examination reveals the enormous scale of savings which citizens can secure, provided they are ready to use a little thrift as the means of thriving.

We can begin in the home. Households consume at least a quarter of all rich nations' supply of energy, two-thirds of it to keep warm or cool, up to 20 percent to heat the water, and the balance for cooking appliances, television, and so forth. We must not, incidentally, talk in abstractions. People do not want "energy" as such. They want warm or cool rooms, steaming baths, convenient ovens, instant lighting up, working appliances, and entertainment. Among all these needs, the biggest savings can be extracted from the biggest user, space heating.

Savings depend, too, upon whether a house is, as it were, being "retrofitted" for energy conservation or whether a new house is being designed. A great deal can be done with existing homes. Savings of at least 40 to 50 percent are possible, not a negligible figure for the users of a quarter of the nations' total fuel supplies. Some of the means of conservation are so simple that it seems almost simple-minded to mention them. There are the many "do-it-yourself" techniques of insulation—filling the attics with thick insulating material, putting anti-draft strips around doors and windows, covering large windows at night with heavy curtains. In some of the leakier houses, the costs of such procedures are offset by lower fuel bills in a couple of years—and in some cases in a few months.

At the next stage of elaboration, windows can be double-glazed and cavity walls filled with insulating foam, with maximum insulation for the main living rooms. The work is obviously more expensive and recouping the cost out of savings on fuel bills may take longer. Yet the estimate is that in a reasonably well built family house in the United States, these methods of retrofitted insulation will reduce annual fuel consumption by 40 percent and pay for themselves in six years. The time will clearly be shorter as fuel prices—inevitably—continue to rise. It is also likely that in attached houses, a joint decision by occupants to insulate in roughly the same way will cut bills even further by increasing the degree of shared heat.

Hot water will demand less fuel if tanks are more carefully insulated. When hot water is needed only at certain hours—for example, in the early mornings and evenings—an automatic timer, turning the hot-water heater on and off at the appropriate times, is an obvious economizer. Then there is the solar panel already described, which can provide a large portion of a family's hot water. For such extra luxuries as heated swimming pools, solar energy can do virtually the complete job. Nor is solar-energy use confined solely to hot water. In a recent survey of a dozen American cities, it was discovered that solar systems could also take over part of the task of space heating and still only require nine to fourteen years of lower fuel bills for the recovery of the costs of installation. And the cost effectiveness of these systems is rising all the time.

Energy waste can also be cut back in our last category within the home—the various electrical appliances. Electricity is the only convenient, economical, or, if you like, "commercial" source of energy for household appliances, audio-visual equipment, and lighting. But improvements are possible. For instance, light bulbs' efficiency can be sharply improved. Fluorescent bulbs use half the electricity of standard ones, and some of the new fluorescent types being developed by the U.S. Department of Energy will reduce electricity consumption while lasting for years. Other energy savings include doing away with pilot lights on gas boilers, cookers, and water heaters and using electric igniters instead. Air conditioners vary enormously in efficiency. Some of them use over two and a half times more energy than other types to do the same work of cooling—a point to be remembered in the labeling of air conditioners for sale.

Finally, there are a couple of devices which affect general efficiency, one almost as old as the camp's first tended fire, the other comparatively new. The old one is simply to ensure that the house's furnace is regularly serviced and its efficiency maintained. The new one is the heat pump, a device which extracts the heat from the air or ground outside the house, upgrades it to a higher temperature, and releases this heat into the building. Its efficiency is improved by putting it in the loft—so it can recycle heat rising from the house below and utilize solar heat trapped in the attic. The heat pump can actually provide two to three times more heat than a standard electric fire or fan heater for each unit of electricity consumed. The recent development of a small, efficient, household unit could ensure its widespread use in space heating for new homes. In some cases, it could replace an old conventional electric heater in a house already built. In the future lies the possibility of a gas-powered heat pump that provides two to three times the useful heat of a gas fire for the same gas consumption.

All the changes suggested so far—and, added up, they are beginning to reach a 50 percent saving in fuels used in the home—can be applied to existing houses. The saving can be up to 70 percent or more when we come to the construction of new houses in which, from the beginning, maximum energy conservation is sought. The toughness and commitment of governments to higher insulation standards is critical at this point—and notably lax in many countries. In general, much of what was retrofitted to old homes can simply be utilized in the new construction—well-insulated roofs and walls, well-sealed and insulated doors and windows, solar panels. It is interesting to notice that in an experiment in Arkansas undertaken by the U.S. Department of Housing and Urban Development (HUD), two hundred houses were constructed with the full array of energy-conserving devices. Their annual heating and cooling bills were 75 percent below those of typical standard houses. Yet they cost not a dollar more than two hundred other houses, built to the old specifications. A group of well-designed and highly insulated attached and detached houses recently built in Britain at Woking have cut space-heating costs for the occupants by two-thirds.

Most of these opportunities for conservation are based on not much more than a common-sense approach to construction. But there are other possibilities ahead—the solar panel, the heat pump, the small fluidized-bed combustor, photovoltaic cells, all likely to become increasingly economic as the flow of customary heating fuels peaks and declines while their prices go in the opposite direction. The photovoltaic cell may be the simplest and most widespread of the new devices. With the very rapid cost reductions expected by 1985, these cells will be sufficiently cheap to install on virtually any building's roof or wall—facing the sun—even in temperate climates. The cells can then feed a direct electric current straight to an immersion heater in the hot-water tank. They could help provide hot water in commerce, industry, and homes. With heat storage they might well contribute to space heating too. In summer, they could power air-conditioning units.

All in all, the chances of well-designed and well-built new homes cutting fuel use to less than half the norm of today is not too unpromising. Retrofitted insulation in existing houses can also achieve spectacular savings. But one thing is certain. Governments could vastly speed up the process if they would give conservation and insulation standards a top priority in building regulations and research. The West German government has announced a two-billion-dollar program for insulation, heat pumps, and solar technology for private houses. This is the direction of the future, and one from which every citizen will gain not only more comfortable homes but lower fuel bills as well.

Is there any comparable hope for the transport sector, which uses fully as much fuel as the home—but is almost totally dependent on oil-based fuels? The United States transport sector accounts for more than half the nation's and one-seventh of the world's oil consumption. Western Europe has not gone quite so far, very largely because it still has fewer and smaller cars and more concentrated patterns of settlement. With 100 million more people, its transport system still demands only half the fuel used in the United States. Even so, present levels on both sides of the Atlantic demonstrate the extraordinarily rapid increase in the number of commercial and private road vehicles and the volume of air traffic over the last two decades. To take the growth in private cars as an example, America began the trend earlier and already had 62 million cars in 1960 and over 100 million by 1975. Western Europe only had 22 million in 1960. Even today, only 10 percent of the households boast a second car. But the over-all number had leapt in 1975 to 88 million cars. And this jump looks modest compared with Japan's exuberance; there car ownership multiplied thirty-five times over between 1960 and 1975. Even the austere Soviets have unbent and the number of cars has more than tripled to 5 million in these fifteen years, a modest figure no doubt in comparison with more than 250 million people, but setting the undoubted trend.

The largest possibility for saving fuel in transport is simply a very considerable return to public means of travel. The figures speak for themselves. With one U.S. gallon of gasoline, a standard automobile with one occupant will achieve some 20 passenger miles, while a city bus or city subway in the rush hour can achieve 90 to 120 passenger miles. An ordinary train with an average load provides 390 passenger miles per gallon. Nor should we forget the modest bicycle, which manages 1,000 passenger miles for the energy equivalent of a U.S. gallon of gasoline. The contrasts in the carriage of freight are as great—although, as we shall see, there are mitigating factors of mobility and ease of delivery. Nonetheless, a small delivery van can use thirty times the fuel of a diesel train in carrying a ton of freight one mile. America's trucking fleet uses around half of all fuel expended on freight transport to carry less than 20 percent of the freight. One should also remember that similar contrasts exist in the air. Jumbo jets consume one-fifth as much fuel per passenger as do executive jets or Concordes.

True, some forms of private transport do rather better. A small private car carrying four passengers is almost up to the rush-hour bus standard. But it remains a fact that if fuel conservation is an overriding aim, a larger use of public transport is the major saver. But of course conservation is not yet an overriding aim for citizens. So it is also not yet a high priority of governments. It follows that our two other means of conservation—based on types of behavior and types of car—will be only very fitfully followed up.

Personal behavior includes a readiness to keep the car in working trim, and its engine properly tuned, by regular examination, adjustment, and repair. It means citizen support and respect for fuel-conserving and life-saving speed limits. It means, at its simplest, courteous and responsible driving. But if these points are obvious, it is only one more reminder that there never will be a conserving society if it is largely made up of careless, wasteful, selfish, and greedy citizens.

For the same reason, although changes in types of car may make a valuable contribution to fuel saving, it does not follow that people are ready to buy them. An extra five hundred kilograms added to a car's weight can add 25 percent to fuel costs. But does that stop the sleek rows of long cars waiting to move diplomats or business leaders or commissars from top-level conferences to top-level dinners? A general shift to the medium and "mini" car could represent savings in the range of 25 to 50 percent, and some governments are in fact trying to change by legislation the mileages which standard models are expected to provide. In the United States, the administration is attempting to ensure that each manufacturer's fleet can average 20 miles per gallon by 1980 and 27.5 miles by 1985. (Incredibly, the average for 1974 was only 14 miles.) Canada is trying to be tougher. The standard is to rise from 17.5 miles per gallon in 1976 to 24 by 1980 and 33 by 1985. All this will entail more compact types of car, more careful styling to reduce wind resistance, a possible shift to wider use of diesel oil (Volkswagen has an experimental diesel car that does 60–70 miles per gallon) and perhaps a general rethinking of the role of the entirely unpolluting electric car for shorter journeys, particularly in built-up areas. Estimates by the automobile industry suggest that average fuel consumption in cars and light commercial vehicles can be cut by one-third before 2000—or even sooner. The electric car—whose future essentially depends on the development and mass production of a cheap, powerful battery—will almost certainly begin to make significant inroads into the commercial-vehicle market in the late 1980s. Both the United States and the Japanese governments are funding major electric-vehicle research programs—and the Japanese even talk of a quarter of a million private electric vehicles by 1986.

Further research may suggest interesting possibilities of lowering costs, reducing oil imports, and incidentally reducing air pollution by mixing traditional fuels with alcohols derived from indigenous fuel stocks, including plants. The Brazilians already mix their petroleum with a 20-percent share of alcohol derived from sugar cane and cassava. All cars for government use are now to employ alcohol only for fuel. In the U.S., the states of Nebraska and Indiana both have programs for developing an alcohol-gasoline blended fuel. A Volkswagen research program estimates that an alcohol-gasoline mixture which includes a 15 percent share of methanol could save 2.4 million tons of gasoline a year in West Germany by 1992. This mixture is economic to produce at present market prices, and it would cost very little to equip new vehicles with the minor modifications needed to make them run smoothly on the new mixture. Volkswagen's research has shown that cars and commercial vehicles can run competitively on pure alcohol, and in addition to its mixed-fuels fleet, the company has experimental vehicles running on pure ethanol and on pure methanol.

Liquefied natural gas may also be a future fuel for road vehicles, with little modification needed in the present design of engines. Similarly, hydrogen may prove to be an inexhaustible alternative fuel, provided cheap methods of breaking down water—after all, a reasonably abundant resource—can be devised from energy-income technologies. Experimental hydrogen-powered vehicles have been running for some years in Japan and the United States. Mercedes-Benz, and others, are experimenting with hydrogen-fueled buses and cars.

The outlook is also not too unpromising in the commercial and industrial sector, for the simple reason that fuel prices *are* going up and this is an area in which cost-benefit analysis is a habit of life. It is also the area of major use of fuels—from the relatively low percentage of 18 percent of all energy consumption in Switzerland to 47 percent in Japan. One can distinguish a number of different activities within this broad sector. Some industries are heavily dependent upon high energy use— iron- and steel-making, metal refining and fabricating, papermaking and oil refining. Other industries are lighter users. The manufacture of consumer goods and textiles, and many forms of engineering, consume much less fuel per unit of output. Then come commercial activities—warehouses, shops, offices, hotels, the entertainment industry— that are far less fuel-intensive than the manufacturing sector. Last of all, come community services.

In all these categories, it can be said at once that some forms of fuel saving are not really very different from the principles of "good housekeeping" for ordinary homes. Switch off unused lights. Insulate walls and roofs. Turn down the thermostats. Do not have lighting systems with units which cannot be individually switched off and which give as much light by the brightest window as in the darkest corridor. (Recommended lighting levels in the United States have tripled in the last two decades without anyone knowing the physiological or psychological basis for the increase.) Do not encourage the office cleaners to leave everything switched on till morning. Set the automatic switches so that the needed temperature is reached at 8 A.M., not 5:30 A.M.—and so it goes. One American corporation achieved a 15 percent drop in fuel consumption simply by asking for a daily report from each department on its use of energy. The Dow Chemical Company discovered after the 1973 "energy crisis" that its standard practice had been never to turn off the de-icing equipment on its service areas and side walks—to leave it blazing away on the Fourth of July.

The degree to which opposite principles still keep their hold can be briefly illustrated by the power companies' practice of offering cheaper rates for higher levels of use. Thus they virtually issue a direct invitation to each member of each firm to leave on as many radiators or lights or air conditioners as habit or laziness may dictate. The "saving" on electricity rates for the firm may seem to offset the waste. One can even encounter cases where it "pays" to leave lights and heating systems on. But the loss of fuel to the national economy—and increasingly to the world at large—simply piles up the costs to the community as a whole and increases local and general inflationary pressures.

The search for saving can logically begin with the business of producing and selling electricity itself. One trend in the last two or three decades has been to encourage the use of electricity, with its cleanliness and convenience, for all purposes in buildings. But this can have two unfortunate consequences. The extra generating capacity required to supply the all-electric house is very expensive. A builder may decide on electric central heating for a new house since it is cheaper and easier to install than oil or gas heating. But the electricity industry will have to invest some $2,000 to $5,000 in extra capacity and then pass the added cost on to the consumers. Over the whole life of his house, the unfortunate purchaser will face heating bills three to five times higher than are in any way technically necessary. This type of mindless waste strongly underlines the need for the general introduction—in both private and commercial building—of the principle of "life-cycle costing." When planning a new building, both private and public interests will tend to accept the lowest bid. They may even be under a legal obligation to do so. But buildings put up at minimum cost tend to have inadequate insulation and inefficient heating and cooling equipment. The capital saving made on an apparently cheaper building is then rapidly lost through higher fuel bills. Life-cycle costing considers in the original calculus all the operating, maintenance, and other recurrent ownership costs. As a result, the most economical, efficient, and thrifty building has some chance of starting where it should—on the drawing board.

The second effect of the all-electric house is further to increase the waste in supplying the needed energy to the consumer. As we have seen, to get one unit of energy in the form of electricity from the conventional thermal power station's furnace to the actual consumer means up to three units of waste heat along the way. Cogeneration (combined heat and power plants) largely eliminates this waste. Industries or cities using cogeneration units also avoid entire dependence upon external supplies of electricity. This is not to say that units servicing industrial complexes or indeed urban areas with both heat and electricity should not be linked to the grid. This would allow surplus electricity to be exported—or grid electricity to be used when, say, a plant was being overhauled. But the grid would then become a subsidiary and not the dominant, wasteful—and vulnerable—channel of all electricity supplies. In West Germany, industry meets nearly a third of its electricity demand from cogeneration plants—and they produce 12 percent of the nation's electricity. In the United States less than 5 percent of the nation's electricity is cogenerated by industry because, by a judicial vagary, it was decided some fifty years ago that first to use a factory's steam to produce electricity and then to use the "waste" heat was an obscure evasion of the antitrust laws. President Carter is now encouraging cogeneration in his energy bill with a 10 percent tax cut, and, one must assume, the Justice Department's concurrence.

The possible benefits of such a change can be gauged by the really remarkable contrasts between the amount of energy used per unit of output in different energy-intensive industries in various countries. The cement industry has already been mentioned. In pulp and paper making the figures are hardly less surprising. Spain and Italy consume around half the energy per unit of output used by Norway, Canada, the United States, and the United Kingdom. In crude steel-making, West Germany and Italy use 40 to 60 percent less energy per unit than Canada and the United States. Admittedly, these figures may in part reflect different ways of collecting statistics, in part the age of the plant and equipment, particularly among the older steel makers, Britain and the United States. It is, for instance, estimated that a thorough modernization of plant in Britain could cut fuel use per ton produced by not much less than 30 percent over the next two decades. But among those efficiencies would precisely be the exploitation of more cogeneration and the transformation of polluting waste heat into valuable process heat, space heat, or hot water for factory use.

This is not the only possible breakthrough. Especially if, in the world's leader in technology, the United States, the ludicrous underpricing of energy and encouragement of its overuse could be checked, a whole new range of energy-saving techniques might be developed. For instance, one of the aluminum companies has developed new processes that re-refine and smelt aluminum more efficiently, cutting energy consumption by 30 percent and, incidentally, cutting water use and polluting emissions. The abolition of subsidies on the use of virgin ores would greatly increase the value and utilization of scrap metal, and when one reflects that recycling aluminum demands a twentieth of the fuel required for its original production, copper a tenth, paper a third, and iron a half, one can begin to sense the scale of energy savings that would be possible in a really determinedly recycling and conserving economy.

Less energy-intensive industries also have a part to play. One of the difficulties in persuading them to see that they have a responsible role lies in the fact that in, say textiles or engineering, energy as such is a much smaller factor in production than in steel-making or metal refining. The bulk of their demand is, in fact, for space heating. But insulating "thin-skinned" workshops and offices and warehouses as though

they were houses, closing doors, controlling temperatures, and introducing heat pumps and solar panels, as one might with a home, does
not appear either a pressing or an obvious requirement. The steady leak
of heat goes on. In commercial buildings, the heights of perversity are
sometimes reached—and ''heights'' is the accurate word, since many of
them are skyscrapers. The large windowed office block, a favored
''prestige'' symbol, represents in terms of fuel consumption about the
stupidest use of materials. Glass intensifies the sun's rays, to make the
summers hotter. It is a poor insulator, making the winters colder. And
new office blocks are often entirely sealed to provide a ''controlled environment,'' so windows cannot be opened for the many days when the
temperature outside is the same as within. Indeed, in the glass monoliths, the cooling system is probably working full time to offset the extra
heat of the sun's rays intensified by the glass, while the temperature
within may well be identical with the temperature outside.

If we add together all the built-in wastefulness of such methods plus
the x factor of human carelessness and ignorance, it is not too difficult to
put the possible savings of fuel, even in older buildings, as high as 30 to
40 percent. New commercial and public buildings, like new private
housing, can reflect a more conserving philosophy. Better siting can use
light or shade from the sun and allow for prevailing breezes. It can use
trees, which in temperate climates have the convenient habit of growing
leaves for shade in summer and losing them in winter, when sunshine is
in short supply. Better insulation can cut both costs and fuel use. Toledo
Edison, for instance, used double panes of glass tinted to reflect sunlight
in a recent building. The extra cost of installation was about $122,000.
But there was an immediate offsetting saving of $123,000, since the
whole building became tolerable with a smaller heating and cooling system. That system in turn proceeded to save $40,000 a year in lower fuel
bills.

Heat pumps can be used very effectively in large buildings. In fact,
they are becoming mandatory in Japan, and their sales in the United
States quadrupled between 1974 and 1978. Heat storage can also
be used. Ontario Hydro has constructed a new headquarters in which the
excess heat from occupants, lighting, and machinery is stored in large
water reservoirs in the basement. In the winter these stores are drawn on
to keep the building at about 23 degrees centigrade. In the summer, they
help to cool it down. The estimate is that fuel consumption per square
foot is only half that of ''traditional'' Toronto buildings put up at the

same time, although Hydro's construction costs were in fact no higher.

Add together all the potential savings—from energy-intensive and other industries, from commerce, from transport, services, and public buildings, from the world of entertainment, and from the farm sector, which we have yet to examine—and fuel savings can rise to match the rise in energy demand. As a result, growth in fuel use slows down or even stops, despite the fact that more is being done. It is on this fact, not on grossly misleading extrapolations from previous wasteful usage, that realistic energy policies must be based. Admittedly, it is difficult for governments to change direction speedily. For at least twenty years, the general expectation in the developed world has been that the demand for energy would continue to grow by 4 or 5 percent a year. Future power systems were planned and ordered on this assumption, and even after the shock of the 1973 oil embargo, the comforting assurance that nuclear power would make similar growth rates possible took the edge off public concern—among both governments and citizens. Today, with rising nuclear costs, and fears, the best description of most official policies is a continued commitment to the nuclear option but with increasing and nagging worries. The result is not exactly an energy strategy, but there is a sort of nibbling away at the edges of the problem.

In the last few years, the old 5 percent mirage has begun to fade. Canada now speaks of a 3.5 percent growth rate in energy—and its Office of Energy Conservation reckons this should be reduced to 2 percent. The United States under the Carter plan would aim at a 2 percent growth rate. Some Western European governments still speak of growth rates of 3 to 4 percent, but British estimates fall as low as 2 percent and the Swedish government is already talking of zero growth for fuels by the 1990s. And some countries are backing these lower predictions with positive inducements to bring them about. The idea of better insulation has spread. Stricter insulation standards for new buildings are being introduced—or more generous grants for installation. The governments of West Germany, the United States, Belgium, Denmark, the Netherlands and Ireland are among those moving into this new field. Yet once we leave insulation, official action is, on the whole, not very coherent. Apart from the mandatory solar panels in northern Australia, only in the United States, France and West Germany have governments taken any real action to encourage solar equipment. The United States federal government is giving tax credits to homeowners for installing solar and wind equipment. It extends tax credits to industries installing the equipment. It is also placing large orders for solar photovoltaic cells, so that larger production runs can reduce unit costs. At the state level, California has offered even more generous tax credits to homeowners and enterprises installing solar or wind equipment.

An interesting flanking attack on energy waste comes from a few states which are insisting that standards of performance be listed on electrical appliances before they are sold. This proposal has run into bitter opposition in the United States, but the Canadians apparently mean to move ahead and legislate a strict disclosure of energy performance. They already have mandatory standards—as have the Italians—for heating systems. Voluntary labeling is being tried out in the Netherlands. West Germany has set standards of efficiency for furnaces, water heaters, and air conditioners. But the list of active Governments is pretty sharply restricted. *Caveat emptor* remains the general motto.

When we turn to public buildings, commercial premises, and factories, the picture is once again fairly disorganized and incoherent. Any government might reasonably begin a conservation program within its own sector. After all, little can so discourage conservationist fervor as to find the taxman's office heated to 24 degrees centigrade. A few governments have such programs—for example the American administration has tried to set energy standards for the running of its own buildings. A 20 percent increase in fuel efficiency is being sought for existing buildings, a 45 percent increase for new ones.

The general pattern of government action in the industrial sector has on the whole a random look. Some governments—the United States, Japan, Canada, and the United Kingdom—are trying to encourage the idea of energy audits and conservation targets for particular sectors. Britain now gives grants to businesses investing in insulation and energy-conserving technologies such as cogeneration. West Germany also has an interest in cogeneration, for which a 7.5 percent tax allowance is given. Austria, Denmark, Norway, and the Netherlands give cheap loans to any industry investing in energy-saving equipment. Belgium will give subsidized loans to any concern that can show a 12 percent cut in energy for each unit of production. President Carter has proposed his special 10 percent tax credit for cogeneration. But, all in all, considering the scale of saving possible in industrial and commercial undertakings, one would have to rate governments' interest as usually modest and in some cases nil.

Finally, one can report some action in the transport sector. The scale of European taxation on petroleum is some deterrent. Italian and Belgian taxes, for instance, are as high as 60 percent of the fuel price. Most Western European nations now impose progressive taxation on automobiles according to their size or power. The worst offenders are the Americans, whose automobile interests—users fully as much as producers—still balk at official increases in the price of gasoline. Even the consequent weakening of the dollar as oil imports and the balance-of-payments deficit rise together has still (in late 1978) had little effect. In fact, the only official conserving step is the one already mentioned—the attempt to increase the mandatory mileage of automobiles.

It is hard to see in all these dissociated and fragmentary approaches anything that really looks like a long-term strategy for saner energy use and conservation. Governments have lowered their projections for future energy use, but they still tend to base these projections on past trends. More highly insulated buildings, more efficient energy appliances, and the trend toward smaller, more efficient automobiles, coupled with a stabilizing population and a steadily less energy-intensive productive sector, simply contradict the notion that energy use must grow year after year. The gradual introduction of the energy-income technologies will also dampen the demand for conventional fuels. Yet no government has said in so many words: we have at least a century of "bridging fuels" in coal, oil, natural gas, and—as a last resort—present nuclear technology. During that period, we can, by conservation, research, and restructuring our institutions switch over to harmless "income energies," and by the middle of the next century, reach a comfortably safe, renewable, and steady state of energy demand and supply. It is surely significant that the official Swedish Secretariat for Future Studies has shown how Sweden's energy supply could be based entirely on domestic and renewable energy sources by 2015. Such estimates make it clear that there is nothing unrealistic about the statement that energy-income technologies can be the future base for energy supplies.

5 THE RECYCLING REVOLUTION

THE REVOLUTIONARY FACT about material wastes in our day is not that we have been throwing them off indiscriminately into air, land, and water. The revolution is simply the scale of the whole exercise. After all, mankind has always used nature as a dump for the wastes produced by daily living. Animal carcasses, household wastes, human excrement, have been abandoned in fields, burnt off into the air, or thrown into rivers and seas. With no very clear understanding of nature's processes of recycling and regeneration, societies seem to have realized that natural systems could be relied on to dispose of most by-products of human existence. Organic materials rotted back into the soil. The winds carried off the burden of smoke. Bacteria and other organisms in the rivers broke down organic wastes, thus restoring their carbon to the biosphere.

The growth of cities was the first major challenge to the throw-away system, simply because the amount of filth, waste water and detritus produced by large concentrations of people began to surpass the capacity of natural cleansers to maintain even minimum standards of health. As early as 2500 B.C., we find sophisticated systems for piping water and for drainage in such ancient cities as Mohenjo-daro. The Romans, with their tastes for fountains and public baths, built elaborate water-supply systems. But these were exceptions, and most European and American cities had to wait until the nineteenth century to be in sight of comparable standards. The other city wastes—household refuse, sewage—were usually dumped into the street or into streams and rivers. Dysentery, typhoid, cholera, were very early signs that nature's cleansing powers can be overloaded and misused.

Inevitably, the industrial revolution transformed all traditional expectations and reliances. It brought together, concentrated in a few square miles, thousands more people with their wastes and excrement; and it began the process of discarding not only a steadily rising volume of wastes but in addition, the effluents of a rapidly growing industrial sector. Sulphur dioxide, ammonia, smoke, and chlorine were pumped into the air, untreated industrial effluent was dumped into streams, canals, and rivers. Chicago's Sanitary and Ship Canal, known as Bubbly Creek, was said to have scum so thick in places that you could walk on it.

This whole process was enormously accelerated after the Second World War, when twenty-five years of continuous boom, rising energy use, leaping material standards, the massive increase in throw-away goods, and the revolution in the use of automobiles poured into the natural environment a flow of effluents and discards representing a wholly new level of scale and disruption. Moreover, these discards included types of material that had never been thrown away before, that had not in fact ever existed in nature and for which the natural cleansers had, inevitably, no ready-made methods of decomposition and recycling. They were not, to use the modern term, "biodegradable." Dangerous concentrations of new types of toxic chemicals could build up, unknown and unseen, in waste waters. Beaches and riverbanks where old spars and sails and sailors' bones had long been naturally recycled began to pile up with plastic junk.

It was precisely the growing evidence of nature's inability to go on standing the strain of cost-free waste disposal that, with gathering momentum in the 1950s and 1960s, introduced a new phase of thinking about the matter. Air in the big cities, saturated by automobile exhausts and emissions from industry, began to be seen as a major cause of respiratory diseases—at times, gas masks had to be worn in Tokyo. Rivers and lakes, their dissolved oxygen exhausted by loads of sewage and industrial wastes, lost most of their organic life, headed off toward the condition of swamps, or fitted the cynic's description of the Hudson River: "If you fall in, you don't drown, you dissolve." Carelessly impacted landfills leaked poisons into nearby aquifers. At about this time, Rachel Carson's *Silent Spring* revolutionized citizens' understanding of the degree to which chemical pesticides and herbicides, more and more freely used in agriculture, were washing off into rivers and estuaries and undermining the life cycle of whole species and ecosystems. The cumulative effect of these new insights was the realization that waste disposal is *not* cost-free, that nature is not an infinitely expandable "spring cleaner" for any degree of waste in human societies, that environmental standards should be seen to have as much validity as, say, educational standards—and someone would have to pay.

In 1969, the United States set up the President's Council on Environmental Quality and also a standard-setting and enforcement body, the Environmental Protection Agency (EPA), with powers to impose the needed standards on wastes pumped into air or water. Japan at about the same time began a program to control the emission of the most common air pollutants—sulphur dioxide, the nitrogen oxides, carbon monoxide, particulate matter—and rigorously controlled the discharge of such pollutants as mercury, cadmium, and polychlorinated biphenyls (PCBs), which had killed hundreds of people and injured many more in the previous two decades. It also imposed the world's toughest controls on automobile emissions. These actions by Japan and the United States illustrate the general trend among developed nations to begin to control polluting emissions within far more comprehensive systems of regulation.

Concern about security against irresponsible dumping of dangerous wastes tended to dominate thinking in the late 1960s and reached its peak at the United Nations Conference on the Human Environment at Stockholm in 1972. But little as the delegates were aware of the fact, the world was about to move with some speed into a third phase in its dealing with wastes and emissions. Two problems—energy profligacy and resource wastes—suddenly began to come together in 1973 after the oil embargo had sunk the day of cheap energy into an uneasy twilight. The result of the collison of two entirely new physical constraints— unacceptable pollution and rising energy costs—had the inevitable effect of changing most of the calculus upon which the earlier environmental policies had been based. Disposal was ceasing to be cost-free just when energy costs were going through the roof. We are still in all the confusions of working out the consequences of this revolutionary juxtaposition. But we can already see a number of consequences which can be said to mark a new phase in our century's dealing with the problems of discards.

For governments, the fundamental change can perhaps best be summed up in a significant readjustment in legislative approach. In addition to regulations and restrictions, government after government has

started to pass what can roughly be called national resource recovery
acts, in which the chief emphasis is placed not only on keeping
wastes—especially toxic wastes—out of the biosphere but on taking a
new and creative look at the wastes themelves. The setting up the EPA
in the United States was followed in 1970 by the passing of the Resource Recovery Act and more recently by the Resource Conservation
and Recovery Act. In 1971, the German Federal Republic formulated
an environmental program and followed it up with a waste-disposal law
which has as its aim to co-ordinate the collection and re-use of waste
materials on a comprehensive basis. In 1974, the British government
passed a new and enlarged ''control of pollution'' bill on the same lines,
and it has since set up an over-all Waste Management Advisory Council
to help secure an integrated approach. Then, in 1975, the French introduced a law on waste disposal and the recovery of materials. Japan
has not only decided to devote more than 2 percent of GNP to the elimination of pollution but is concentrating more and more attention—for
instance, through its new "Keep Japan Clean" center—on the latest
techniques of waste management and recycling. This tide of legislation
does not, inevitably, wash over all the vexed points of jurisdiction and
responsibility—who collects the wastes, where they go, what is the best
use to be made of them—but it marks what is probably an irreversible
trend among developed governments.

Conceptually, at least, the treatment of pollution, the acceptance of
the need for conservation, have entered a new phase. The intention and
effect of this new approach are, of course, the same. The elimination or
re-use of potential wastes can prevent their being discarded to contaminate soil, air, and water. If production wastes cannot be eliminated, the
system accepts the principle of nature's own methods of recyling and
seeks to apply them to as many forms of discarded materials as lend
themselves to recycling and re-use. It is hardly surprising that this
change has been forcefully encouraged by the sharp rise in energy
prices. Although most basic materials—apart from oil and natural gas—
are not yet within a hundred years of being in short supply, the transfer
to the use of leaner ores often demands more energy, and many of the
substitutes for present metals, such as materials based on silicon or
plastics based on coal or even cellulose from renewable woodlands,
demand larger inputs of energy to transform them into durable, working, lightweight substitutes for steel or copper or tin. If we remember
that the energy saved by re-using metal scrap can be as high as 90 per-

cent, we confront a not exactly unimportant economic rationale for a new look at recycling.

Inevitably, the degree to which governments have succeeded in encouraging a new mood of thrift is still uncertain. Both consumers and the productive sector have far too many varied interests for any set of regulations or costs to have anything like uniform effects. Take, for instance, the general conflict between the producers of original raw materials and those who wish to substitute recycled residues. There is likely to be a strong logging lobby anxious to avoid too large an expansion in the use of recycled paper. An estimated 300 million trees a year could be saved in the United States through tripling the amount of paper recycled, but very likely some loss of work and profit for the pulp industry would be entailed. Paper companies tend to turn to the recycled material only to cover temporary shortages or surges of demand. The result is alternating glut and famine for secondhand-paper dealers and often complete discouragement for civic-minded groups collecting the paper for the public good. In 1974, both the French and the British authorities found themselves all but buried under mounds of unwanted used paper. It is for this reason that a number of governments, including the French, the Japanese, and the Norwegian, are setting up orderly guaranteed markets for recycled paper through such measures as subsidized collecting centers, storage space, and guaranteed prices. If the next step is to tax the original timber, then the real conflict with logging interests begins. Nor is the dilemma confined to wood and pulp. In the United States, for instance, depletion allowances and special transport rates give a strong economic advantage to the use of virgin ores. In a world of increasing resource shortages, the policy makes no sense at all.

There is similar difficulty in assessing the effect of government efforts with another very powerful body—the motor industry. A number of governments are now proposing that the disposal cost of cars—in Sweden it is three hundred krone—should be included in the original price and, rather on the principle of a returned bottle, be paid back to the owner if he turns his car hulk in at an approved receiving center. Since the company passes on the cost to the buyer, since no competitive differentials between companies arise, and since, at the same time, the money is finally returned, this procedure should surely rate as "supportive" to all concerned—especially if the disposal fee is suitably indexed. But some corporations are uneasy over the whole approach.

In another field, the West Germans have imposed a disposal tax on lubricating oil that covers the cost of collecting and refining the wastes. As a result, they can afford to re-refine twice as much as does the United States with its very much larger road fleet. Another proposal, pioneered in Canada, would also seem likely to reduce some of the detrimental impacts of car use. This is that the big car carriers which deliver new cars round the country might pick up the hulks and turn them in at collecting centers, where the remains would be shredded, separated, and turned into useful scrap.

The advantages to be gained from using recycled material in the productive process have encouraged a number of countries—notably the Scandinavian—to give official support to business corporations to take on the whole business of collection and re-use. The Swedish company SAKAB recovers chemical wastes and oils. Norway thinks of using public corporations to secure dangerous products. Finland has established three collecting centers for recycling used paper. Then, for all the other industrial wastes which turn up and for which, unlike paper or scrap, there are no organized markets, some countries—all the Scandinavian nations (in their Nordic Wastes Market), the Netherlands, West Germany, France—are beginning to introduce "waste exchanges" which attempt to bring together more miscellaneous buyers and sellers. The United States set up its first experimental exchange in 1975. The frugal Chinese incidentally operate a very wide range of waste-purchasing departments. In a single year (1972) they claim to have collected 2½ million tons of scrap iron, 760,000 tons of used paper, and large quantities of used rubber and scrap metals.

There are therefore at least four ways in which a government can actively promote the reduction or re-use of wastes. The first is to ensure that manufacturers pay the cost of disposing of their products—as with the West German tax on lubricating oils and the Swedish tax on new cars. These taxes can then fund the needed programs to re-refine the waste oil and recycle the metal from the junked cars. This principle could find far wider application. For example, it should be applied to all nonreturnable containers and to packaging, so that the manufacturer would have to pay a tax to cover the cost of their eventual disposal. This would encourage the manufacturer to use far less packaging and, where possible, to use returnable containers. And a tax exemption given for the use of recycled paper in packaging would boost the wastepaper industry.

A second approach is to stimulate the markets for recycled products. A couple of indirect ways of achieving this have already been mentioned—waste exchanges and support for paper-storage schemes that allow gluts or sharp rises in demand to be accommodated. It can be achieved more directly through a government's ensuring that part of its own needs are met with recycled material. Conservationists might feel happier about their tax returns if they are completed on 100-percent recycled paper.

A third approach is simply in certain instances to ban nonreturnable containers. We shall see in chapter 7 how several states in the United States have considerably eased their waste problems and drastically cut litter by banning nonreturnable carbonated-beverage containers. Then, finally, governments can extend grants or other incentives to aid municipalities and industries in installing innovative equipment that reduces or recycles wastes. All in all, with so many alternative procedures, one can only conclude that governments which take no action lack not the knowledge or the means, but the needed commitment.

6 INDUSTRY: REWARDS AND RISKS

IT IS PERHAPS not surprising that some of the speediest reactions to the problem of reducing or recycling wastes have come from industry itself. It has, of course, always recycled a good deal of its own internal scrap and waste without much fanfare. It is also most accustomed to careful cost-benefit analysis. The first effect of environmental controls, particularly where the principle "the polluter pays" has been strictly enforced, has therefore been to encourage industries to take a new look at their own disposal policies. A lot of the productive sector's opposition to new environmental regulations was based on the fact that adding equipment to cut down polluting air emissions or building a treatment plant to ensure that effluents met prescribed standards was expensive. It did put up operating costs, since the disposal costs were no longer handed on to nature.

In efforts to reduce these new costs, industries began to look for new solutions. The most obvious approach was to see if the wastes previously dumped might have some value as resources, instead of needing expensive treatment. An American corporation, Westvaco, began converting its polluting pulp and paper discards into a variety of salable chemicals. Within a few years, it found it required a subsidiary chemical division with four reprocessing plants and a research center employing eighty scientists. In only five years, sales doubled to $45 million. Yet the whole raw-material base for these operations had simply been dumped in the years before.

An alternative solution to using waste products is not to produce the wastes at all. A Canadian company, the Great Lakes Paper Company, has evolved a new, closed-cycle paper mill which, using its own patented salt-recovery process, reclaims and recycles the water and chemicals that with a traditional plant would have dumped into the nearby Kaministikwia River. The mill now passes on only clean water and, at the same time, has reduced operating costs and produces higher yields. Another highly significant example comes from the food industry. This is, incidentally, one of the really serious sources of pollution, since its effluents consume particularly large amounts of dissolved oxygen in any water they are thrown into and thus threaten every species of the river's natural life. Distilleries can be particular offenders, and many Scottish rivers were beginning to show an alarming tendency to run out of salmon. But the distillers, under the shadow of imminent prohibitions and sanctions, realized that much of what they had been throwing out in the way of grain husks, sugar, starch, fat, yeast, and protein could be dried out and turned into valuable cattle feed. North British Distilleries, in Edinburgh, found they could sell cattle feed to the value of over a million pounds sterling with a profit of £687,000—a transaction which more than covered, in a single year, the cost of setting up the needed machinery for conversion.

The French have done some interesting calculations on the actual cost/benefit to be gained from replacing traditional pollution-control processes—which tend to have both high capital and high operating costs—with processes that use the wastes as a resource. The SILF factory in Strasbourg found that new methods of recovering protein and potassium from the wastes of its yeast production required half the investment that conventional pollution-control equipment would require. It was also discovered that the recovery process covered all its operating costs by sales of the recovered products. The whole operation made a clear profit of 155,500 French francs a year. A steel works (Salicor, in the Moselle) began recovering iron dust, and at twice the investment needed for conventional pollution control, found that sales from the recovered product paid for operating costs and gave a profit of 800,000 French francs a year.

Perhaps one of the most remarkable success stories comes from an oil refinery—Raffinerie Elf Feyzin—which set out to recover and sell waste hydrocarbons. It would have cost some 2½ million French francs to dispose of these every year. But with an investment of 11 million francs, sales from the recovered products soon covered operating costs and yielded a profit of more than 5 million francs a year. Such examples can be multiplied—from soap factories, from glue and gelatine manufacturers, from dairies, even from modest fruit processing plants. The experience is uniform.

A more borderline case involves the point of extraction of raw materials. Few of us need reminding of the ravages of mining and quarrying—the bare mountains of tailings round Johannesburg, the stripped and ravaged lands of central Illinois, the vast Welsh tips which at Aberfan slid down to cover and kill the children in a whole primary school. But here, too, environmental insights, controls, and penalties are changing the old unheeding pattern of neglect and squalor. Opencast coal areas in West Germany have been restored not simply to previous but to higher standards of agricultural productivity. Land once stripped for mining can have its productivity restored by the judicious use of sewage sludge and composted refuse. In some areas, properly compacted wastes have been landscaped, reafforested, turned into hillsides and picnic areas—one thinks of the 150-foot Mount Trashmore (or Mount Hoy, to give it the official name), near Chicago, with its adjoining lakes made from abandoned gravel pits. Its success has prompted a new project in the Greene Valley, with two 250-foot hills for skiing and hiking.

In fact, provided regulations scrupulously prevent the disruption of the steepest gradients, most mined land can be successfully restored. It can even make a profit. Along the Thames, vast gravel pits were gouged out, largely for road building. But one of the companies concerned, Ready Mix Concrete Company, has turned the ugly, gaping holes into pleasant lakes, where yacht marinas have been built and where in 1975 the world water-skiing championships were successfully held. The entire recreation complex makes a profit, and the lakes shine beside a Thames they no longer shame by their dirt and disorder.

Yet in spite of all that is promising in the area of industrial conservation and re-use, it must be admitted that in one vast and central complex of production, the toughest regulation and the most profound caution appear to be the needed approach. No industrial sector has expanded so rapidly as the chemical industry. It has become a giant among America's many giants, producing products worth $100 billion every year, and is now one of the United States' most valuable exporters. In the Soviet Union, great emphasis has been placed on expanding the chemical industry—production tripled between 1960 and 1975, and the present five-year plan, up to 1980, aims to expand production by a further 60 to 65 percent. Japan and West Germany have chemical industry sales which exceed $30 billion a year. This diverse industry supplies the process chemicals for the extraction, refining, and conversion of all natural minerals into final products. It synthesizes all plastics and man-made fibers. It also synthesizes most of the fertilizers and other chemicals used in Western agriculture. The petrochemical section of this industry has grown steadily in importance, since its feedstock enjoys the immense advantage of being a relatively cheap by-product of another highly popular and salable commodity, petroleum.

No one can deny the uses of this gigantic business network. Housewives will not easily abandon drip-dry shirts and detergents. Agriculture could not abandon all artificial fertilizers. The chemical industry plays a critical role in virtually all industrial production. And given the numbers of people already consuming synthetic fibers and plastics, and the two billion more who will be looking for clothes and basic consumer goods by the year 2000, it is not easy to see whether wool and cotton and wood—the natural substitutes—would be available in sufficient quantities without encroaching on the world's shrinking supplies of the land needed for food and for forests giving fuel and fundamental environmental protection. In short, the products of the chemical industry are useful and seem irreplaceable. These advantages are quite sufficient to explain its world-wide surge in the last fifty years.

But at what real cost? Here lies the shadow. Already, the scale of toxic wastes carelessly dumped before any introduction of stringent pollution controls is beginning to show a dangerous legacy. At Niagara Falls, an old canal used as a dump for industrial wastes was filled in and houses built around it. Unusually heavy rains caused the underground canal to overflow, bringing with it more than twenty toxic chemicals, including eleven known or suspected carcinogens. Nor is this an isolated incident. In Massachusetts, seventeen thousand barrels of toxic chemicals had to be moved when some were found to be leaking into the Merrimack River, the water source for several communities. In Michigan, the state had to clean out completely a site in Pontiac when the authorities were warned that a spell of hot weather might be enough to cause some of the old dumped chemicals to explode and send a toxic cloud over the city's suburbs. The regulations on the disposal of hazardous wastes have been tightened, for all disposal sites, but there are 100,000 sites in the United States, and many may still have inadequate safeguards. Disposal sites set aside for hazardous wastes, as at Niagara

Falls or Pontiac, may number as many as four hundred. How many are more secure?

Industrial risks are not confined to the legacy left by careless industrial dumping. We can take one central group of chemicals from the petrochemical industry—the organohalogens—to demonstrate how the advantages of chemicals now on sale have to be weighed against the costs. The basis for this group is the bonding of carbon, the basic ingredient of organic life, with chlorine or, more exceptionally, with iodine, fluorine, or bromine. (Since their collective name—the organohalogens—is virtually impossible to say, write, or remember, we shall refer here to the basic carbon–chlorine bond, recording only that there are also other types.) Compounds with the carbon–chlorine bond are widely used as solvents, degreasing agents, fuel additives, fumigants, and dry cleaners in industry. They appear as biocides to protect crops from pests and disease. They are used in medicine, where the relief of pain, the palliation of mental diseases, the control of physiological imbalances, and even the treatment of infections and malignant diseases would be mortally reduced without them. Chloroform, which is made up of carbon, chlorine, and hydrogen, was one of the first anesthetics to be mercifully used in medicine.

But the carbon–chlorine bond is exceedingly rare in nature. It is as though, in the planet's three billion years of organic life, selective evolution had largely rejected this set of bonds as uncongenial to further development. The bond is comparatively stable, so the bacteria and other organisms that break down all natural wastes cannot easily break down carbon–chlorine compounds. Much of the worry about DDT and PCBs—both with carbon-chlorine bonds—centers around the fact that they break down very slowly. As a result, human beings and animals in environments contaminated by DDT or PCBs can accumulate more and more of these compounds in their bodies. No one knows what effect this will have. But could evolution be giving a salutary hint?

Nor is this a theoretical apprehension. Some of the worst environmental risks and disasters of recent years can be traced back to compounds with the carbon–chlorine bond. Probably the most widely used—and useful—plastic is PVC. But vinyl chloride, the gas used in its manufacture, is now known to be cancer-causing. It has produced liver cancer among dozens of workers in PVC factories, and birth defects in adjacent communities. In Michigan, in 1976, the muddling up of bags of fire retardant with those for cattle feed caused PBB contamination in the people who ate the cattle who ate the feed in the first place—and no one can be sure what the final toll in ill-health for the millions affected will be. In the same year, at Seveso in Italy, a contaminant produced in the manufacture of chemicals for cosmetics and herbicides (a dioxin called TCDD) caused disease and birth defects—and contaminated an area of some seven hundred square miles—despite the fact that only two kilograms were released. A herbicide containing this same material was banned from use in Vietnam because the TCDD was known to be a most potent agent of birth defects.

When Kepone, a carbon–chlorine product used to poison ants and roaches, leaked from a carelessly operated factory near Hopewell, Virginia, it gave scores of residents incurable ailments and contaminated more than a hundred miles of the James River. And this case is a reminder of the earlier message of *Silent Spring*, that massive emissions of DDT and its successors, dieldrin and aldrin, could work total havoc among the whole range of natural species they contaminated while attacking mosquitoes and other pests. True, it cannot be proved that DDT is directly carcinogenic. It causes tumors in mice but perhaps not in men. The trouble is that there is no longer any way of setting up a control group in the developed world. So great was the early enthusiasm for DDT that nobody is without some DDT in his or her body. Thus there is no way of telling whether the cancer some people are suffering from has come from DDT or from any of the other widespread cancer-causing agents—asbestos, smog, smoking. What is certain is DDT's toxicity to natural species. It becomes concentrated as it goes up the food chain—say, from plankton to minnows to needlefish to ospreys, which at the end of the process either produce no embryos or else eggs with shells too thin to protect them. Since every cause of human cancer has caused similar malignancy in animals, even the evidence of the mice must be taken cautiously. The links *could* be dangerous in both directions.

What then should be done about this potentially devastating group of chemicals that are being continuously released into the biosphere? To ban chemicals having the carbon–chlorine bond, and with them an enormous range of products, is a step no society—private, mixed, or collectivist—is likely to take, because of the many vital uses of these substances and the apparently insoluble problem of providing alternatives. The answer must therefore lie in much stricter controls at every stage of the productive and distributive process. The more dangerous chemicals must of course be banned, or their use restricted. Then the danger has to be examined at the manufacturing stage. For example, once the plastic PVC is made, it is not toxic to those handling it. PVC waste can even be recycled for use in factories making anything from bicycle saddles to shoe soles. The dangers arise from the gas vinyl chloride, from which the PVC is made. In the United States, the EPA rates vinyl chloride in toxicity with such well-known poisons as mercury, asbestos, and arsenic. In 1974, the U.S. Department of Labor fixed one part per million as the maximum permissible exposure level for workers in the industry, and it aims to put an end to 90 percent of this gas's emission into the atmosphere. In 1977, the European Commission introduced new regulations limiting the exposure of factory workers to three parts per million and set stringent standards for the level of vinyl chloride contamination allowed in materials coming into contact with food.

And this regulation illustrates a wider problem. How many of the potentially dangerous compounds used in the chemical industry have in fact been effectively identified and controlled? There are more than four million chemicals, with tens of thousands in general use. As many as five hundred or more new compounds are introduced by industry every year. How many of these are cancer-causing? How are adequate controls, in any case, to be introduced?

Part of the answer lies, of course, with governments. The U.S. Congress has now passed a Toxic Substances Control Act which lays on industry the obligation to test every new compound and requires the EPA to be given ninety days to examine the evidence of effective testing and determine whether it is adequate. The West German government's initiative in 1978 to tighten controls on dangerous chemicals includes a similar provision to place on industry the responsibility of testing new chemicals before they are brought onto the market.

As great a responsibility rests on industry itself. No self-respecting management should wish to introduce, by inadvertence or indifference, death-dealing substances into the biosphere. But possibly, in open societies (where, incidentally, virtually all the research and the control for chemical toxins have been carried out) an alert public opinion is also an essential safeguard. Union leaders have pointed out, with grief and irony, that some toxic substances aroused public dismay only after they affected penguins or ospreys. Yet they had been killing workers for half a century. It took five years' haggling to get the Toxic Substances Control Act through the Congress—a fact which reflects favorably neither on management nor on public opinion. The path of testing, control, and where necessary, prohibition has to be followed by developed societies. It is a poor commentary on both business and public concern when one sees how much kicking and screaming can accompany the process.

Yet the path of prohibition leaves some problems unmet, particularly in the vital field of protecting against pests in food production. One can admit that DDT, dieldrin, and aldrin are too long-lived and their long-term effects too uncertain for them to be generally used. The use of DDT is either banned or carefully restricted in all Western nations. Sweden was among the first to ban or restrict biocides with the carbon–chlorine bond. The United States has now suspended or restricted the use of six biocides with the carbon–chlorine bond and has several more under investigation. But can the same level of food output be secured without the retention of a number of carbon–chlorine compounds? Here perhaps the answer—akin in a sense to that of better testing—lies in much more scrupulous care in the use of all agricultural chemicals. There are a number of shorter-lived alternatives to DDT—for instance, the natural plant substance pyrethrum, or new synthesized pyrethrum-like biocides—that have none of the dangerous side effects of the carbon–chlorine biocides. Organophosphates are less persistent than DDT—although they must be very carefully handled since they are far more toxic than DDT to the human user. Herbicides have been shown to be less dangerous if they are used in small exact quantities (no slosh-on spraying from aircraft). The chemical must also be as closely related as possible to the particular pest. In some areas, planting seasons can be varied to avoid the potential predators' hungriest periods, and by using different varieties of seed or crop or companion plants that repel pests and harbor their predators, the chance of a massive overkill by a particular pest can be much reduced.

Now that the ominous "cancer maps" of nation after nation show the degree to which chemical contaminants are among the most potent carcinogenic agents, the need for careful and conserving practices—at every stage in the manufacture and use of chemicals—is the first imperative of the chemical industry itself, of governments responsible for the public welfare, and of the concerned citizen.

7 A ROLE FOR THE CITIZEN?

BUT HOW CONCERNED *is* the citizen? It is not perhaps surprising that industry, keenly alive to costs, has started to react with some force to the rising expense of waste treatment and the increasing attraction of substituting recycling or alternative use. But the actual production of goods is only a part of the problem. Once the goods are manufactured and sold to the consumer, the problem of waste disposal passes directly to the public authorities and, at one remove, to the citizens themselves. And citizens, it must be confessed, still seem to have few innate control mechanisms—such as industry's almost instinctive cost-benefit analysis—to encourage them to less wasteful habits. In fact, one can argue that the phrase "consumer good" gives away the whole story. Most citizens do genuinely believe they *consume* goods. But they do not. They simply use them for a spell of time—a second for the flick of a match, perhaps a lifetime for a brass bedstead—but at the end of it, all the materials in the goods they have "consumed" are all still in being, waiting to be collected. Yet how many citizens have any clear picture of the consequences of their own throw-away mentality? If you really think you consume something, then it is hard to get excited about recycling it, because in your unconscious mind, it is no longer there. It is therefore hardly surprising to know that in the United States just before the energy crisis struck in 1973, only 7 percent of the citizens' garbage was being recycled. At the same time, the European Economic Community (EEC) estimated that the proportion of material recycled from the 40 million tons of metal, glass, plastic, rubber, and cloth discarded by the community's citizens every year was not much higher.

But just as the growth of environmental consciousness in the 1960s was, to a very considerable degree, a movement of citizen awareness and responsibility, we have no reason to suppose that, if workable strategies are evolved to go on dealing with the consequences of the movement, citizen interest and support will not continue. At present, a sense of helplessness often plays an inhibiting role. It can be very difficult to achieve and sustain a commitment to a cleaner, more appetizing and attractive environment if the scale of the problem is felt to surpass individual efforts while no collective clues or guidelines to an answer are provided. So far, this has been all too often the case. Municipalities have provided habitual waste-disposal services. They have not suggested how the increasing volume of wastes could be reduced—or put to good use. There have been a few exceptions—for instance, Leningrad and the many composting plants in the Netherlands. But until recently these were as rare as good sewage systems in the 1860s.

But as we have already noticed, the reactions of the public authorities are changing, in some cases, as drastically as industry's. Not only business firms but municipalities are beginning to assess the gains to be made from turning residues into real resources. For instance, in the United States the EPA has made the estimate that at least a billion dollars' worth of recoverable metals and a billion dollars' worth of potential fuel are thrown away in household garbage every year. Japan has made the estimate that if paper recycling could rise from 40 percent to 60 percent, three million tons of pulp could be dropped each year from the import bill. These are the kinds of calculations that were simply not being made even a decade ago. They can hardly fail to become the basis for a fundamental rethinking of waste-disposal strategies in which the concerned citizen can play an active part.

Some of the most marked changes are occurring, not surprisingly, where there was a little previous experiment and experience to build on. The Leningrad plant, which now takes the metal scraps out of nearly 600,000 tons of garbage, composts the organic wastes—food scraps, rags, dirty packaging—and then sells them to surrounding farmers. By 1985, the city fathers hope to bring the entire flow of municipal wastes into the system. Holland has been providing garbage-based compost for the last fifty years—about 200,000 tons of it every year. The Czechs plan to have a composting plant in every community of over fifty thousand. The model can, incidentally, be followed at any level of citizen activity. The individual gardener can repeat the experiment on a mini scale by putting food and rags and garden wastes into containers where they turn into compost. Tenants in housing blocks have been known to club together to create compost for their own surrounding gardens.

Even in so apparently unpromising a neighborhood as the South Bronx, a local community-development corporation is making compost out of seven hundred pounds of waste collected each week from the local vegetable market.

Another alternative open to municipalities is to use the trash as fuel. Some two hundred plants in Western Europe burn wastes to provide heat for buildings or industry and in some cases generate electricity too. Munich gets both district heating and electricity from burning its garbage and derives 12 percent of its electricity from this source. Trash-fueled district heating is common in Sweden and Denmark, and one plant in Copenhagen uses the refuse from 500,000 people to heat twenty thousand homes. Plants in Paris burn 1.6 million tons of city waste every year to produce electricity and district heating. There are garbage-for-fuel schemes in Amsterdam, Düsseldorf, Vienna, and Frankfurt. In Nottingham, in Britain, refuse is incinerated together with locally mined coal to provide district heating for part of the city center. Another British instance comes from Imperial Metal Industries and Associated Portland Cement Manufacturers, who use shredded household waste to supplement coal in some of their factories' boilers. Although the United States has been slower to use household wastes as fuel, several plants are now in operation or being built. One at Saugus burns 1,200 tons of waste a day, from ten neighboring municipalities, to provide steam for a General Electric factory.

All these uses are relatively direct. But there are more sophisticated processes that can separate the garbage into different categories, allowing a more efficient use of the various wastes. A pilot plant in Yokohama separates paper, metals, and plastics from city garbage for recycling and produces compost from the residue. A fifty-thousand-ton-a-year plant in Stockholm will also recover plastics, paper, and metals, and produce compost, when it goes into operation in 1980. A pilot plant in St. Louis shreds incoming garbage and separates out the metals, glass, and other heavy materials. Ferrous metals can then be reclaimed for resale, and the light combustible fraction of the refuse can be used as a fuel supplement in power stations. The pilot project has been so successful that a new plant is being built with twenty times the turnover.

This St. Louis example points to a tendency in the United States to take a greater interest in fuels derived from garbage than in directly burning the garbage itself. The largest contract now under consideration is of this type. It involves New York City and a private corporation, Combustion Equipment Association. The company has developed a process of converting raw garbage into fuel (Eco-fuel II) by first separating out metals and glass and then turning the remaining wastes into a brown powder of which one ton is roughly equivalent to 2.6 barrels of oil. After operating a plant in Brockton, Massachusetts, transforming nine hundred tons of garbage a day, the company is now negotiating a three-thousand-ton-a-day plant with the municipal authorities in New York City. The price—seven dollars for every ton of garbage disposed of—is fifty cents cheaper than present disposal costs. The city also gets a share in any profits from the company's sale of its products—from metal scrap to the final fuel. Since the proposals cover only 15 percent of the city's garbage, success could lead to more and bigger contracts.

Other methods of producing fuel include pyrolysis—the process of heating garbage in the absence of oxygen to break it down into salable gaseous and liquid fuels. Various other chemical and biological processes can also be used to produce liquid or gaseous fuels or even proteins for use in animal feed. A pilot plant is planned for Pompano Beach, Florida, which will use city garbage with sewage sludge to produce methane.

All these processes, inevitably, require the removal of metals first. But at this point we encounter a number of dilemmas of choice and institutional arrangement. Clearly, the cheapest thing to do with bottles is to return them, with paper to recycle it. Furthermore, if the garbage arrives at the fuel plant or composting point already sorted out and cleaned up by citizen action—bottles and glass removed, tins and containers and metal scraps set aside, newspapers stacked elsewhere—the next stage of transforming the usable organic remains will be much less complicated. This is important, since the technology of automatic separation, such as the use of shredders, air classifiers, and magnetic separators, and of complex refuse-to-fuel conversions on a large scale is still relatively new and there have been some considerable breakdowns. In Baltimore, for example, a pyrolysis plant failed to meet environmental emission standards and was still operating at only half its capacity four years after its supposed date of completion, owing to a series of technical failures. In fact, its builder, Monsanto, paid up under the penalty clauses and moved out. There are other examples. A Nashville garbage-incineration plant had to keep on going back to conventional fuels because of inadequate emissions control and deterioration of the boiler tubes from corrosives in the solid wastes.

There are thus problems at the "high-technology" end of garbage separation which lead people to propose with all the more enthusiasm that citizens should accomplish the first phase by sorting their own trash, and thus simplify the later stages of technology required to produce the fuel. Their advocacy has been strengthened by a couple of cases in America where a private garbage-collection company agreed to sign a contract with the municipality only if it guaranteed *not* to reduce the flow of garbage. This, as a method of reducing waste, borders, to say the least, on the irrational.

Here we confront a critical and unresolved problem in the whole citizen approach to waste, garbage, dirt, and neglect. How much trouble are individual people prepared to take? There is no dispute about the fact that all mechanical recycling schemes would function more cheaply and reliably if some of the sorting were done before the mass of material arrived at the depot. The three components in most garbage that lend themselves easily to citizen sorting are bottles, cans, and newspapers. Can we really say that, taking these most straightforward examples, citizens are reacting in a way that makes their long-term co-operation a reasonable hope?

Bottles and cans are uncertain cases. The litter on roadsides, beaches, and picnic sites is enough at times to turn the most staid and conservative citizen into a momentary convert to the radical belief that there *is* a "criminality of affluence" when the careless, thoughtless, and lazy leave such waste to destroy others' pleasures and tarnish the land. But there are some hopeful pointers. The most conserving use of a glass bottle is to return it. There is nothing very magical about the idea. It is done several times a week for virtually every householder in Britain as the milkman delivers fresh bottles and removes the empties. But the task may be easier in most countries if a simple financial incentive is introduced. Since 1972, the state of Oregon has effectively banned nonreturnable beer and soft-drink bottles, requiring a two-cent deposit on every standard bottle and a five-cent deposit on other types; the money is recovered from any retailer when the bottle is returned. The number of bottles in household garbage has fallen by 80 percent, and collection costs have fallen, too. Vermont, Maine, Alaska, Iowa, and Michigan have since followed Oregon. Latest reports suggest that in Oregon, over

90 percent of the refillable containers for soft drinks are now being returned and 85 percent of those for beer. Vermont claims a return rate of
95 percent and a corresponding fall in litter on highways and tourist
sites.

In other parts of the world, Norway has introduced compulsory de-
posits on bottles, and Switzerland, where bottles for a wide variety of
uses are standardized to a single size, semiautomatic receivers in super-
markets repay the deposit—a convenience to the many shoppers who
tend to do most of the week's shopping in one or two visits and can
offload their accumulated bottles at the same time. The Swiss also arrange for collecting bins in each neighborhood for nonreturnable bottles
of different colored glass, which citizens are left to separate out themselves. Apparently a 50-percent return is achieved.

Controls on the use of cans were also part of Oregon's "bottle bill."
The use of pop-top beverage cans was banned to prevent manufacturers
from simply switching from nonreturnable bottles to nonreturnable
cans. Restricting the use of cans is thus part of the answer. In addition,
cans could be made more easily recyclable by the universal use of standard materials. The great variety of metal mixes in the cans now sold
commercially makes their recycling far more difficult.

The third category—wastepaper—depends as we have seen on
available places (or markets) for disposal. No one can blame the citizen
for burning or throwing away old newspapers when the back door will
hardly open because of carefully conserved and still uncollected edi-
tions of last month's *Times*. But where the markets have been set up, a
measure of citizen response has been the result.

So we can perhaps give a cautious but not altogether discouraging
answer to the question of whether citizens are prepared to help their
neighborhoods to become and remain clean. The answer perhaps lies in
three directions. The first is to find ways of making separation finan-
cially attractive to citizens. The experience of Oregon shows that even
two cents counts. Rent and tax reductions for co-operating communities
could be considered. And if such schemes seem too crassly self-in-
terested and also to underestimate the civic spirit of the neighborhood,
boy scouts and komsomols could collect the rewards and devote them to
work for the elderly or the handicapped or anyone nearby who needs
help.

A second line of approach could lie in making special and flexible
arrangements between citizens and collecting agencies. In Sweden, for

instance, the government has empowered a private corporation, PLM, to work out its own techniques of collection with co-operating citizens. Something like 176,000 households have responded. Half of them separate paper, glass, and tin cans; another 40 percent take out wastepaper only. The price inducement provides a stable bond between the company and the co-operating citizen.

The third path, especially appropriate perhaps to larger communities, is to begin, as in New York, with a high-technology approach for a part of the garbage separation, and then extend the system or not according to the degree of citizen participation. The response—motivated either by the prospect of payment or by a sense of civic duty—can be gauged, and facilities planned to match it. The evidence, inadequate as it still may be, does indicate that people are readier to do things for their community than much of the popular denouncing of apathy and carelessness may suggest. So often inaction simply reflects ignorance of what to do. Citizen education, clearly organized collection systems, some down payments if necessary, might before too long produce a busy, co-operating, garbage-sifting community. And since the cost of self-help schemes is very much lower than the investments for high technology, the path of wisdom for municipal authorities would seem to lie in resisting the bureaucratic temptation to rely solely on the large plants of high technology, which can be ordered and installed according to known procedures, and which, unlike the unruly citizen, neither vote nor answer back. A mixed system, vitally involving the community itself, is at least worth a first attempt. Its further expansion and development can then depend upon citizen response.

8 WATERS AND WASTES

THERE IS AN analogy between the citizens' reaction to water and its uses for human benefit and the recent careless "slosh-on" approach to energy. At its core is the virtual impossibility, in most developed lands, of believing that there is any reason for conserving water. Most developed nations are in temperate zones which have quite simply all the water they need. True, the *fresh* water available for all human uses, evaporated and desalinated by the sun from the land and the oceans (which contain over 97 percent of the world's water) and then returned to the earth's rivers, lakes, and ground water through rain and snow and hail and dew, is only a tiny portion of the earth's fresh-water reserves, since most of the planet's fresh water is either frozen at the poles and in permanent glaciers or lies too deep in the ground for human use. But the minute percentage nonetheless adds up to over 25 quadrillion gallons every year.* It also falls most reliably in the temperate zones, and even the most confirmed pessimist would find it hard to worry about the availability of millions of billions of gallons on such a scale.

The results of this abundance are predictable. Modern developed societies use water as lavishly and wastefully as they have been using fossil fuels, and have seen themselves as possessing even more cogent economic reasons for doing so. Water costs virtually nothing. On the average, water makes up no more than 0.5 percent of industrial costs. Industry uses almost unbelievable amounts—up to 125,000 gallons for a ton of printing paper, 200,000 gallons for a ton of aluminum. A ton of synthetic rubber can require 500,000 gallons. Another symptom of disregard lies in the remarkably different amounts of water used in industry for identical processes. In making soap, for instance, precisely the same

---

* This figure is for the total precipitation falling on land in one year.

unit of output and the same type of product can use anything from 1,000 to 37,000 gallons.

Yet all these millions of gallons inevitably pick up poisons and chemical impurities along the way, and as they reach rivers, lakes, and estuaries, add to the filth of inadequately treated sewage and fertilizer runoff—a load of contaminants already threatening most major rivers and inland seas. The 150 billion gallons used every day in the United States for cooling thermal power stations are not so prone to direct pollution, but they can increase the temperature of lakes and rivers and thus drastically distort the aquatic ecosystem.

Domestic use of water presents an equal number of inconsistencies and stupidities. The water needed in a house for cooking, drinking, and bathing, the uses where total cleanliness is essential, amounts to only about a quarter of all that is in fact used. The rest goes to watering lawns and washing cars, to the laundry and the toilets (in any one year a typical user contaminates 13,000 gallons of clean water to flush away only 165 gallons of the body's wastes).

In temperate zones, agriculture relies overwhelmingly on rainfall, not on specially diverted irrigation water. (Big exceptions to this rule, such as California, confront problems which occur more often in the Third World's arid lands.) But even in temperate farming, a particular form of wastage cannot be ignored. Overuse of fertilizers or biocides leaves behind in the fields more nutrients and toxins than plants need or the soil can absorb. So the surplus is washed off into the watercourses. Fertilizers stimulate the growth of aquatic plants, upsetting the ecological balance, and can so overstimulate the growth of algae that the decaying plant life consumes virtually all the water's dissolved oxygen, leaving a virtually dead, foul-smelling swamp behind. Biocide runoff can, as we have seen, cause massive fish kills—and all agricultural chemicals can poison water downstream or underground and thus contaminate other people's potential supplies of drinking water. Although in theory (and usually in practice) ground water is renewed by the cycle of raining days and months, there are cases of pumping levels which so far exceed any replacing flow that the result can be severe subsidence of the ground itself. London is said to have sunk by six feet in the last three hundred years. Things are brisker in Las Vegas, which has dropped by four feet in only twenty years and in some areas is literally beginning to crack open. In some coastal zones, pumping up too much ground water has allowed salt water to begin to seep into fresh-water aquifers.

Another symptom of overuse—already briefly mentioned—occurs when a watercourse like the Rhine or the Hudson has to sustain such multiple "insults"—industrial effluents, untreated sewage, thermal pollution—that it reaches a stage at which the possibility has to be faced that no affordable retreatment process will make its water reliable for drinking. Another form of overloading can be found in the Colorado River, which is dammed and diverted again and again to provide irrigation and drinking water for America's southwestern states and arrives in Mexico in a condition of unacceptable salinity

Then there remains the lack of any real reserves or fallback positions in the case of drought. In Western Europe in 1976, even the British Isles, with their traditionally weeping skies, endured a four-month interruption in rainfall. France's hydroelectric flow was so sharply reduced that a billion dollars had to be spent to import extra oil. Again in 1977, the American Southwest—admittedly on the dry side of the temperate zone—had to introduce water-conservation schemes and pump up what could be a dangerous quota of extra ground water in order to survive a dry spell. Few meteorologists will hazard any very exact predictions about future weather. Yet in the last year or so a consensus has developed that weather systems appear to be on the way to becoming more "unstable." Within the range of instabilities must be included the possibility of further and perhaps longer droughts. To be without reserves or alternatives could threaten every sector of society—industrial, agricultural, or domestic.

The response most congenial to contemporary attitudes is simply to decree that there shall in fact be larger supplies of water and that engineers must set to work to provide them. But the issue is not so simple. Something like 89 percent of the developed nations' sites for large water reservoirs (usually combined with hydroelectric installations) have already been used up, and there is already competition for what may remain. Valuable farmland, areas of great natural beauty, historic sites, cannot be carelessly engulfed. The size and the cost of some schemes are already daunting. One thinks of Denver, which taps runoff from the Rocky Mountains through a 1,500-mile distribution system to provide water for its very rapid recent growth, or of the vast interchanges which bring the waters of the San Joaquin and Sacramento rivers from northern California to supply the bulk of the population who live in the southern part of the state. And these are dwarfed by some of the more ambitious proposals for the future. Some plans discuss the possibility of bringing huge volumes of water from Alaska and north Canada all the way down through seven Canadian provinces and three or four times as many American states—with even perhaps a small bonus for Mexico. On a similar scale, the Russians are discussing turning round Siberian rivers which flow into the arctic and bringing them southward to irrigate the arid lands of central Asia. Similarly, in China, some of the waters of the vast Yangtze River may be turned to the drought-prone north.

The cost of such vast schemes is not the only question that remains in doubt. What effects would follow for wider climatic regions? Are the Siberian and Alaskan rivers essential to some heat balance in arctic waters which, if once disturbed, could unpredictably spread regions of uncultivable permafrost or exercise a wholly unforeseen impact on marine currents and marine life?

Cost is the difficulty with one other possible method of expanding water supplies—desalination. The process requires large amounts of energy, and although there are a number of relatively inexpensive sun-powered distilleries in tropical areas and oil-powered ones in the Arab oil states, to obtain water on anything like the scale required for a large urban region would inflict unacceptable increases in energy costs. (And a lot of salt would have to be harmlessly disposed of, too.)

The conclusion is obvious. As with so many other human uses—and abuses—of the earth's materials, a *conserving* strategy both provides more of what is required and does so at a much diminished cost, occasionally even at a profit. If we take our three divisions—domestic, industrial, and agricultural—each offers its own particular opportunities for less wasteful use. We can begin with industry since, in developed states, it is the largest consumer of water supplies, in fact using between 60 and 80 percent of all the water employed. The largest single saving is, of course, to stop a once-through-the-plant process and begin the internal recirculation of the water. It is this fundamental change in tactic that accounts for the extraordinary variations that have already been noted in the volume of water used. Another critical advantage of the conserving and recycling techniques is that they make possible far more control over noxious wastes and chemicals (or even their recovery and re-use), so the water flow can be prevented from simply carrying them off into the nearest watercourse.

One of the most polluting of industries—pulp and paper making—has been transformed in Sweden since the late 1960s. When quite tough environmental standards were first applied, the industry had the choice of setting up waste-treatment plants to deal with the effluents once they were released or to re-use the water, with internal cleansing processes, inside the plant. It was soon discovered that this conserving strategy not only made the maintenance of environmental standards more reliable but cut down the use of water so sharply that the industry estimates that when all plants have adopted the most modern methods, the amount of water used may well be only one-third of the 1971 level. In another area, the Soviet Union, it is reported that a new recycling design for an ammonia plant cut water use by 90 percent, reduced energy consumption to a degree which allowed the managers to dispense with a 70 megawatt electricity generator, and still made ammonia at one-third of the conventional cost.

The most straightforward way of encouraging the change-over to more conserving methods is to introduce water charges and end the myth of cost-free disposal. These charges can also be accompanied by tax rebates and depreciation allowances to cover part of the cost of the necessary changes in process equipment—a particularly important point wherever new water charges threaten to knock out the small plant while being comfortably carried by the large.

But less use of fresh water can probably be made even more effective in some areas by the relatively simple procedure of using for factory processes not the river's pristine flow, but recycled water from the city's sewage-treatment plant. We come back to the point that not all water needs to be at a standard fit for drinking in order to do its work. Partially treated water (say, with the grit and sediment removed, as in primary treatment) can be used for the town's factory system. This is already happening in Kawasaki, in Japan, and near Naples, in Italy. Within such a dvision lies the germ of a new idea, at least for new settlements—to establish a dual system, providing two qualities of water: one meeting prescribed standards for drinking, cooking, bathing, and certain high-quality industrial needs; the other for general use in the factory or in domestic lavatories and garages, recycled through its own second-grade circuit.

Such a dual system could have obvious domestic importance. The toilet systems and primary cleaning would use the less treated water— water closets in Hong Kong use sea water now—while water at drinking standards would be supplied (and metered) separately. However, short of the complications and expense of introducing new sanitary practices into old communities, a lot of water could quite simply be saved by the straightforward principle of making people pay for it. It is also perfectly possible to save water by inserting a brick or a plastic gadget into the toilet tank. The Japanese have an ingenious invention which releases varying amounts of water, according to need, depending on the direction in which the handle is turned. There has still not been the fallout of new sanitary arrangements—chemical toilets and so forth—which space travel seemed at one time to promise, but experiments are being made with pressure and vacuum systems to see whether the amount of water passing through domestic drains cannot be drastically reduced. Meanwhile, country districts and suburbia offer possibilities for new experiments. The composting toilet uses no water at all. Its bulkiness—it needs a large composting chamber—makes it unhandy for existing houses and generally inappropriate for high-density city buildings. But it could find more widespread use in rural areas and in low-density urban dwellings, especially since kitchen wastes can also be disposed of in the chamber and a usable compost produced.

Discussion of the use and saving of water in agriculture belongs to a later chapter, since it is especially important for developing countries in the hot and often arid zones. Most developed countries lie comfortably in the temperate belt; the crops pick up the water they require from the falling rain, and the rest flows off into rivers and lakes and aquifers. But there is one particular aspect of water use that is relevant for developed agriculture—the role that the employment of partially treated waste water could play both in increasing productivity and in purifying the water supply.

One of the difficulties with the various stages of sewage treatment is that even secondary treatment leaves the nitrogen and the phosphates in the water. Yet these are just the nutrients that farmers need to produce high crop yields. If, therefore, like fertilizer runoff, they are left in the effluent and dumped into rivers and lakes, they provide a banquet for the algae, which "bloom" and then use up the water's dissolved oxygen in their decay. The final result can be lakes or rivers with virtually no oxygen at all. This is a serious drawback to the whole development of better treatment plants and lower pollution, for it does not make much sense to spend billions of dollars on secondary treatment and still lose the dissolved oxygen by another route.

But in Paris, treated water is used to irrigate market gardens. Methane produced by the waste treatment powers the pumps. In Muskegon County, Michigan, in the United States, over two thousand hectares of farmland are irrigated with waste water that has gone through secondary treatment. The land gains all the nitrogen and phosphates which it needs and the water is purified for return to rivers and aquifers. The irrigated croplands flourish—in 1976, the crop yield was 60 percent higher than the average for the county. Downstream users find their water in better condition. To crown everything, the system produces its own profit. In a sense one can say that instead of the high expense and complex technology of such tertiary-treatment plants as have been built—one remembers Lake Tahoe in the United States—the soil itself is the safest, cheapest, and most useful purifier. Once again, working with and not against the needs and functions of natural things produces not only a better environment but a profit as well.

9 FUEL FOR FOOD

NOTHING IN THE developed world since the Second World War has changed so radically as agriculture. The simplest description is to say that it has become industrialized at an unprecedented speed. Even as late as 1958, there were still as many farm horses as tractors in Britain. Now there are about 500,000 tractors—part of Europe's pool of nearly 7 million—and the number of working horses on the farms is negligible. Another measure of the change is the incredible speeding up of farm operations. Some American estimates suggest that it took a farmer 150 minutes of human labor to produce a bushel of corn in the 1900s. By 1955, the time was down to 16 minutes. By the mid-seventies, it was less than 3. Another index of the cataclysmic speed of change can be taken from the figures of those working in agriculture. As late as 1945, American farming still required 20 billion man-hours a year. By the mid-seventies, the figure was not much above 3 billion. In France, the number of people in agriculture has remained comparatively high, but their proportion has fallen from 25 to 10 percent of the work force since 1950. Even in Switzerland, where urbanization is still relatively modest, the share of the wage bill for farm workers has fallen from 17 to 2 percent since the last war.

The whole process can, of course, be seen as the final absorption into technological society of a still relatively preindustrial sector. The 100,000 farms that disappear in America every year are part of the same historical evolution that has brought 80 percent of the population in most developed lands into urban and suburban ways of life. But there is no doubt that the revolutionary speeding up of the whole process after 1945 had at its root the fantastically low cost of oil. This encouraged an extremely rapid substitution of mechanical power for labor and a vast increase in the use of fertilizer derived from fossil fuels. Where land was cheap and labor expensive, as in North America, the emphasis has been on increasing "labor productivity" through mechanization—in other words, getting rid of the men and putting in the machines. As a result, output per worker is now very high, but output per hectare almost certainly lower than it would have been had "efficiency" been measured by total food production rather than by output per man-hour.

Japan's farming shows the other extreme, with expensive land and cheaper labor. The stress there has been on getting the most out of small farms with high fertilizer applications and intensive farming. Output per hectare is very high, but output per worker relatively low. Countries in Western Europe fall between these two extremes. Land and labor costs are more nearly in balance and give reasonably high outputs for both hectare and worker.

But a rapid increase in the use of fertilizers is common to all industrial nations. The figures tell the tale. Between 1960 and 1975, Holland and France tripled, Canada quadrupled, and the Soviet Union increased eightfold, the production of nitrogen fertilizer. Since the war, Britain has taken to using five times more nitrogen fertilizer and eighteen times more phosphates and potash. Fertilizer use in the United States has multiplied sevenfold in the same period.

This combination of increased mechanization and higher fertilizer use has helped to put the agriculture of the developed world into the heavy-industry class as a user of energy. In Britain, in 1972, each full-time worker was backed by a direct energy input of nearly twelve tons of oil equivalent each year.

But, of course, this average figure per worker does not include energy that is applied once the food has left the farm. Indeed, agriculture has to be seen now in the wider context of the whole "food industry." In 1970, in the United States, for instance, the farms themselves accounted for only a quarter of all the energy used to grow the food and get it to the table. Food processing and packaging accounted for a quarter. Transport took 15 percent. Finally, households and commercial caterers, between their freezers and their cooking stoves, absorbed the remaining 35 percent.

These figures represent to a considerable degree another lightning change—in the way in which the developed peoples eat. Increasing affluence appears everywhere to bring with it an increasing desire for such high-protein foodstuffs as meat or poultry or eggs. Even Japan, once an almost vegetarian country, tripled its meat consumption between 1961 and 1974. The bounding (and sometimes unmet) demand for grain from Soviet farms reflects not only a nation of tremendous bread-eaters but a steadily rising demand for meat. Another change, made possible by a vast expansion in refrigeration, is the expectation of eating, all the year round, the vegetables and fruit—the peas and beans, the peaches and strawberries—which once were for summer sale. A last change, linked to new patterns of domestic life, with wives and husbands both at work, is the expansion of precooked "convenience" foods, ready for instant defreezing or decanning and heating up, in place of the long tasks of cleaning carrots, peeling potatoes, and basting the meat. One might also add that in the United States more than three-quarters of the food is prewashed, precooked, or otherwise preprocessed.

Nor should we forget the degree to which all these changes of diet have contributed to the rapid growth of self-service stores—super-markets and hypermarkets—where the whole new range of choice is laid out, in refrigerated cabinets and open shelves, for the busy house-holders who have just time to park, rush in, seize their prepackaged steak and sausage and frozen eggplant, queue to pay, and drive home again—with perhaps five kilograms of food in a two-ton motorcar.

No one can deny the many benefits of this revolution in food sup-plies. Food output has grown quite steadily—about 2 to 3 percent a year, with much of the expansion due to higher use of fertilizers, im-proved seed, fewer weeds and pests, and in countries of uncertain cli-mate, the speed with which machines can get in the harvest in sudden spells of good weather.

Nor should we forget the number of citizens who have neither the time nor the preference to cook and home-cure and home-bottle in "the way my mother used to." Anyone decrying prepackaged food must honestly face his or her readiness to wield the vegetable knife. No market could have grown so quickly against a background of indifferent customers. No, it is not the convenience or even the acceptability of the food revolution of the last thirty years that is in question. It is simply its profound wastefulness, its almost total dependence upon cheap energy and its liability to a number of subsidiary effects—on human health, markets, and institutions.

We can look at the waste from three points along the food process—production, distribution, and consumption. The actual mechanization of many operations in the field has not been wasteful in itself. Indeed, we should remember that farm horses used to require up to a third of the land for fodder growing and also a larger work force to take care of their harnessing, cleaning, and bedding down. Land has been released for growing crops, while manpower needs have fallen as a result of mechanization. But there are one or two points of difficulty. The very rapid rise in oil prices has been a key factor in sharply rising food prices, and until alternative fuels are found, future increases in fossil-fuel costs (dictated inevitably by shrinking reserves) will be reflected at once in the food markets. We should also remember that such energy-intensive food systems do not provide a workable world model. If the American habit of using not much less than a ton of oil equivalent for each citizen's food every year—with Western Europe not far behind—were adopted on a planetary scale, the process would, of itself, absorb *half* the world's present level of energy use. As it is, the high-energy food system is one reason why the United States, for 5 percent of the world's people, is now consuming nearly 40 percent of its nonrenewable energy resources.

Where cheap oil produced undoubted waste was in the rapidly growing use of agrochemicals kept cheap by the low cost of power and oil feedstocks. They could be sloshed on without particular regard for the crop's needs or its growing cycles. Biocides killed off pests and their predators indiscriminately. Agriculture become a major polluter of developed water supplies. Nor were these the only pollutants encouraged by cheap energy. To satisfy rapidly rising demand for meat and poultry products, farmers began applying "industrialized" methods to meat, fowl, and egg production. Herds as large as 100,000 cattle have been brought together under cover, stuffed with cereals, mass-produced for the markets while their wastes simply slop off into the nearest water body. Battery hens are processed on the same principle. The waste is twofold. The operations themselves depend upon heavy uses of fuel. But, in addition, the animals are fed grain fit for direct human consumption and convert this grain to meat very inefficiently. Something like five to ten pounds of grain have to be put into the beast to produce one pound of meat or eggs. These are the production methods which have made it possible for human consumption per capita of "grain equivalent" in North America to grow to nearly a ton a year (with only 150 pounds directly in cereal) while the Soviet Union and some European countries are not far behind. Yet the average Indian diet is an annual four hundred pounds of grain, largely eaten as grain.

When we turn to distribution costs, we find that some of them are simply due to the newly satisfied desire for all-the-year-round foodstuffs. It is quite impossible to fly in avocados from Kenya or Israel without incurring a stiff fuel bill. At a more mundane level, general dependence upon the Great Plains of North America for the grain surplus which underpins a high-protein diet means that steady and, in times of Russian shortage, large transport costs absorb energy and must be added to food prices.

With anything that fluctuates as much as grain harvests, storage costs are inevitable, but the decline of the mixed farm and the growth of the large single purpose unit has meant that one of the cheapest and most useful forms of storage—spare grain fed to pigs and poultry on the farm itself—has seriously declined.

We should also not forget one form of waste already mentioned, the food-packaging explosion. According to the EPA, the consumption of food in the United States by weight per person grew by only 2.3 percent between 1963 and 1971. But the tonnage of wrapping and separate packets went up, one by over 33 percent, the other by nearly 39 percent. No rational explanation has yet been given for this astonishing addition to the fuel and food bill.

Inside the home, the balance of waste and use is difficult to assess. The deep freeze, for instance, is a small user of fuel and can be a vast conserver both of food and of human time. It is practically impossible to do a cost/benefit contrast between the amenity and acceptability of older cooking habits and the new kitchen of devoted "energy slaves," all the way from the oven to the parsley chopper. Too much depends upon personal interest and preference, too much on the pressure of time. But the kitchen does not seem a major culprit—save in one respect. It is the place from which extravagant amounts of usable food are simply thrown away. A recent congressional report discovered that the United States throws away every year enough food to feed fifty million people.

This waste is part of wider and, if the world grows hungrier, increasingly unacceptable aspects of developed diets. One cannot claim that the late twentieth century is a time of very general hard physical labor in the developed world. The car and the television set and the growing volume of office work may well have produced the most literally sedentary population human society has ever known. But at the same time, diets stuffed with the proteins and calories needed for a lumberman or a professional boxer have become prevalent. Everywhere, high meat consumption demands grain-fed animals. Meanwhile, what little grain we do eat through bread usually has little nutritional value and roughage, since these are removed when the flour is refined. Thus the human bowel is deprived of the fiber it requires to function easily. The eating of fresh vegetables—which also give necessary fiber—has fallen off by between a third and a half in the last half century. Processed, defibered products have taken their place. The results are literally apparent. In all developed nations, obesity and diet-related illnesses are now a major medical problem. In West Germany, 2 percent of GNP (seven billion dollars) is spent each year helping people to recover from overeating and overdrinking. And lest this should be thought a wicked capitalist vice, the figure for East Germany is 1 percent of GNP, with 40 percent of the men and 20 percent of the women overweight. Many medical experts are now agreed that with fat, sugar, cholesterol, refined grains, food additives, and the general absence of roughage, modern citizens are literally —*via* heart attacks and cancer—eating and drinking themselves into the grave.

10 SAFER DIETS, WISER MEANS

CAN MODERN SOCIETIES be weaned from patterns of eating which are inherently unhealthy and at the same time wasteful, polluting, and in some instances destructive of the very soil in which the food is grown? In the short run, the answer can only be discouraging. It is difficult to doubt that United States habits have a way of infiltrating other cultures, and with one in every three food dollars already spent on eating outside the home, with hamburgers absorbing at least half of the nation's meat supply and McDonald's and Kentucky Fried Chicken becoming universal high-street attractions, the future looks all too safe for industrialized, energy-intensive forms of food production. In view of the steady rise in the demand for meat, a future of this kind certainly looks much more probable than, say, one characterized by the one-third reduction in meat eating which the American Medical Association has recommended in order to reduce the United States' pandemic increase in coronary and vascular disorders.

However, one possibility of reduction may well lie in the simple brutal fact of cost. The changes in diet and the increased eating of animal products over the last twenty years have been based upon two factors—neither of them repeatable. The first was a very great increase in the production of cereals made possible by new strains of cereals, fertilizers, and new machines. So much grain over and above human needs was produced in North America that it led to the usual consequence on traditional farms in years of grain surplus. More grain was fed to animals—to pigs, poultry, and cattle.

The second factor has been the bedrock cheapness, right through the food-production system, of fossil fuels. In the years ahead, the gains from new "breakthroughs" in cereal and fertilizer research may well be less. Fuel costs will steadily rise. The combined effect is likely to press most heavily on those foods which demand high inputs of cereals and energy. Our bodies are fueled by food, and the energy we get can be compared with the energy required to produce the food (in the form of labor, fuel for machines, fertilizers, and so on). A householder's vegetable plot—or an urban allotment—usually has an energy output of two to four times the amount put in to it. A Chinese farmer, with his intensive farming, can get an energy output forty times larger than his input. Wheat produced in Britain contains three to four times the energy it takes to produce it. In contrast, for intensively reared animals, the equation is reversed. Milk takes more than twice as much energy to produce as the consumer gets back in calories. Broiler meat passes on to the consumer only one-tenth of the energy invested in it. So does beef from feed lots. Commerical fishing operations can give back as little as a hundredth of the energy input. Such figures show how intensively raised animal products and ocean fish must be much more drastically affected by rising fuel prices than, say, wheat in the field or vegetables grown in the back garden.

Reinforcing the certainty that rising food costs will be linked to rising fuel prices is the fact that many farm sectors have already reached the stage of diminishing returns. In other words, the cost of more fertilizer is not recovered through the sale of the increased yield. The Dutch get 20 percent more wheat, 25 percent more potatoes, and 16 percent more animal produce from each hectare of land than do the British. But they spend more than twice as much as British farmers on fertilizers and lime, nearly twice as much on fuel, and four and a half times as much on feedstuffs. In terms of returns to this investment, the Dutch are a long way along the road at which an extra kilogram of fertilizer costs more than any increase in yield it may produce. In short, further "intensities of production" will not offset rising fuel and fertilizer costs because nearly all of these intensities have already been realized.

Some switch to less energy-intensive food may thus be a result of market changes. Simply because of the pressure on their pockets, people will give up some intensively produced meat. This does not in the least mean enforced vegetarianism. Lamb or mutton or indeed cattle raised on open pastureland unsuited to arable farming represent an extremely efficient, uncostly transformation of inedible grass into meat for human consumption. The raising of pigs on food wastes is a comparably unwasteful transformation. Both are more or less immune to rising costs for grain, fuel, and fertilizer.

But clearly the pocketbook need not be left to do the whole job. There are a number of steps that governments could take to encourage the change to cheaper and healthier diets. One would be to stand firm against demands from livestock farmers for any kind of subsidy in buying feed grains. This could be backed up with support for schemes that turn wastes into livestock feed. For example, a recent estimate in Britain suggested that at least half of Britain's pigs could be fed on processed institutional food wastes. This would save 1.5 million tons of grain a year and cut pig farmers' feed costs. Another approach could begin with the basic process of education—in schools, in the press, on television. Both Norway and Sweden have undertaken public-education programs on the basic facts of diet and the danger of unbalanced eating and drinking.

The pricing of food constitutes a wide area for experiment. There is not a government in the developed world that does not, in one way or another, manipulate the prices paid for at least some farm produce. From 1934 to a brief interregnum in 1975, the Americans fixed the price of wheat and food grains (as well as cotton and tobacco) and were ready to buy up all yields on offer at that price. To prevent this guarantee from creating unmanageable surpluses, farmers had to keep a proportion of land out of cultivation, and in the 1960s successive governments also reduced reserves by supporting needy countries abroad with cheap food under the so-called Public Law 480. For a time, in the seventies, the great Russian grain raid cleared out stocks to the point at which both price support and cultivated-land limitations in the name of the "free market" were dropped. As a result wheat prices tripled. But harvests are too uncertain for any prolonged reliance on market mechanisms. Record harvests in 1976/77 brought back both the pressure for guaranteed prices and the possibility of retiring land. They also, as we shall see, make at least possible the creation of global grain reserves on a more rational basis.

The EEC has no dietary policy. The aim of its commodity price-support system has been simply to obtain the highest economic returns to farmers, which in the days of expanding cereal production and cheap fuel meant encouraging the trend to highly mechanized farms and more concentration on animal products. But these days are passing. Given the practice of annual target fixing for prices, the EEC at least has a mechanism for examining the possibility of subsides and restraints which encourage the direct eating of grain, fresh fruit, and vegetables while lowering the consumption of animal fats generally.

But is hard cash to be the only educator? Developed peoples have increased their demand for grain by a third in the last couple of decades (largely to feed it to themselves through animals). Behind them a number of other countries, notably in the Communist bloc, are beginning to demand more ''affluent'' diets. Other developing countries are moving up in the growth league. Yet North America is the only area capable of producing a rising supply of surplus grain. At this point, is it irrational to ask whether there may not be an argument not in cash but in conscience for Western diets to become more restrained in their supercereal consumption? The time has come to establish the kind of reserves of world grain that prevent damaging swings from plenty to penury, that unsettle world food prices, promote hoarding when harvests falter, starve the poorest, and add inflationary pressure to food prices even for the well-off. No farmer minds a ''free market'' in time of scarcity. The trick is to get the kind of control over reserves that guarantees him an income in times of plenty and protects the consumer—who is now the world-wide consumer—in times of dearth. At the United Nations Conference on Food in Rome in 1974, a reasonably comprehensive scheme was proposed for this type of world system. It included a small immediate reserve for instant use in disasters like the Bay of Bengal typhoon. It added a larger reserve, turned over each year and equal perhaps to sixty days of world consumption, to stabilize grain prices. Most vital of all, it demanded quite new levels of investment in developing world agriculture.

If this scheme was carried out, it would be possible to plot the needed scale of reserves against the increase in food sufficiency in deficit areas like Bangladesh. Meanwhile, the North Americans, who alone can fill the storage granaries, should not be left to carry the full cost of providing the world's system of food insurance. All wealthy countries should contribute, say, through a sum fixed in proportion to their GNP. The difficulty with the scheme is the unreadiness of the Europeans (let alone the Arabs) to bind themselves to contribute to this ''ever-full granary'' and the uneasiness of the American farmer, who tends to see a reserve as permanently depressing his grain price.

However, if citizens on both sides of the Atlantic began, for conscience's sake, eating less cereal-stuffed meat, governments in Europe

A Thames gravel pit

The same pit restored

Hot water in the city, 70 percent from the sun

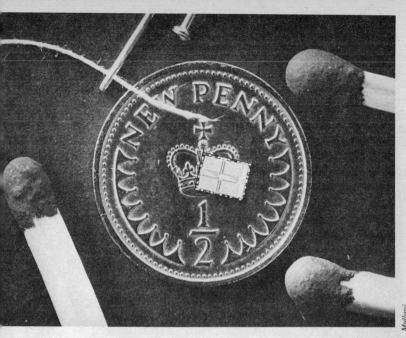

Silicon chips, obsolete workers?

High-rise living—how far can a child reach?

and North America would come under pressure from the farmers to keep up grain production, and this pressure, politically, would help the setting up of an adequate grain reserve—internationally financed, renewed, and regulated. Citizen conscience, the need for healthier diets, and the cereal farmers' interests in production and income would begin to move in the same direction. Combined, they could provide a period of world control of cereal reserves long enough to allow the Third World better to satisfy its own needs and meanwhile ward off the risk of mega-famines.

When we turn from diet to the problems of processing and distributing food, clearly we are enmeshed in all the changes, vast and small, brought about by the industrial revolution. By bringing large numbers of people together in manufacturing cities, industry by its very nature broke up many of the old food networks—from farm to market to village shop—which had been based very largely on local self-sufficiency (in good years, but near famine in bad). There could be little idea of bringing food from great distances—save for the spices which launched Europe on its colonial ventures and gave some taste to salty and often maggoty meat at the dead end of winter. Tea, coffee, and cocoa were added as colonial products later. The steamship and the train expanded the whole scope of supply. Refrigeration followed. Cheap foods, imported from fertile, temperate, largely empty lands, reduced British agriculture to virtual stagnation from the 1870s to the Second World War. Imports of cheap food kept wages low, low wages produced cheap manufactures which were then sold to purchase the cheap food in a circuit that kept people fed but at the cost of slack times in farming and, for an island, some strategic questions about possible interruption of supply.

The real surge of change followed the 1950s. Cheap fuel and fertilizer had their inevitable effect. They kept cereal prices low while draining more and more people to the cities, where they would—inevitably—live still farther away from local food supplies and depend more and more on processed food obtained increasingly through integrated marketing and processing units. Often these were co-operatives (with federations at regional and national levels) which organized both the input and the marketing of the produce. Such co-operative organization remains strong in many nations. It dominates Japanese and Danish agriculture and in Sweden handles most of the milk, livestock, and egg production. Marketing co-operatives also handle Soviet and Eastern Eu-

ropean food sales. In other countries, corporations increasingly play this
role. In the United States, co-operatives remain strong for a few agricultural products, but corporations control more and more food production
and have a virtual monpoly on food processing. Similarly, in Britain, a
handful of firms control much of the processed-food production. One
reason is the simple one of scale of markets. The Tokyo conurbation has
more than twenty million people, New York City nearly seventeen
million in its metropolitan area. Such vast markets must have means of
organization and distribution on a very considerable scale. This is not a
question of ideology or varying economic structures. The Russians face
the same problems in Moscow. Even in smaller lands, like Sweden, the
various co-operative movements have had to integrate their activities
"vertically" to remain competitive both in buying supplies for their
members and in disposing of their produce. But there is a question
whether the extraordinary cheapness of the cereal and fuel inputs has
not led to some distortions, so that new directions should be sought.

Such directions could include a reconsideration of the universal validity of the concept of "comparative advantage." No one supposes that
coffee beans can be grown in Essex or near Hamburg. But do the tomato
growers of New Jersey have to be knocked out of local markets by
Florida corporations that use gases to "ripen" the fruit and have perfected a hybrid with a skin that has a tensile strength comparable to standards laid down by government for the front bumpers of a motorcar?
True, it has long "shelf life." But that can hardly be counted as an
ingredient in the body's needed budget of fresh fruit and vegetables.
Additives are another drawback of these centrally produced foods and
long-distance supply systems. The American federal government is
having to re-examine over two thousand additives in processed food on
the grounds that they may pose significant risk to health. Some of the
most alarming are the antibiotics which are added to animal feed to encourage growth and uniformity but which risk a build-up of immunities
in potentially dangerous bacteria and thus a lack of protection for
humans in times of infection.

These questions of processing and distribution in industrial society
have no single or even simple answers. The big cities are facts. The
convenience of packaged foods is a fact. The past cheapness of cereals,
fuels, and distribution has helped to make them facts. What one must
perhaps envisage is a partial undoing of the disadvantages and dangers

by means of a wide range of different policies and above all, over time. Most of the changes that have appeared since, say, 1750 have taken thirty to forty years to become apparent. Even the consequences of the sudden postwar fuel explosion were not fully realized for nearly twenty years. There will not be any sudden answers now, but there can be a variety of changes and trends.

Some we have looked at already. The food-processing industry is one of the worst waste producers. Strict environmental controls to check the very polluting effluents will promote a rethinking of the processes of food production and the handling of wastes they generate. Many food-processing firms now convert their wastes into animal feed, since this is more profitable than submitting the wastes to the levels of treatment they require in order to meet mandatory pollution standards. Using waste water to irrigate and help fertilize croplands is another alternative attractive enough to be used by such giants of the industry as Campbell Soup. Standardized, recyclable cans, returnable bottles, packaging taxed by weight, can be required by governments to preserve use while preventing profligacy. Subsidies for fresh and healthy food also fit into the category of possible public action.

Sharply rising fuel and transport costs may well have the effect of encouraging regional centers of distribution for goods like meat and dairy products, fruit and vegetables, where comparative advantage is a particularly fuzzy concept and the value of the fresh produce particularly high. In South Carolina and Georgia, a government program helps small farmers to organize "food fairs," bringing their produce to city consumers. In North America and Western Europe, direct farmer-to-consumer marketing through such food fairs and through roadside stands, is becoming increasingly popular, as are "pick-your-own-food" operations that give the added bonus of a little unexpected exercise.

But perhaps one of the most interesting pointers to a possible future change lies in some of the things citizens want to do for themselves. One such symptom is the popularity of consumer food co-operatives in North America—the originator and chief exponent of the standardized food industry—and these are also increasingly common in Western Europe. Rather on the food-fair principle, families and households join together on a street or district basis and establish direct links with wholesalers and with farmers at not too great a distance. They arrange bulk contracts and then resell locally among themselves.

Another pointer lies in the degree to which urbanized people retain the desire to grow some of their own food. Something like two-thirds of Russia's fruit and vegetables are grown on the peasants' minuscule private plots. A small farm in China, Taiwan, or Japan, cultivated with garden-like intensity, produces the highest yields in the world. There is no reason why a certain "labor intensity"—in other words, men and women digging their own plots—should not have the same result in the developed West. In Britain, the municipal authorities are supposed by law to provide allotments for would-be gardeners. There are over 700,000 urban allotments and a waiting list of over 100,000. Urban allotments are common in Holland. The capital city of Canada, Ottawa, is experimenting with a "rent-a-garden" scheme to create five thousand small lots within easy reach of the city center. As we have seen, many Dutch communities sell waste-derived compost to a whole ring of market gardeners. In the United States, nearly three million people now work on some thirty thousand community-owned garden sites. The government put three million dollars into urban gardening programs in sixteen large metropolitan cities for 1978—and from New York City comes the comment that "the gardens have improved and revitalized many blighted areas of the city. We didn't just grow vegetables, we actually grew hope." The retail value of home-grown vegetables in the United States was more than fourteen billion dollars in 1977. Nor is all this a capitalist quirk. In East Germany, one family in eight has an allotment—and these produce over 200,000 tons of fruit and vegetables a year as well as most of the honey and half the eggs.

Another aspect of the same readiness of many citizens, especially young ones, to provide the calories for food production out of their own energy can be seen in the growing popularity in Britain and North America of "weekends on the farm," where young people go off and for no pay, in return for their keep, hoe and clear and muck out, and do all the other jobs which accumulate on labor-scarce farmsteads. Some estimates suggest that as many as half of the households in the United States produce some of their own food, and certainly one of the most effective appeals of suburbia is not the shaven lawn in front but the vegetable patch at the back.

The amount of land lying neglected in urban areas—lying between demolition and rebuilding, in speculative expectation of the next land boom or simply in the un-care of an indifferent municipality—is on such a scale that the question arises whether developed governments (rather like the Chinese round Shanghai) should not establish market gardens, orchards, and even small mixed farms in such areas. Nothing could do more for public amenity than to see the decaying neglected haunts of weeds and old cars and abandoned chicken coops turned back into productive land. Admittedly, the disintegration of urban life in some areas means that such enclaves of high and orderly production might simply be robbed and vandalized. Yet allotments on the whole seem secure. School children could receive training literally on the ground in growing—and not destroying—plants. Local surveillance need not be oppressive. Above all, perhaps, order breeds order, and it is precisely the images of neglect and squalor given by abandoned land that lead on so easily to the corresponding temptations to violence and abuse.

But when we reach the level of systematic farming in urban belts, it is not really the part-time citizen gardener who is in question but the productive system itself. Can this, in a larger sense, be made more truly fruitful and conserving?

11 FARMING FOR TOMORROW

THREE OF THE most exceptional features of developed farming in the last thirty years can now be summed up. The first is an input of energy which can put food production in the heavy-industry class as a user of fossil fuels. The second is a scale of grain use for animal feeding for which there is no precedent in history. The third is a scale of chemical input and a disregard of the natural fertilizers produced by the processes of farming itself which make the agricultural sector one of the largest water polluters, even in societies where over 90 percent of the work force are not engaged in agriculture at all. As a picture of "unconserving" practice, it is formidable. But it is equally formidable to reverse trends which have behind them so many of the economic and technological postulates and so many of the consumer preferences of our day.

However, whatever the often unconscious drives, images, and aspirations of "advanced" societies, change will come, if not by choice then by necessity. As we have seen, the kind of massive grain reserves for export that marked the postwar years is unlikely to be a lasting agricultural phenomenon. Diminishing returns on the farms are beginning to appear in North America, the only true surplus area. World demand for cereals is rising and with it the risk of as steadily rising prices. There are uncertainties over weather systems which have only to cut, say, a week of good weather for ripening and harvesting in Canada and Russia to make the 1973 grain rush a renewed possibility. At the same time, fossil fuels and all their derivatives in the shape of fertilizers and biocides will not become cheaper. The changes that lie ahead, affecting both grain and fuel, can and may be managed—ill or well. They cannot be avoided. So what can be done?

Fuel for tractors and agricultural machinery is a rational place to begin the search for an answer, since it is the major energy cost on the farms. A first point must be made. A world with a population to be fed now in excess of four billion can abandon forever any neo-Arcadian dream of ending reliance on modern technology and returning to the man behind the oxen—or, more likely, the woman with the hoe. As we have noted, draft animals can use up to a third of the available arable land for their own upkeep, and they cannot pace their work to the vagaries of weather. The tractor, on the contrary, requires no precious soil and works at the necessary tempo.

What is less clear is whether all forms of farm machinery have the use and adaptability of the tractor. The combine harvester, which is often comfortably unused for some 330 days a year and then supposed to work flat out with no mechanical interruptions for the remaining month, seems a particularly unhandy piece of machinery. Its uncertain performance, according to some analyses, goes part of the way to explain the fluctuating and disappointing nature of Soviet harvests. At any one time, on any one collective farm, 50 percent of the machines have on occasion been reported to be out of order. In any economy, a combine harvester involves a very large capital input for any but the "big man," and co-operative structures do not help much since inevitably everyone wants to harvest at the same time on the same day of uncertain sunshine. What would appear to be necessary is a wider range of machines and manpower, available at harvest time but flexible enough for other work throughout the year. The Japanese have made a variety of experiments in what one might call garden-sized tractors for their very small farms—and have achieved among the highest yields per hectare in farming anywhere.

Similarly, experimentation may be necessary to determine the most efficient way to use artificial fertilizers and the various chemicals which counter pests, weeds, and fungi. More careful application of nitrogen fertilizer can prevent half of it from never being taken up by the plants at all and so seeping off to pollute watercourses. In the future lies the possibility of producing grains that fix their own nitrogen or techniques of stimulating the growth of nitrogen-fixing bacteria in the soil. The use of nitrogen fertilizer could then be greatly reduced.

The higher costs of chemical fertilizers should also encourage a much more careful estimate of what can be achieved by using vegetable and animal wastes on farms both for fertilization and for preservation of the soil's quality. At the height of squalid waste is, of course, the United States feed-lot farming, with grain fed to the beef cattle with a tenfold loss of calories and the manure dumped into whatever river or lake happens to be nearby. In these wholly artificial conditions, there is one possible solution—to compel feed lots by law to install "anaerobic-digestion" plants which transform their manure wastes into methane and a concentrated residue which is a valuable soil nutrient. All units in which animals are intensively reared have a major problem in disposing of the large volumes of liquid slurry the animals generate. But this slurry is an excellent feedstock for methane-generating plants, and one huge 100,000-cattle feed lot could supply the natural-gas needs of around fifteen thousand people. An alternative is to use composting plants to convert the liquid slurry from the massive feed lots into compost, making it far easier to handle, store, and spread on the fields.

But a wiser solution, encouraged by higher prices for grain, is to return cattle to their most conserving use in mixed herds for milk and meat, raised on pastureland—including hills, with sheep alongside (the two do not compete)—and fed with special fodder only during the winter months. Mixed farms guarantee the return of the manure and straw bedding to the soil—an essential part of the cycle which eliminates the leaching of essential nutrients from the soil. At the same time, they produce what is, on balance, a perfectly adequate meat diet, with lamb and mutton consumption increased and considerably less consumption of beef. Farm wastes, animal feed derived from the organic material in urban and industrial wastes, and in good years, spare grain can also keep up the farm reserve of poultry and pigs. The latter would return, with great advantage, to their traditional role of consuming wastes and acting as surplus store bins for grain. They would therefore no longer demand a steady year-round supply of grain as feed.

Wastes can have one further role, especially in warmer climates. They can be converted into fuel. Organic wastes will spontaneously yield methane in the absence of oxygen—the production of methane from cattle manure, mentioned above, is one example. Organic wastes such as inedible crop residues, like stalks and chaff, can also be fermented to produce ethanol, which then provides fuel for tractors and other agriculture machinery. Straw can be used as a fuel when grain has to be dried—or compacted into briquettes for solid fuel.

So valuable and various are the potential uses of natural fertilizers and organic wastes that some farmers have abandoned the use of chemicals altogether and turned to what is known as "organic" farming. The return of organic wastes to the soil, careful rotation of crops, and the use of "green manures"—legumes planted in the winter and plowed back into the soil before spring sowing—can produce yields comparable to those of "conventional" farms. One intensive study, conducted over two years in the United States corn belt, comparing organic and conventional farms on similar soils for similar products, came to the rather mixed conclusion that of the two the organic farms did rather better in bad weather, that in a good year the output of the organic farm was somewhat lower than that of the conventional farm, and that demands for labor were about equal. The really significant feature was that the organic farms were one-third as energy-intensive as the conventional farms. And since they often supply local food stores, mills, or food cooperatives, they can also greatly reduce the energy costs of food distribution.

At the same time, more careful, sophisticated, and often more labor-intensive methods of dealing with pests and weeds have begun to appear. For instance, if the life cycle of a particular pest is fully understood, a pesticide designed only to eliminate this one organism can be applied at a particularly vulnerable point in its life cycle. This means far less pesticide is needed. It also means that a wide range of species, including all the predators that help control the pests and other beneficial organisms, are not also killed by the pesticide. Another example of more careful use is the ultra-low-volume (ULV) sprayer—also known as "controlled droplet application"—which allows the farmer to deliver a very fine mist of concentrated pesticide to deal quickly and effectively with a pest infestation. This greatly reduces the amount of pesticide required.

Very large amounts of research have gone into producing chemical killers—with attendant risks of dangerous runoff, of devastation to many local species that are not pests, and of possible carcinogens concentrating up the food chain. But comparatively little research has been done by governments and farming institutions on biological control, in which pest predators are specially bred and released to control specific pests, or naturally occurring insect diseases are used for the same purpose. Both these techniques tend to be effective controls for the particular pests but harmless to all other organisms. The Australians were completely successful in eliminating a plague of cactus by importing the cactus moth (*Cactoblastis cactorum*) a South American moth whose larvae killed off the cactus. Another example is a disease of the cotton bollworm which is now being marketed—and should protect the cotton crop without the very heavy levels of pesticides in contemporary usage.

There also exists a wide range of other techniques, such as sterilization of male insects, breeding crops which are resistant to pest attack, cultivation of companion crops which repel pests, and the maintenance of hedgerows and shelter belts which provide alternative food for pests and house their natural enemies. The reintroduction of shelter belts in northern Germany has apparently increased crop yields by up to 20 percent. But one reason the big "spray-on" continues, in spite of the known and suspected risks and damaging effects, is that it demands very little manpower and virtually no attention at all to working with the enormous variety of soils, plants, and insect and animal life that make up a farm's ecology. Methods suitable to structural-steel production are often used on substances that are living, changing, developing—and dying under misuse. In fact, if one weakness more than any other can be attributed to "industrial farming," it is that a farm can never be a factory for the simple reason that one is alive and the other is not.

All these possible changes in the direction of a more conserving agriculture have one thing in common. They imply more care, more attention, more individual concern, more complex decision-making, and this is simply another way of saying they require more trained manpower with genuine agricultural and indeed managerial skills. The wholesale departure of workers from the land in developed countries has reflected in part a wage system which discriminates in favor of the organized industrial worker. But it was also a reflection of the fact that the fuel-cheap machines and chemicals could produce more for each man employed and thus considerably increase the over-all return on the farm. Now, thirty years later, direct costs in fuels and chemicals, and indirect costs in waste and pollution, are changing the equation. The possibly growing pressure on food supplies points in the same direction, since more labor-intensive farming is almost universally more productive by the standard that counts for the hungry family—not output per man but output per hectare.

We shall examine on a later page whether this changed relation of costs and benefits on the farms may not be coming at a time when both the industrial and the service sectors (and the "quaternary" sector) are beginning to show symptoms of structural unemployment. What begins to be significant is the evidence from a number of countries, including

the United States, that many young people would, if they thought they had any chance, like to become farmers. Self-sufficient food-producing communes are naturally not the answer to feeding a planet. But the number of them springing up suggests a readiness among the young for new experiments and new ways of life, if only the opportunities were felt to exist on a sufficient scale. At present, there is virtually no institutional support in any country for an enlargement of the farming community. For would-be trained farm workers there is quite simply no training at all in the places where they now are—in urban schools, possibly about to emerge into a jobless center city. For potential farmers, prohibitive costs for land—American farmland more than doubled in cost in the early seventies—lack of credit, lack of potential co-operative support, are equally widespread. Nor are they helped by the rapid expansion of "corporate farming," which brings food production, processing, and distribution into the kind of vertical integration that has given American corporations control of nearly 90 percent of the vegetable crop.

Admittedly, the size of possibly viable holdings is uncertain. It may well be that the German average—13.8 hectares—is simply inadequate to provide a living wage for highly developed farming. The Japanese manage a reasonable income and the highest productivity on 8 hectares. But in Europe the economic size, depending upon soil and types of cultivation, may well be larger (its average is now 15.5). In the United States, very large ratios of land to population exist—one citizen to every 129 hectares compared with virtually one for one in Japan. The prairies are prime grainlands and the world's only present insurance policy against the risk of famine. Four hundred hectares is perhaps a rational size here at the present stage of world food supplies, while in other areas, much smaller farms could provide adequate incomes for new farmers.

What does seem clear, whatever the scale demanded by types of output and densities of population, is that the most productive farms tend to be owner-occupied or farmed by tenants with very secure rights of tenure. The reason is obvious. If managerial skills are the final key to productivity ("the best fertilizer is the farmer's boots"), the more direct the interest and involvement, the better the chance of good husbandry and high yields. This does not mean that farms run as a sideline (often for tax advantages) are necessarily ill managed. Farm managers can be devoted servants of the land short of actual ownership. But any use of

land for speculative purposes or with little intention of long-term occupation must interfere with managerial continuity. (The absentee feudal landowner in developing countries reaches the acme of irresponsibility in this line.) And certain widespread forms of commercial
exploitation—for instance, the vertical integration from farm to frozen-
food company—do not necessarily give the farmer the freedom and
flexibility he needs to balance his books, keep his land in good heart,
and allow for the weather, especially if he is only permitted to produce
peas for freezing. This is not simply a problem of market economies.
Soviet agriculture has struggled since collectivization with the proper
balance between overdetailed instructions from the distant planners and
the need to give local farmers more flexibility. The shuttle of decision-
making has gone backward and forward, now stressing central instructions, now more local initiative.

But there is more than efficiency and effective food production in
the balance. In all systems, it becomes a social evil if those who do the
final work are too divorced both from the later gains their work makes
possible (the "value added") and from any creative say in how the
whole enterprise should be conducted. It is possible both in America's
type of "agribusiness" and in Russia's type of bureaucratic control to
underprice the work of the farmer at the base of the pyramid, leave him
out of the decision-making process, and by insisting on fixed deliveries,
often put undue strains on the productiveness of the land and the sensi-
tive management of particular sorts of ecosystem. We shall encounter
the problem of divorce of the producer from the processors in another
form in the developing world. But within developed societies, there are
creative alternatives—above all, the co-operative movement, which
permits farmers not only to share in the whole cycle of food production
but to exercise some control over distribution and general management.
One should not exaggerate. Well-managed, stable, commercial or collective farms on a sensible scale are to be found in all developed lands.
But it is certain that even at their best, they do not necessarily reach the
combination of productivity and conservation that marks the finest
farming and alone secures the long-term preservation of the land itself.

More conserving patterns of farming have effects that go beyond agriculture. Greater attention to types of soil, local flora, the natural ecosystems, can often bring back into use land that has been written off as
marginal and like the brecklands and heaths of East Anglia before the
Second World War simply abandoned to rabbit warrens and bracken.

Now they sturdily support mixed farms. People tend to leave remoter regions simply because they are, in modern transport terms, "remote." If more conserving patterns of farming were to bring back to the countryside skilled men and their families—one can estimate perhaps four extra people for every returning worker—a number of regional centers would revive or grow up, and, "remoteness" being a relative concept, the result could be that mixed farms, market gardens, orchards, hill farms, and even intensive restocking of fish in local lakes and streams might be combined to produce an environment at once more productive, more desirable, more attractive, and above all, more populated, than results from the present imbalance between concentrated urban and suburban areas and declining land and emptying villages everywhere else.

We will return to this issue of a better distribution of a nation's population in a later chapter. Here let it simply be asked whether between high-pressure commuting to cities whose centers may be slipping toward decay and expanding country towns surrounded by returning farmers, with small agro-industries springing up, services starting in schools, co-operatives, banks, and markets, and new communities coming into existence and experimenting with new social choice, there may not exist attractions, decisions, and opportunities to which in over a century of industrialization, the nations' rulers and planners have simply given insufficient thought?—or possibly no thought at all? In France, at least, in the most comprehensive rethinking of urban structure in any developed country, the fate of the small traditional centers is being at least considered. Could it be that reviving rural communities is one of the clues to the hope of a much wider revival of employment, social vitality, and the good life?

12 THE LAUNCHING PAD

WHEN WE TURN to the third category of change mentioned in the Prologue—the particular historical background of modern technological economies—there is an immediate paradox. When one considers traditional societies, with their backbreaking labor, killing plagues, high infant mortality, early death, and recurrent crises of near famine, it should have been a safe prophecy that the application of science and technology to man's and perhaps especially woman's daily work would bring with it a vast material improvement in the human condition. Some of the world's greatest thinkers certainly expected it. "When the looms run themselves, there will be no more slaves," said Aristotle. In the earliest days of the industrial revolution, the foremost commentator on the nascent system, Adam Smith, believed that provided all outmoded royal monopolies, obstructive bureaucracies, "circumlocution offices," tolls, levies, and the obsolete safeguards of the old craft guilds could be taken off the backs of the enterprising men who actually wanted to try out the new techniques, a whole new tide of energy and productivity could be released. Rational principles of demand and supply, operating in an unimpeded market, would lead to a unique and exemplary increase in the flow of goods at the citizen's disposal.

Yet in fact the first impact of industrialism was to produce some of the vilest conditions ever endured by a humanity not wholly inexperienced in the realities of misery. The fundamental point is that markets are not abstractions. They occur within social frameworks, and in the late eighteenth century there could be no question of "unimpeded entry"—in other words, more or less equal bargaining power in a free market. The whole society was tilted toward the power of land and its natural resources and toward capital—the savings required to cover the time needed to build the machines and the factories and get them to work. One thinks of Mary Davies, who as the technological revolution was starting up, brought a few hundred hectares of swampy land by the Thames into the Grosvenor family as a dowry. But these included Belgravia and Pimlico, and when London grew to engulf them, the value of the land—the "unearned increment"—created by the community's growth rose to give the Grosvenors an effortless inheritance which even today has been put as high as half a billion dollars—a position not without market power. This was, no doubt, an extreme example. The mass of savings, increasingly channeled into business by a growing body of enterprising bankers, often came from artisans and craftsmen and small traders who used their own savings—and their friends'—to launch a new machine or service. Many failed. But the key to success was the ability to mobilize savings—the greater the mobilization, the larger the market power.

Against these forces, the third and indispensable factor of production, labor, had little chance. Cottagers driven off the land by enclosures, the urban poor, hand workers disfranchised by the new machines—where could their countervailing bargaining power be found? They had none. By competing with one another for the new jobs, they drove wages down to the smallest sum required to keep a worker in existence. Under this "iron law of wages," a Lancashire laborer had an expectation of life of seventeen years, women worked underground on all fours in coal mines, pauper children went manacled to the mills. One can gauge the scale of their drudgery by one of the first pieces of corrective factory legislation passed in Britain in the early nineteenth century. It limited children of twelve years and under to an *eighty-four-hour week*. As William Cobbett bitterly remarked of the new working classes, no medieval serf had had to labor "in a heat of eighty four degrees [Farenheit] and be liable to punishment for looking out at a window."

As for the urban environment of the new factory towns, we can quote Friedrich Engels writing to his friend Karl Marx in the 1840s about Manchester's chief river: ". . . a narrow, coal black foul smelling stream full of debris and refuse . . . which gives forth a stench unendurable even on the bridge forty or fifty feet above the stream." It was at about the same time that a public commission of enquiry admitted that in all Lancashire there were no parks and only one public bath.

Within a market so biased by power at the top and abject defenselessness at the bottom, the "bargain" gave the entire surplus gained by the productiveness of the new machines to land and capital and thus produced an unexpected instability in the whole system. The poverty of the mass of the people was such that they lacked the purchasing power fully to absorb the new flow of goods. A new process or invention would be introduced. Eager entrepreneurs competed with one another to produce it. Ambitious bankers put up the credit for its financing, and the expansion in the supply of money set in motion inflationary pressures. (When in the 1840s, the state government of Michigan tried to check these trends by insisting that banks keep a certain fixed relation between their reserves of bullion and their scale of lending, a coach containing the bullion regularly preceded the inspectors from bank to bank!) The surge of investment then produced more goods than an impoverished market could absorb. Inventories began to pile up, bankruptcies increased, banks closed their doors, speculators took discreet boats to America. Then, when prices had plummeted sufficiently and producers and products fallen away, a new invention or market or raw material would trigger a new expansion. These "trade cycles" so contradicted the concept of natural balance in the market as an all-pervasive automatic and progressive mechanism for automatically balancing supply and demand that some economists even attributed them to sunspots. The truth was and remains that a market system alone cannot produce the balanced bargain of an equitable system since it has no self-correcting tendency toward a more equal balance of power. The point is of interest not simply for the nineteenth-century record but for our own day, where, as we shall see, we are trying to conduct our interdependent planetary economy primarily on a market basis—with almost precisely the same consequences, power to the rich, misery to the poor, and instability for the entire system.

It is important to remember that early industrializing society was not compelled by strict technological rules to follow this path. There were various social alternatives. Robert Owen educated his work force and made them not "hands," but co-operative partners in his Lancashire venture. His profits and surplus for reinvestment were not impaired. In Denmark, early land reform gave the small farmers their land, grouped them in co-operatives, introduced technical high schools to educate them, and turned them by the mid-nineteenth century into the most efficient farmers in Europe. But the sheer weight of the postfeudal society confined these creative examples to outside exceptions. The first stages of industrialism must be counted, in terms of the genuine "conservation" of men, women, and children, among the most inhuman phases of the historical record. Workers lost—at a cost we still pay for—the variety, gaiety, and relative autonomy of earlier traditional societies in which, between saints' days and church holidays, few people worked more than half the year, and the record of folk songs, costumes, dances, tales, and pilgrimages still brings us echoes of a merrier life.

Nor need we look backward. To this day in the more fortunate states in Africa, traditional communities work hard preparing and bringing in the harvest but spend the rest of the year in every kind of social activity—games, festivals, dances, endless conversation, and above all, the rhythms of a music which, in the shape of jazz, has captured the ear of humanity more than any other kind of rhythm. Few breaks in human experience have been as great as the industrial revolution's introduction of total work. We are still trying to recover from its merciless effects of human stultification.

For, of course, there have been steady attempts at change and reform. Otherwise no social order at all would have survived—as indeed the social order nearly failed to do in 1914 and 1939 and in the total revolutions which stormed down on such irreparably unreformable societies as czarist Russia and nationalist China. There were several strands in at least a century of reform.

We can pick out three main strands in the effort to "conserve" people in the maelstrom of the new industrialism. One was to improve the hopeless bargaining position of the poor. In liberal societies the power of an egalitarian tradition (going back ultimately to the Bible) would not permit "civil liberties"—the rights of assembly and free speech and voting in secret ballots—to be confined in perpetuity to the noble or propertied classes. Free speech allowed the horrors of Dickens's slums and tenements to reach the conscience of the more fortunate. The extension of the franchise to the mass of the people inevitably increased their chance of swapping votes for drains and houses. The right of assembly established trade union movements with the specific aim of *us* bargaining from strength against *them*—the managers and the wealthy.

This concept of a more equal bargain also took political forms, which constituted the second significant development. It may be doubted whether, in market economies, the concept of redistribution of the rewards of the economy by progressive taxation would have been achieved so relatively speedily if two world wars had not vastly increased tax rates to pay for the armaments, and created a community feeling that made it possible to keep both the idea and the practice alive after the struggle was over. Even so, it was weak enough after 1918. The basic concept of the welfare state—that no citizen should fall below a certain level of sustenance—was driven into the nations' imagination by the comradeship at Dunkirk, on Guadalcanal, on the beaches of Normandy. But however catastrophic the psychic origins, the great wars marked a permanent revolution in the concept of a transfer, by taxation, of a measure of economic power from rich to poor. That this transfer also mitigated the trade cycle by ensuring that *all* mass purchasing power did not dry up at the bottom of the cycle was an unintended but, as we shall see, critical by-product of the change.

Clearly, the various forms of wealth transfer in this mixed system were not enough for tougher reformers, who, following Marx, put the whole trouble down to the possessors. Transfer all "means of production" to the community, they argued, and the resulting flow of goods can be divided impartially between workers of hand and of brain. The poor are raised up, inequalities abolished, and at last, the state itself, the "managing directorate of the bourgeosie," will wither away, since it will no longer have need for coercive and restraining power.

That the economy might become, in such conditions, the "private property" of the managers who controlled it did not occur to the original propounders of communism. After fifty years of practice in the Soviet Union, it is a key issue. One consequence is to strengthen the convictions of socialists who, without losing ultimate confidence in communal ownership, are giving more thought to mixed economies, workers' co-operatives, small business, and decentralized decision-making. No political movement of any validity today accepts the profile of wealth distribution tolerated in the nineteenth century. The means and scale of redistribution are in dispute, but not the principle. The result inevitably reinforces the first historical change—the political influence of the mass voter and the power to combine in protection of the workers' interests. No striker faces starvation. There is a cushion under every bargain.

And this extra security was reinforced in the mid-twentieth century by the third critical development. It is important to remember that the political gains of universal suffrage, the introduction of a small measure of redistributive taxation and very modest social insurance or welfare, were quite insufficient to defend the world economy against the tornado of 1929. Then without government regulation or intervention or high taxation or recalcitrant unions or rising raw materials prices or any other of the bugbears of traditionalist thinkers, the whole industrial system seized up. And it was in the wake of this giant upheaval—with stockbrokers raining down from skyscraper windows and millions upon millions of citizens on a wholly inadequate dole—that Lord Keynes formulated his basic theory, which in a sense repeated Marx's prediction that industrial society would be racked with crises of overproduction which would, in fact, be crises of underconsumption.

There simply were no inherent automatic market forces, created by economic necessity, to ensure sufficient purchasing power to mop up all the goods capable of being produced by the economic system. There was, first of all, the essential instability we have already noticed. Since capital goods such as railways and steelworks take time to complete, they are "lumpy." They can concentrate a very high level of investment over a certain period of time, creating widespread activity. If industrialists, who tend to be influenced by the same trend, all invest together, the boom swings up, creating jobs and wages (and often a good deal of hopeful speculative activity as well). But when the "lump" of investment is complete, there may be no countervailing investments on a comparable scale to offset the completion. Then the reverse process begins. With jobs falling, wages fading, purchasing power vanishing with them, the slide into "bust" accelerates. In 1927, the first signs of the slide had started with a falling off in primary prices all round the globe. Consumption began to fall. When the decline reached United States farmers, the bottom began to drop out of America's markets. The amount of speculation in the earlier expansion now made contraction all the more violent. The bust was on—and there were no countervailing mechanisms to steady the economy. There were not even any ideas.

This was the bleak condition in which Keynes formulated the concept of "aggregate demand"—the amount of purchasing power required to keep an economy at a reasonably high and steady level of investment and hence of employment. Since the market itself could not provide this guaranteed demand, it would have to be the task of the public authorities—through minimum wages, countercyclical public works, inducements to investment and research, and a general commitment—actually and formally incorporated into an act of Congress in 1946—to the maintenance of full employment.

It was on the general acceptance of this theory after the Second World War that the "golden years" in part were built. In fact, one can argue that the visonary decision of the United States to give away 2 percent of a GNP half its present size for several years under the Marshall Plan was an inspired application of the Keynsian principle. Europe, shattered by war, its colonial systems flattened by conflict and neglect, simply lacked the purchasing power for recovery. This the vastly expanded and undamaged American economy provided through the vision of its government and the unexampled generosity of its people. And in the event, the rebuilding of Europe and the "trickle down" of some of its growing wealth through aid to the rest of the world was the first foundation of the mid-century's twenty-year boom. There were others. Some we have noticed—the rock-bottom cheapness of energy, the low capital costs for industries which covered none of their environmental degradations. Other factors included a fluctuating but relatively low level of prices for primary materials, and spin-offs from wartime technology—bigger aircraft, jets, the development of electronics. In these conditions, as a result of a massive substitution of machines and energy for human labor, productivity as a measure of what a worker could produce rose by 4 or 5 percent a year. Yet so sustained and rapid was the over-all expansion of the economy that what might have meant growing redundancy among workers in farming, mining, and manufacturing as the machines moved in simply released manpower to new sectors—for more services, for communications, for the whole "knowledge industry." Thus the percentage of the work force in primary and secondary employment began to fall and the age of the tertiary and quarternary sectors dawned. At the same time, the general rise in wage levels—the cost offset by cheap fuel and new technology—actually underpinned and stabilized the market by constant increases in consumption and if, in any one year, demand faltered a little, a timely government deficit (and the perpetual spending on arms) helped to pick up the slack.

One should notice how much of this expansion was sustained by the extra-market forces already mentioned—the new power of the unions to bargain (matched in some countries by a considerable concentration of business control, which lessened competition and made it easier to pass costs on to the consumer), the postwar levels of redistributive taxation (much of it going into a really large increase of investment in education and the housing sector), budget deficits, and arms spending. However

uncertainly and, sometimes, even bashfully, governments were all prac-
ticing forms of "demand management." And the new system seemed to
work. If the conservation of human beings could be said to consist of a
steady job, a roof over one's head, ample diet, a reasonable mortgage,
television and a car on the installment plan, then it must be said that in
1973, a majority in the industrialized nations were nearer to human conservation than at any time in their history. But at just that point, once
again, the roof began to fall in.

13 BACK TO FULL EMPLOY-MENT?

THE CRISIS which struck the world economy had a variety of causes. One was simply a version of the traditional nineteenth-century boom. In the late 1960s, all the industrialized nations had expanded their steel-making and their shipbuilding and their car plants and their machine tools at the same time, inspired no doubt by all the splendid extrapolations which showed the growth of the decade extending until kingdom come. But then, in 1972, bad weather intervened, taking Russia into the great grain raid which cleared out America's reserves and tripled prices throughout the whole interdependent world grain market. Within a year, the Arabs' oil embargo quadrupled the price of their single wasting resource, and with this move, up went the prices of most other goods as a result of the energy incorporated in their production and distribution. This combination of potential overcapacity and bounding costs led everywhere to a slackening in the expansive drive and consequently to a sudden jump in unemployment.

The exceptional growth of the sixties had masked the degree to which (as we have seen) many parts of the economy had been steadily substituting machines for humans and, with the computer revolution under way, were promising to do so at a still faster rate. One should also add that unemployment has been—and will continue to be—exacerbated for some developed nations by the entry of the postwar baby-boom children into the job market. North America, with its earlier baby boom, began experiencing this rapid growth in the labor force in the late 1960s, with unemployment rates two to three times higher than those of Western Europe. Now it is Europe's turn. In addition to factors dampening the creation of new jobs, Western European nations will have to cope with labor forces generally growing far more rapidly in the 1970s and 1980s than in the immediate postwar years. A far higher entry of women into the labor force should also not be overlooked.

But one cannot push the analogies with old-fashioned booms and busts too far. Organized trade unions on the one hand and large corporate management on the other proved powerful enough to prevent the earlier consequence of "recession"—a massive shake-out of wages and prices, with bankruptcies and failing banks adding to unemployment, and a lowering of costs all round in potential preparation for a longer-term recovery. On the contrary, since food and fuel prices were rising, and with them the cost of living, the stronger unions could bargain for higher wages, and their opposite numbers in management could again hope to pass on the rise to the consumer. Prices rose further, and economic activity fell; wages climbed, and jobs declined. In fact, some economists began to argue that since after every fallback in activity, there would be no corresponding fall in wages or prices, a sort of "ratchet effect" had been introduced into the economy, whereby the starting point of every new recovery would always be at a higher price level than before, and the economy would therefore be inherently more prone to slip into early inflation.

We have therefore to consider some very divergent possibilities for our economic future. But perhaps the clearest approach is to examine two of these in some detail. In the first scenario, the underlying structure of the industrialized economy does not change. As in the United States, the five hundred top businesses, representing less than a fiftieth of 1 percent of all businesses will go on producing over 60 percent of all the goods and services. As in Britain, less than 150 enterprises will continue to account for more than half the nation's manufacturing. On the side of labor, the strategic sectors—power workers, teamsters, steelmen, miners—will have enough clout at least for long confrontations, at most for unassailable bargaining strength. In the second scenario, the economic landscape will have changed—toward more dispersed power, new forms of association and co-operation, toward greater local autonomy combined with the possibility of reaching some critical nationwide and indeed international bargains. What can be done about unemployment, the misuse of human resources, the boredom and irresponsibility of work—in short, the conservation of human beings—will be rather different according to which of the two futures predominates.

We will look first at a virtually unchanged condition. In 1973, no one foresaw the effect of the economy's rigidities on the ability of governments to offset unemployment by Keynsian applications of demand management. But it was to become the dominant theme of the long, dragging semirecession of the following years. What was new was in fact an obvious consequence of the new structures in society. Since recession had done little to reduce costs, if governments now attempted a general reflation—to increase employment and raise effective demand—they would find themselves almost at once faced with further inflationary trends. Those in work would bargain for higher rewards. Energy costs would—it could be safely surmised—spring up again. Thus capital costs would go on rising. As a result, industrialized governments tended to back away from earlier concepts of stimulating the economy with budget deficits or even tax cuts. At the other extreme, only comfortably tenured professors suggested, as an alternative, a return to the savage deflationary disciplines of earlier and harder times. So market economies seemed stuck in the new phenomenon of "stagflation," in which low activity combined with continued inflation while the planned economies went $50 billion into debt, in part to contain their own inflationary tendencies. The Third World's debt figure, excluding the oil producers, soared to $200 billion in 1978. In these conditions, there began to be ominous undertones of the 1929 crisis, with nations muttering that the importing of other peoples' goods was keeping down employment and they would be better off protecting their own production—the argument which in 1929 cut world trade by three-quarters in less than a year and made certain the final collapse of 1931.

But, in fact, we are not in any necessary deadlock. Even taking the first scenario of virtually unchanged market power, there are a fair number of new policies to be considered which meet the admittedly new conditions of our times and do not necessarily trap us in stagflation. We must distinguish at once between policies for developed societies and for the poor of the world. An element of conservation and restraint must be a first emphasis in developed (or overdeveloped?) societies, an emphasis on expansion and growth in the lands of the poor world. This distinction will be taken up in a later section. Here we are concerned with what can be done about the stagflation of the rich.

Greater conservation, because it involves less energy and lower inputs, provides more jobs but does not immediately crank up the inflationary engine. We should be clear about this point of unemployment. In America few factories have closed for failing to meet environmental regulations—the EPA puts them at 102 between 1971 and March 31, 1977, affecting 20,318 employees. They tended to be the older plants that would probably have closed soon on other grounds. In any case, their closing is more than offset by the million or so new jobs created by the need to produce, install, and operate environmental protection equipment. To this could well be added whole new industries based on a massive and rising demand for such essentially conserving technologies as heat pumps, solar panels, and photovoltaic cells. The Project Independence Solar Task Force in the United States has suggested that a serious national program of manufacturing and installing solar-heating and -cooling equipment in the nation's buildings to cut down oil imports would create more than a million new jobs by 1990. Improving insulation in buildings also generates a lot of work. The American Institute of Architects has estimated that a conservation program for new and existing buildings would create from half a million to more than a million direct jobs through 1990. Materials conservation achieved by recycling paper and metals, legislation for returnable containers, and the use of city refuse for fuel or compost also creates jobs. All these conservation schemes could stimulate the demand for labor while actually reducing resource consumption—an almost classic definition of uninflationary growth.

But when we take up the issue of directly conserving a balance between the full use of labor (with the risk of unemployment) and an extra deployment of capital resources (with the risk of inflation), there *are* a number of limited economic and social changes which, without retreat to the Stone Age or advance to Star Wars, can help to secure a better balance of resource availability and resource use and conceivably, in the process, produce a society more truly conserving of human values and human beings than the lavish but uneasy decades from which we have just emerged. These measures do not amount to a complete answer. The more fundamental changes must wait for our second scenario. But they are useful in themselves and could prepare the way for wider reform.

If we take a structural change first, the most far-reaching decision would be, until social conditions have changed a good deal, to approach with considerable caution the notion of *general* reflation as a means of countering unemployment. Given the semimonopoly positions of many corporations and unions, a general increase in activity can lead to a quick rise in the wages of already employed, protected, and normally skilled men, rapid increases in energy use (and price), and the passing on of costs to the consumer. In no way do these processes help the most seriously affected groups of unemployed—ill-trained adolescents trying to enter the job market, untrained women, immigrants, minority groups. (One thinks of the 40 percent unemployment rate among America's young black workers.) On the contrary, the successful wage-push of the stronger workers' groups increases the cost of labor and by that fact alone encourages further mechanization and automation. The outcome can be even fewer jobs. Under these conditions, general refla-tion could become the recipe first for rapidly renewed inflation and then for stagflation at an even higher level of stagnancy.

But such broad strokes of the economic brush are not the only an-swer. There are a whole series of particular policies which, partial in themselves, can add up to new and more favorable economic condi-tions. A first set of expedients can be summed up in the description "a leaner use of energy and capital"—in other words, rather more reliance in the processes of production on labor, which is in reasonable supply, and less on fuel and capital goods, which are becoming subject to price rises and other potential constraints. It must be emphasized that this is not a return to the pretechnological society, but a relatively small and socially useful modification in the mix of factors of production. We can look at two sectors as examples, cars and housing. In both, a more labor-intensive approach, more conserving of the scarce factors of pro-duction, is undoubtedly possible.

The French motor industry is a good example, since few industries have shown such a frenetic pace of substitution of energy for labor over the last decades. Between 1960 and 1973, energy consumption rose more than sixteenfold while production increased by only 157 per-cent and labor by a mere 50 percent. In the main, the bulk of jobs remaining involve unskilled work on the assembly line. There is also some suggestion that capital investment in the larger car plants has been growing far faster than output per worker. Diminishing returns have been setting in.

The average life of the car produced seems to have been ten to eleven years, and an interesting study prepared for the EEC by the Bat-telle Geneva Research Center has examined how the various factors of production might be modified if industry aimed to produce not a ten-year but a twenty-year car. A first advantage of such a car is that al-though it demands more energy in its immediate production—to ensure a more rust-resistant body and a generally more sturdy machine—its energy input for each year of car life over the full twenty years is little more than half that of the typical ten-year vehicle. Another possible saving in capital cost lies in less frequent scrapping of dumped cars. But the biggest change is precisely in the area of employment.

Between 1960 and 1973, jobs in the French car industry grew by little more than 100,000, an increase, as we have seen, of about 50 percent, while the value of output nearly quadrupled. But during this same period, the number of repair and maintenance jobs appears to have doubled, and it is now in fact not much smaller than the total number of workers employed inside the factories. Twenty-year cars, designed from the start for careful but uncomplicated maintenance, would, according to Battelle, increase the labor input for each year of car use by 50 percent. Moreover, the work of maintenance, repairing, and refurbishing is so essentially more interesting and creative than the appalling monotony of the assembly line that the French report a return of workers out of more highly paid factory jobs back to garages and workshops simply to get away from the deadening routine. (It will be no surprise that 80 percent of the assembly-line jobs are done by migrant labor and recently a violent strike broke out at some Renault factories on the simple issue of the boredom of work.)

Another illustration of this point comes from Sweden, where the Kalmar plant, designed by Volvo, attempts to overcome the monotony and depersonalization of the assembly line by designating workers to a series of organized "work spaces" (with their own rest and tea and changing rooms) to which the incomplete car with the next batch of components is brought by a computer-guided carrier. In each area, a team can devise how it will add these components, and arrange its work. Productivity has not increased, but absenteeism—as high as 19 percent in some plants—has fallen, and although Detroit dismisses the experiments as unproductive and hence unprofitable, Fiat is experimenting with a version of the decentralized work pattern.

The same story of mass applications of capital and energy with diminishing use and amenity of labor is repeated in the construction and construction-materials industries. On the materials side, there was a nearly 300 percent increase in output in France between 1960 and 1973, a 250 percent increase in capital stock, a 65 percent growth in energy consumption, and in the labor force, a 12 percent increase, all of it before 1966, when growth virtually ceased. This massive "industrialization" of materials production has been matched by a corresponding change in construction itself. The mechanization of the process can be gauged by the near tripling of energy use in the French construction industry between 1960 and 1973 and the substitution of energy for labor at a rate of 5.8 percent per year, rising to a remarkable 11.8 percent per year between 1969 and 1973. All this is mirrored in other changes, such as the shifting of labor from building sites to assembly-line factories making prefabricated components, a more than thirteenfold increase since 1955 in West Germany's use of tower cranes, a steady rise in total demolitions everywhere, and in France, an extravagant increase in the production of ready-mixed concrete—an eighty-two-fold increase (admittedly from a very low start) compared with a less than twofold increase for bricks and tiles, in just twelve years after 1960.

Yet the result of this whole shift has been that the new capital-intensive processes demand the construction of very large complexes to cover their costs—vast office blocks or the kind of ugly, impersonal, monolithic high-rise housing which has proved to be one of the social disasters of the postwar developed city. It is only now that government after government is beginning to realize that a cheaper and more human solution to the housing challenge would have included a massive element of rehabilitation of existing communities, and that the range and variety of jobs—for plumbers, masons, bricklayers—such schemes would have required could have been one of the means of preventing the disastrous collapse of manual employment in the big city centers. By getting the mix of capital, land (all too often at inflated values), and human labor hopelessly skewed, modern city planners have helped to use up what is scarce—reasonably priced land and capital; to neglect what is available—urban labor; and to produce what is all too often a socially disastrous result.

Another range of options, primarily for public authorities, lies in substituting for general reflation specific aid to offset local or regional unemployment. The approach avoids over-all expansion of investment. It carries financial and technical assistance on a much smaller and more precise scale to places or groups of people in special need. Such schemes can take the form of modest subsidies to encourage early retirement by older workers—provided the young are employed instead—or to keep redundancies down by giving subsidies to maintain the payroll. They can go all the way up to such large disbursements as the European Regional Fund gives to run-down and usually peripheral communities in Europe. Combined with local plans, these grants can be on a scale to ensure very widespread revival. Ireland, for instance, added 120,000 new factory jobs between 1971 and 1977, many of them by persuading new industries into the country. These in turn will create new jobs in the many sectors serving industry.

But there is one danger in these selective policies which has yet to be fully gauged, let alone overcome. If subsidies are given indiscriminately to troubled areas, may they not be simply subventions for industries which should be allowed quietly to die? It is a truism to say of Europe and North America that many sectors in textiles, clothing, steel, shipbuilding, and leatherwork, and even some electronic sectors, have become too uncompetitive to be anything but a drag on the community. Propping up declining enterprises may simply perpetuate an overlong decay. The need is for the specific public subsidies and forms of technical assistance to attempt either to meet genuine local requirements or to support new ventures and new ideas. Neither task is impossible, and there are several working models of what can be done.

Take first of all local needs. In any community—but especially in communities tending toward decline—there are people, often elderly, who cannot entirely cope, and there are services which are beginning to run down. Under such programs as Canada's Local Initiative Programme (LIP), now renamed Canada Works, jobless people— especially the young—can be recruited for those jobs which the *local* community feels need most urgently to be done. The work may be cleaning up and renovating homes for elderly couples or running a hot-meals service for the aged. Jobs in the Canadian program included work at day-care centers, as hospital assistants, as auxiliary firemen, even as operators of puppet theaters for children. The effort was made to get those employed, the young people especially, out into the countryside for active conservation—cleaning up state parks, building trails, reafforestation, stream clearing and monitoring, and in the winter, snow removal, so that everything else could move.

This is only one example of a national program with the distinguishing mark of local choice and initiative. The U.S. Office of Economic Development has had the same policy of putting the initiative in local hands (not always a popular policy with local politicians), and the community-development corporations it funds, in spite of some adverse publicity, have generally contrived a higher rate of success in the enterprises they finance than have local independent businesses. These

corporations aim to develop their local economy by helping to set up
new enterprises on a sound financial footing and, in some cases, undertake programs to improve housing, infrastructure, or social services.
One example is the East Los Angeles Community Union, which has
provided services ranging from housing and jobs to the creation of
businesses and financial institutions that serve the residents in its area
and the surrounding Mexican-American communities. It has recently
purchased land from a company that closed its East Los Angeles factory, and is building an industrial park to attract new enterprises and to
provide work for as many as 2,500 local residents.

From the United States, too, we can cite another interesting variant
of local initiative. A scheme in Hartford, Connecticut, allowed unemployed and low-income residents to volunteer for local service jobs and
be paid through a reduction in their local tax bills. Time spent cleaning
up a neighborhood or a local park reduced property taxes or the car tax
by $2.50 for every hour worked. The inclusion of the local park is not
unimportant. In every urban conglomeration in the developed world,
true "civilization"—the word, after all, like "urbane," comes from the
concept of cities as good places to live in—has faded before the decay,
the destruction, the vandalism of so many inner cities. Jobs which
renovate housing, restore parks, clear playgrounds, build skating rinks,
and even, as in Holland, provide funds and studios for local artists,
begin to reverse the dreary, decivilizing cycle of decay.

But perhaps one of the most important selective interventions of
government throughout the industrialized world, the one which is most
likely to help the poorest and most helpless citizens, lies in the creation
of opportunities for job training or retraining. To go back for a moment
to the example of the twenty-year car or the renovated house, again and
again, work at this level of complexity has been dismissed on the
grounds that there are not enough skilled craftsmen to do the job. So in
sets the vicious circle. We lack craftsmen, so we automate. We automate, so we train no craftsmen. It is possible that one of the indispensable keys to a more active and less monotonous future lies in the readiness of governments to put punch and drive into their programs of
re-education. The United States had over two million people under
training in 1977. The British government multiplied its schemes seven
times over between 1971 and 1976—although the proportion of the
labor force being retrained each year is still low, less than 0.5 percent.

Canada managed a 3 percent retraining rate in 1977. It is significant that the Swedes, those pioneers of social-democratic inventiveness, had as many as 5 percent of their labor force undergoing retraining for new work or upgraded skills.

But training for what? Some of the needed skills—for draftsmen, mechanics, plumbers, and carpenters, and for some increase in farming and forestry techniques—have been mentioned already. The jobs connected with social services should not be regarded as temporary. After all, up to two-thirds of the working population in developed countries are now in what are called service industries, and there can be little doubt that in many cities the public services—with their need for police officers, firemen, sanitation engineers, day-care assistants, hospital aides—are gravely undermanned. In many areas, too, the number of pupils in classes, and their intellectual unevenness, make smaller classes and more individual attention a virtual precondition of ending the illiteracy with which all too many young people are leaving school. Now that America's "baby bulge" has moved on and up and all but out of the school system—a phenomenon Europe is now experiencing in primary schools—the response should not be a sharp reduction in the teaching force and socially disruptive graduate unemployment but a determined effort to decrease the size of classes and increase opportunities for individual coaching with whatever new aids the computer revolution makes available in the shape of learning machines with a beguiling smack of science fiction and hence of stimulus and fun.

This whole question of a wider provision of needed social services must not be seen as a temporary expedient for a passing recessionary phase. During the eighties, as work forces continue to grow and the manufacturing sector to shrink as a direct employer of labor, the tertiary sector has to expand. It can do so by providing genuine and needed services of the kinds envisaged, for instance, in Canada's LIP. It can be made more flexible by a larger provision of part-time jobs. Shorter working weeks have to be considered. The alternative—the 40 percent unemployment among black youths in America for instance—is the recipe for social disruption and civic collapse. Admittedly, the growing unwillingness of better-off citizens to accept high taxation has yet to be worked out, since the consequences of cutting vital civic services have still to be fully experienced. But whatever the adjustments, the underlying fact remains. In societies as well provided with material goods as the developed West, services are the sector where need is greatest, deprivation most demoralizing, and long-term vision most required for a genuine re-creation of a civilized society.

One further range of specific and creative possibilities could lie in reconsidering the role and needs of small- and medium-sized businesses. They are, by their very nature, "leaner" users of capital and energy for the simple reason that they lack the resources and the fraternal links with friendly bankers to be lavish in this field. They are also formidable generators of new ideas and new forms of labor-intensive skilled employment. One estimate has put at over 50 percent the share of individuals and their tiny enterprises in the seventy-one key inventions of this century. Indeed, the tendency of large corporations to grow by "agglomeration" has often been admitted to spring from the need for innovation that is no longer provided by giant bureaucracies but is readily bought up from small entrepreneurs who lack the resources for further growth.

What some of these small businesses can do on capital so lean as to be all but invisible is well illustrated by a 1977 winner of Britain's Queen's Award for Export Achievement. In 1971, Arthur Organ invented a machine for the automatic weighing and packing of bolts and nuts. The large firm he worked for was not interested. This lack of interest in innovation often springs from the amount of capital already tied up in existing machines and processes (the "dinosaur syndrome"?). But Organ was not deterred. With no more capital than a month's salary, he built his machine in a shed in the garden, took it in his wife's small car to various packaging firms, and used the proceeds of the sale of the model to build two more. The explosion began. By 1976 he was employing ninety-five people, with export orders of over a million pounds.

How many more such entrepreneurs would break through on minimal capital and maximum skill is hard to calculate. In most areas, they lack financial backers at critical points of potential advance. Disgracefully, in a number of cases, they are not paid promptly by the big firms they supply and in fact provide the dinosaurs with a cash reserve. One of the most secure and creative ways of lowering unemployment without increasing inflationary pressure would be to subsidize jobs in a wide range of small enterprises and to set up for these enterprises co-operative banks or special accounts in local banks. The United States, for instance, has its Small Business Administration, the Netherlands its Special Bank.

In West Germany, decentralized credit institutions supported by the government give especially generous help with small-business overdrafts. Britain has a Council for Small Industries in Rural Areas which has lent some two million pounds a year over the last ten years and has provided technical assistance to small firms in communities of less than ten thousand people, thus helping to establish profitable concerns which now employ seventy thousand people. The government has even started a scrutiny at Cabinet level to see what more can be done for the small man in business.

Most remarkable of all, Poland, Yugoslavia, East Germany, and Hungary are all attempting by a variety of inducements to coax many would-be bureaucrats or assembly-line workers back into the risks (and delights?) of running their own restaurants, bakeries, butcher shops, garages, tailoring and shoemaking establishments, and all the other services of immediate need to the citizen for which—it is more and more freely admitted—large state enterprises cannot properly provide. At both ends of the ideological spectrum, the economic scene seems to be dominated by the Goliaths. Perhaps the ordinary citizen would be better off if myriad Davids were provided with better slings and stones.

14 TOWARD "PRIVATE SOCIALISM"

FEW OF THE expedients outlined in the last chapter have not been tried out in some form in one community or another. They imply no heroic changes, no historic turning points. And for that very reason, they may not be enough to meet the future, since it would take a bold prophet indeed to affirm for the next decades Falstaff's disgruntled forecast of "a calm world and a long peace." Suppose that all the retraining and regrouping of labor, the conserving of energy and resources, the direction of aid to specific groups and regions, the new emphasis on smaller and leaner units of production, still left millions unemployed and millions more below the poverty line? It is not an unreasonable question, since the economies of the Western world have been trying out a variety of mixes since the blow struck in 1973, and there are still at least fifteen million people out of work.

Yet if this stagnant side of the work–prices equation is broken by the kind and scale of stimulus required to give all citizens what should be their birthright—a reasonable income and the chance of work—are we not back in the inflationary spiral, aggravated, by the time we reach the 1980s and 1990s, by shortages of some critical resources and by the certain rise in energy costs?

It is therefore possible that we are in the contradictory position of needing the Keynsian instrument of demand management, yet being unable to use it without results which, either from stagnation or inflation, lead to profound social dislocation and unease. Deadlocks of this type belong historically to the types of dilemma which demand more radical answers.

One way forward could lie in taking a new look at the Keynsian solution. Government, union, management, and consumer representatives might meet in a "grand assize" to assess the scale of resources and production required to satisfy present claims and also provide sufficient income and work for every citizen. Then the task would be to judge whether the economy, internally and externally, could produce the needed scale of goods and services. In a sense, this could almost be called "supply management," leading to a clearer picture of just what opportunities for creative action—or even inaction—the economy must face.

There are possible models here in the use made by both the Japanese and French governments of "indicative planning." Their plans, it is true, were not precisely geared to the basic needs of the citizen, but rather to the effect of certain rates of economic growth on different sectors of the economy. They also proved most effective in the booming fifties and sixties, when distribution could be left, it was thought, to the "trickledown" effect. The key points were to achieve balance between different sectors and between imports and exports. Yet comparable techniques of forecasting could be used to assess the scale and pressure of demand that would result if, in addition to those citizens now adequately supplied, everyone else had a good diet, good health care, good schools, a reasonable home, and access to work. Then, in theory at least, this "aggregate demand" could be compared with the likely profile of output and foreign trade. Decisions, of the indicative-planning type, could be taken to stimulate various sectors, increase investments in big areas of shortage and, where necessary, transfer skills and capital from fading to increasing needs. The scale of over-all stimulation could then be open to public discussion and even become the focus of what might be called a "social compact" between government and citizens. After the public debate, all would agree on a certain scale of demand management of personal reward and of productive response, to be maintained for a fixed period—a year, or two or three.

There are, after all, analogies from past experience. In more expansive times, the representatives of industry, in both Sweden and the Netherlands, did negotiate with government the annual wage bill on a synchronized basis, in order to keep demand from outstripping likely production. The periodical meetings in West Germany at which representatives of the unions, management, government, and the central banks come together to analyze the economy and its prospects have had something of the character of a "grand assize." In the fifties and sixties, common understanding of what the economy could and could not afford was one element in West Germany's remarkable record of social peace, agreed deployment of labor, and growth of new industry. In another instance, the British government was reasonably successful in 1976 and 1977 in setting a standard—a six-pound-per-week rise, a 10-percent increase—beyond which, in their view, inflation would begin to rise again. The relative paucity of these illustrations shows how far mixed economies are from any effective practice of genuine demand management, but the reasons for the weakness also give a clue to where a second set of reforms, that are also more far-reaching, might be introduced to strengthen the central idea of a "social compact."

All have to do in some measure with what can be not inaccurately described as "overmighty subjects"—industries which have grown too powerful and concentrated to be checked by competition (or allowed to fail by the public authorities), unions which have the particular muscle of indispensability, large government bureaucracies which have grown up to exchange letters and unintelligible regulations with equally large private bureaucracies, nationalized industries which live comfortably off the citizen's pocket—whether in London or Moscow. To them we should add the citizens themselves always on the lookout for another rise in income.

The list is long. It has a special significance. It shows clearly that scale is *not* the road to the kind of flexibility needed in responding to creative concepts of economic management. It is not the small firms and unions which break guidelines, manipulate prices, hold out in the longest strikes. In fact, in Britain, a community not noted for total industrial peace, in 98 percent of the manufacturing plants, there are no strikes at all in an average year. The record of the nationalized industries shows on the contrary what disruption a sense of undisputed power can encourage. It is surely significant that in the latest bid to save Britain's car giant, Leyland, the solution sought is precisely to make it less of a giant by restoring autonomy to previously absorbed firms. This trend, in fact, is general in most conglomerates. They establish decentralized "profit centers" or businesses with a large measure of local autonomy. Holland and Scandinavia, as we have noticed, have a far lower proportion of large conglomerates, and although concentration is growing in Germany, it is very much lower than in Britain. Small is efficient, it seems.

Governments can encourage the trend by strict antimonopoly laws, by commissions to prevent too much domination by one firm in any particular sector, and by specific policies. For instance, excessive advertising expenditure could be discouraged. Some firms which sell such goods as toiletries, soaps, and soft drinks spend 15 percent or more of their sales revenues on saturation advertising; in the case of one United States firm, more than a third of its sales revenue was being spent on advertising and other forms of promotion. This practice could be restricted by limiting the amount of advertising deductible from tax as an operating expense, especially for firms that dominate any particular market. The consumer would hardly suffer if all the extolling of lotions and pet foods began to have to be paid for in this way. Nor would smaller companies have too much difficulty in taking up the new opportunities. In fact, some giants, such as Westinghouse, have already got out of a whole range of small consumer goods because they are too specific and the demand for them is too varied for a large "run" from the big assembly lines.

But the policies favoring smaller enterprise need not be all negative. As with the Small Business Administration in the United States, it can be made a matter of policy to secure a certain percentage of government orders for firms below a given size. Insurance companies and pension funds could, with proper safeguards, be encouraged to invest in small firms part of their enormously expanding capital funds. (Pension funds control savings worth fifty billion dollars in Britain alone, and insurance companies slightly more.) Tax relief might also be given to firms which, like a group of a hundred small businesses in California, now share a number of common services and offer each other counsel and support.

This theme of co-operation carries us beyond the corporate sector. One of the roots of the indifference so many workers feel toward the larger issues of inflation is their concentration on their own wage packet. Their inability to see any connection between the two lies in the whole hierarchical, one might almost say, postfeudal organization of most business enterprise. "We," the workers, earn our wages; "they," the managers, run the show to their own advantage and that of abstractions called shareholders whose chief distinction is, the workers believe, that they are better off. Wage bargains conducted basically on an adversary basis accord ill with any idea of a "social compact" at a higher level, and it is very probably within industry itself that the critical steps away from uncheckable price pressure and unquenchable demand will have to be made.

Clearly the most obvious way to make the link between earnings and profitability is to permit and encourage workers to share in the profits. The first really successful pioneer was Sears, Roebuck and Company, the legendary American retailer, which in 1916 started up a scheme devised to share profits, encourage savings, and cushion retirement. This scheme is, incidentally, still one of the largest in the world. Like many later American imitators, Sears based the plan on the distribution of shares which are held in trust until the worker retires or leaves. Many American companies have followed this pattern, for it gives the workers a secure vision of their future but leaves the funds with the company. However, this also entails the risk of leaving all the employee eggs in the single company basket, and especially since passage by Congress in 1974 of the Employment Retirement Income Security Act, management has been compelled to diversify its workers' holdings—a practice Sears began as early as 1941.

The United States is not alone. West German legislation has encouraged deferred-savings plans, including share ownership, but the level of participation is still only a third of that in the United States, in part because German shares have to be in public companies and only five thousand of Germany's 1.5 million companies are public (another example of relatively small but efficient scale). In France, in 1967, General De Gaulle's enthusiasm for worker participation helped through a law for the setting aside of reserve money in companies for worker participation, but the scale so far has not been large enough to offset a strong ideological malaise among the unions, which see profit-sharing as "co-operation with the class enemy," even in nationalized industries.

Britain has both share and cash schemes in a wide variety of (highly strike-free) companies, including Marks and Spencer, Barclays Bank, and the John Lewis Partnership. The figures are even higher in Holland. Just over half the workers enjoy some form of profit sharing. On balance they prefer to take it in cash.

Some countries—Sweden, West Germany, Denmark—have gone rather further and discussed a national plan for legal trade-union control of profit-sharing funds. The difficulty in this approach is the divorce of the scheme from the staff actually involved at the working level and the potential strengthening of a remote union bureaucracy.

This potential divorce is a point of vital importance. Unless a measure of identification between company and worker self-interest is achieved, financial gains may be secured. Social changes are less likely. Perhaps the clearest way to illustrate the issue is by looking at a more detailed description of a particular example. In a Breman BV factory sixty miles east of Amsterdam, in the Netherlands, employees elect their bosses, take a direct part in decision-making through a workers' council, and share among themselves one-third of the company's profits. Within five years of Breman's worker-control plan coming into existence, annual sales had grown from six to twenty million dollars and the number of employees had tripled. Nor can the success be dismissed as an example of Dutch conservatism and hard work. An equally significant example can be found in France; indeed, in this instance success came in spite of the unions' official ill will. A leading toy company, Majorette, employs about six hundred people in the Rhone valley. After six months, each worker becomes a shareholder and receives shares according to his or her level of pay. In 1976, half the company's net profits went to the workers. The only rule is that they keep their shares for five years, but even that is being modified. Today, nearly 20 percent of the company is worker-owned, and the firm has invariably shown a profit.

Such schemes have a double advantage. They involve the worker directly in the fundamental ability of the firm to pay its way by producing a salable article at a price that covers cost. If all firms are meeting this criterion, then demand management is no longer a problem. But the plans also make some dent in the unsolved social problems resulting from most modern structures of work. Take for instance the vastly different levels of reward in industrial societies. This is not an issue simply in market economies. High privileges, including access to restricted shops, mark the top bureaucracy in "people's democracies." But it is a nagging concern in open societies, where stock options, business expenses, the "three-martini lunch" are added to the basically still feudal differences in levels of pay, say, between a black doorman and the head of General Motors. How can any "social compact" survive such advertised and perceived divergences, especially when—as may become the case within half a century—there are less and less disposable material goods to go round? Already some of the ambitions of "catching up" in material terms are unobtainable. If everyone can have a holiday in Majorca, the place ceases to be worth a visit. Motorcars in center cities are almost in the same plight. To reward extra effort and extra responsibility simply by more money unleashes the avalanche of competitive wage demands—a problem unsolved in any market economy and fudged in planned ones by restricted material privileges and considerable "under-the-counter" activity. Yet share ownership, a sense of parity of esteem within the company's property relationships, is perhaps one part of the answer, especially in times when "rationalization" (the substitution of capital for labor) is being strongly pushed and a share of the company's stock can be set against the risk of redundancy.

High redistributive taxation without too many obvious loopholes has proved to be another underpinning of relative social restraint. But the time may be at hand when the issue will have to be publicly canvassed, and agreement obtained. If, as in California, middle-class voters turn to rejecting the taxation which supports vital public services, it may not be enough to wait for the lack of policemen and sanitation engineers and firemen to turn the tide. More open, reasonable, and informed agreement on rational levels of reward may have to be included in basic discussions of the scale and role of the public services.

All societies may, in return for a working "social compact," have to consider some more formal upper and lower limits of material reward, perhaps with a multiple of the lowest wage serving as the upper limit for the highest. In this regard, Japan and Sweden already have a better "profile" than the Soviet Union. Spain's Mondragon co-operative movement has even settled for a mere three-to-one ratio. A solid chance of institutionalizing the "social compact" in open societies may depend upon more obvious progress in these directions.

But are they enough? In a sense, they still belong to the Adam Smithian concept of the economy of buyers and sellers, with rewards earned by market performance. One of the psychological difficulties of this approach is that it leaves out so much of the human interest, responsibility, and dignity which are required to conserve a full humanity. The "serfdom" William Cobbett rebelled against in the Manchester of the 1830s was not simply inadequate pay in poor conditions. It was utter lack of control over every decision that affected those conditions. It was not a community of work but an assemblage of "us" and "them" which brought trade unionism to birth in a largely adversary position and symbolized and perpetuated the differences which good fortune, good education—and good family—could epitomize in society. To believe, as Marx did, that this class trap could be sprung only by abolishing its economic basis in unequal property relations was not really a surprising conclusion from contemporary facts. But the continued subservience and lack of autonomy of the workers under state capitalism is one more example of how far beyond purely economic rewards and inducements the problem of civilized human working conditions must be seen to go.

There is a further reason for re-examining in some depth the involvement of all workers in the enterprise. Profit-sharing and cash bonuses are an easier part of the answer in times of steady expansion, when the economic cake to be shared seems capable of continuous growth. But by the 1980s, the precondition of effortless plenty may need radical reconsideration. In Europe the work force should be growing more rapidly than at present—although such growth will be slowing down in the United States and Canada. At the same time, we shall begin to see the full effects of a technological change as potentially vast in its consequences as steam power itself. This is the mini-computer, made possible by decreasing costs and size for data-storage systems, and the development of the silicon chip with its infinitesimally small circuits which can contain enormous computing power. The result is a range, control, and accuracy of work, either on the assembly line or in the office or in communications of every sort, which can spell a new wave of redundancies in occupations which vary from car assembling to transatlantic telephone operators. Robot electronic welding machines are displacing skilled welders in many automobile production lines—for instance in the Renault plants, in the Chrysler plant at Belvidere in the United States, and in the Toyo Kogyo plant in Hiroshima. Automatic assembly and testing of electronic consumer goods such as stereos and televisions can compete with the Asian-based factories that have long relied on cheap labor to keep their costs down. "Numerically controlled machine tools" are coming to dominate modern production-machine factories. The next wave of industrial investment in West Germany is to be directed in a major way toward rationalization—the substitution of machines for workers.

The impact of the "electronics revolution" can be just as dramatically in the service sector, with electronic equipment replacing many kinds of unskilled work. Automated sorting of mail already threatens many jobs in the postal service, and electronic transmission of funds, messages, and data can only accelerate this trend. The automation of both national and international telephone systems is greatly reducing the demand for telephone operators. The new electronic switching equipment which telephone systems are now installing needs far less labor either to manufacture or to operate. Automatic check-out machines in retail stores and automatic pay-out machines in banks directly replace people. Electronic inventories and data-storage systems can take the place of many clerks who now keep a check on stocks and maintain the files in offices. Automatic ticket-vending and collection machines are increasingly being used for public transport and may also be used in cinemas and other places of entertainment. Television sets can be linked through the telephone system to data-storage banks which provide up-to-date information on local or national news—or on copper prices or the temperature in Karachi. They allow the user to book hotel rooms or airline tickets or hire cars—or even order goods from local stores—without involving any human being in the operation. In every office, an enormous variety of devices—advanced typewriters with mini-computers and large data-storage systems, dictaphones, and telephones that take messages, redirect calls, and automatically redial engaged numbers—may well reduce the more utilitarian needs for secretaries and virtually eliminate the typing pool.

The replacement of people by electronic machines will be partially offset by the increased demand for workers to build, program, operate, and repair these devices. Between 1960 and 1976, a third of all new jobs in manufacturing in the United States were created by expansion in the electronics industry. This in turn stimulated demand in other sectors—for instance, for batteries to power the new, portable electronic consumer goods. The world market for computers is likely to reach $150 billion by 1980. Some 400,000 people are now employed in the United Kingdom alone in the computer and telecommunications industries.

And no one can deny the enormous benefits the mini-computers can bring with them. Boring and repetitive tasks are the most easily automated. Mini-computers can make sure that industrial boilers or indeed whole production systems work with maximum efficiency and minimum waste of resources. They can help provide education and training. Advances in the telephone system can give greater flexibility to patterns of employment. They allow more and more people to work at home yet remain in close touch with colleagues and with the firm's information system.

Yet the advantages are offset by the unsolved unemployment problem. The electronics revolution itself is unlikely to generate all the jobs needed to cover the work that is displaced. One of the reasons the cost of many electronic goods is falling is that they require less and less labor in their manufacture. By a further unlucky twist, the electronics revolution will be displacing many more unskilled jobs than it creates. Yet it is the young and the unskilled that make up the hard core of the unemployed. A science-fiction world of robots producing the goods for which no one has the wages to pay—since there is no human work—may still be science fiction. But the Western world's fifteen million unemployed are one corner of this picture.

There are two sides to this new and possibly drastic reordering of the economy. One is the conern of the community at large. It is to ensure— by a guaranteed annual income, by a negative income tax, by increased social security—that the falling away of wages as machines replace human beings is not matched by a corresponding collapse in the community's purchasing power. If a concept is conservative enough for President Nixon to think of introducing it, we need not rush off with cries of "subsidized slacking" or anarchy let loose. No doubt a few people may prefer not to work. It will harm them no more than it already harms the often unhappy children of the very rich. But most people will prefer work—full time or part time—and here the social inventiveness of the community is required to provide, as we have described in the last chapter, the range of jobs in social services, in small-scale industry, in community efforts, which would not only take up the slack of possible unemployment but also extend a civilizing influence throughout societies.

Here we come to the second aspect of the needed new working arrangements—that the work force be associated in full responsibility with the redeployment of activity. Only then can there be any hope of social peace for the nation or decent self-respect for the people concerned. And here we can perhaps say that the last two decades have started to bring forward new models and methods which could help in the search to conserve human beings in an age of incalculable transition. As a summary of the new trends, we can hardly do better than take the proposals put forward to European managers in 1977 by Wine Kôk, president of the merged Social Democrat and Catholic trade union confederations of the Netherlands. At the center of his agenda for action was a steadily wider acceptance of "co-determination," the running of an enterprise by managers with workers as fully responsible partners. To this he added the workers' right to share in the capital growth of the company. As a reassurance to possibly hostile managers, he pointed out that such suggestions were already accepted doctrine in some countries and firms and that they represented an organic and evolutionary growth from present conditions toward a more just, acceptable, and peaceful industrial order.

How far was Kòk ahead of his audience? Some way, no doubt—yet, without question, there is a growing direct involvement of workers in what one would call the managerial aspects of running companies. It is no longer a matter merely of their decisions about canteens or washrooms. The scale and kind of investment, the way of dealing with possible redundancies, the actual organization of work itself—serious and responsible discussion of these issues is the most striking new development in Western society since the general acceptance of the welfare state. Here, West Germany, almost without meaning to, is the pioneer. When the occupying powers, particularly the British, consulted with the Germans on the structure of a revived trade union movement, they not only created an immensely powerful central organization, the Deutsche Gewerkschaftsbund (German Labor Federation), with sixteen member unions representing major industries and service trades (thereby avoiding the continual squabbles about jurisdiction which bedevil older craft unions based on different trades and skills); they also proposed that workers should be formally represented on supervisory boards overseeing the enterprise as a whole. The supervisory bodies were to have real powers, though not dealing with day-to-day problems. The two-tier system provided authority at the top and flexibility at the working level.

The Germans led the way. Since then, within the EEC, the Netherlands, Denmark, Luxembourg, and Ireland (for the public sector) have introduced legislation to produce variants of this co-determination. Norway and Sweden have their own variants, and Britain, after the report of the Bullock Commission, is considering the change, although the report has plumped for a single supervisory board, relying on traditional works consultation for day-to-day problems. But there is one point in this experiment which the British may be approaching from the wrong angle. Basically, the British proposals leave the choice of delegates to the official trade unions. Yet independent polls have shown that over 90 percent of the workers questioned want to elect their own representatives. There is a danger of official trade union leaders becoming as divorced from the rank and file as managers are supposed to be.

It is significant that in the model draft company law drawn up by the EEC to simplify and encourage the process of forming transfrontier companies, the proposed co-determination is obtained by the election of a third of the council directly from the works' floor. However, the passage of this law is marking time. The strength of Communism in France and Italy has prevented much experiment either there or in the EEC at large because the unions feel that in co-determination they would run the risk of "co-operating with the class enemy".

It is not only the more radical workers' leaders that are disturbed by some of the implications of co-determination. The traditional thinking of management is still, to a considerable extent, conditioned by both economic and hierarchical tradition. The managers are the people responsible for keeping the firm solvent, for encouraging its growth, for taking the decisions on products, on work patterns, or on manning which make growth and solvency possible. This inward-turning vision explains why even today, many managers still tend to feel that such larger social issues as environment, pollution, and the effect on a community of closing a plant are not really part of their responsibility, even though they are central actors in the drama. Shareholders have, by tradition, intervened not at all in solidly managerial decisions, for they too are content with solvency and growth or a decent price for a takeover. The managers have therefore not been much used to the kind of "responsibility" implied in becoming more answerable to anyone, let alone to their own staff. "We" and "they" exist at both ends of the spectrum.

Take, for instance, the largely negative reaction of the management of Lucas Aerospace, part of the British-based Lucas multinational, when representatives from all the company's separate units got together in the face of possible redundancies and worked out a joint plan for alternative products. The new products suggested were suited to the skills and facilities that Lucas Aerospace already possessed—and their production could have replaced work that was threatened by the contraction of aerospace and defense contracts. These new products included fuel cells, heat pumps, electrical and fluid-control systems for solar collectors, windmills, remote-handling gear to improve the safety of undersea rig maintenance, mining, and fire fighting, advanced medical aids—in short, a mixture of products which were believed to be salable and socially useful. The overall reaction of the management was to stress aerospace as the company's main concern but to refer parts of the plan back to local worker-management groups in each plant for discussion. The development of the suggested products as an alternative to redundancies was not backed by management when layoffs began to look threatening in early 1978. Management's real concern was not redundancies, but the possiblity of a work force taking over managerial functions.

The same concern has made many Dutch and Swedish managers look with uncertainty at formal plans to increase the workers' share in capital growth. Would they by this route become dominant both as workers *and* shareholders? In that case, where would management's future lie? Admittedly, this is already a confused issue. With insurance companies and workers' pension plans already appearing as major stockholders in a whole variety of companies and institutions, it can be argued that many firms are nearer to being "co-operatives" than they are ready to recognize and that, provided participation is conducted by workers thoroughly versed in accountancy and the facts of financial life and profitability (a training precondition which most managers would like to lay down), there is no reason why workers who are also part owners should not be just as effective a "court of last appeal" as a shareholders' meeting.

And how successful such developments can be is illustrated by the remarkable achievements of the Mondragon co-operative movement in Spain. There, beginning, significantly, with a training and educational establishment (and with no doubt a spice of Basque nationalism), workers' co-operatives have grown from the first firm (Ulnor), set up to produce oil stoves in 1956, to a network today of eighty-two co-operatives, employing fourteen thousand workers. Fifty-eight of the co-operatives manufacture a wide variety of industrial goods, such as electronic components, excavators, steel-mill equipment, and washing machines. Sales of industrial goods in 1975 reached $336 million, with an $82-million export trade. In addition, the group has its own bank, the Caja Laboral Popular, which aims to attract new money and hence new co-operators—all those who are prepared to put in sixteen hundred dollars to buy a share in the movement. (Those who invest without joining receive a fixed 6 percent interest.) A high proportion of the co-operatives' profits has been consistently reinvested to make expansion and more jobs possible. Management is appointed on the basis of efficient performance, but some of management's traditional responsibilities—for instance, discipline in the plant—are exercised by the membership, with sacking as the final threat for "very grave faults." Strikes are all but unknown. In fact, in 1974, when twenty-seven men tried out their grievances against the management, a general assembly of two thousand workers voted to have them dismissed.

The fundamental point of the Mondragon example is that provided workers are involved enough and indeed investing enough in the enterprises they work for and, through them, in banks that both support the enterprises and spread the risks, they are no more of a threat to management than is a shareholder base. It is surely clear that management, whose survival depends upon the firm's profitability, has nothing to lose by gradually reducing the stiff division between "factors of production," and seeing labor, capital, and resources fused in the common interest, and may indeed very greatly gain by fuller participation on the part of the workers who understand the same imperative. Then by an evolutionary process entirely in keeping with the habits of open societies, the harsh disfranchisement or undignified paternalism of early capitalism could give way to what one might almost call "private socialism," the dispersion of wealth throughout the community and the involvement of all in their factories and offices—an involvement which more than anything else can dissolve perhaps the worst aspects of traditional industrialism, the alienation of the mass of workers from their community of work.

It is perhaps an ironic postscript that in the so-called Communist countries, the maverick Yugoslavs are the nearest to having developed a comparably devolved and co-operative "worker-director" structure, while the Soviet Union has remained inextricably caught in its own centralized bureaucracy. It is much more than a postscript that the largest developing country in the world—China—is beginning to show a lively interest in the Yugoslav experiment.

15 CITIES: SURVIVAL OR ELSE?

IN THIS CENTURY, it is perhaps above all in society's breathtakingly rapid switch to an urban base that we can see most clearly that strategies for conservation, for less waste and disorder, for more general standards of decent citizenship, depend not only on particular policies, actions, and decisions but upon the whole basic social context within which change takes place.

Mankind is, inevitably, not very good at stage-managing cataclysmic change. It took at least 100,000 years for the planet to house its first half billion people. Now we can add a couple of billion in about twenty years, and we are doing so in the pattern of steadily larger concentrations in cities. The Athens of Alcibiades, the Philadelphia of the Founding Fathers, were "big cities" with their fifty-thousand inhabitants. But we shall have 273 cities of over a million people by 1985. Perhaps as many as seventeen will exceed the ten-million mark.

The coming of industry and the linking of the world by train and steamship in a single great web of trade were, of course, the unquenchable energies behind this explosion of ports, manufacturing centers, and capital cities. There was no trace or hint or idea of carefully picking out suitable sites for expanded urban settlement. The cities grew near mineral reserves, in and around existing settlements, or beside promising estuaries. They crowded the workers in and provided the minimum accommodation for survival. Among the noisome factories, behind railway stations and docks, the tenements grew and were extended round and about by the vagaries of land sales and speculation. Few writers have described the process more vividly than Charles Dickens in *Dombey and Son* when he writes of London advancing as though "a giant in his travelling boots had made a stride . . . and has set his brick and mortar heel a long way in advance; but in the intermediate space . . . is a disorderly crop of beginnings of mean houses, rising out of the rubbish, as if they had been unskilfully sown.'' This unskillful sowing left the poor to live within smelling distance of Engels's polluted Manchester river and the new middle classes to plan their own retreat to fresher air and spreading suburbs, from which, first by carriage and later by train, the husbands returned to the center for work while the wives embroidered the boredom of Putney and Brooklyn and Alderly Edge.

The divorce in the city had begun, between a center divided between the rich in old, often ex-royal quarters, and the working poor—London's typical West End/East End split—and the surrounding expanding suburban rings of the newly growing and prospering middle classes. No one planned anything so shapeless. On occasion, the engulfing of a strong existing community—a Chelsea, a Greenwich Village, a Trastevere—left townlike nodes intact within the wider undifferentiated urban tissue. But the general effect was incoherence, inconvenience, and until the great sanitary revolutions of the latter part of the nineteenth century, disease and death as well.

Other pollutions, above all the fog bred of continual coal combustion, were simply endured. In short, nineteenth-century cities were on the whole profoundly ''unconserving.'' Most of their beauties and dignities came from a simpler or more aristocratic past. Their extent and incoherence bred perpetual and tedious movement. Their pollutions bit into skin and stone. Many of them inherited lively traditions of both cultured and popular art and drama. But between tenement and railway track, smoking chimneys and darkened skies, underpaid drudges and commuting clerks, they hardly offered their majority a reasonably urbane existence. The steady expansion of suburbia showed how strong was the impulse to get out of the urban mess as soon as rising personal prosperity made it possible.

Urban upheaval did not end with the first great century of industrialism. Two portents were on the horizon as the nineteenth century came to a close. One was the invention, first in Chicago, of the bastard child of technological arrogance and uncontrolled urban land markets—the skyscraper. This enabled the owner to recoup in high-density renting and selling the inordinate price he had paid for urban land, but inevitably increased central-city densities and, as we shall see, lessened housing amenities and city services. By crowding in more people, many of

them as determined as ever to come and go, the skyscraper also helped
to exaggerate the scale of the commuter flood, which by the middle of
the twentieth century, was taking in and out of New York City each day
the equivalent of the inhabitants of central Paris, all three million of
them.

And some 25 percent of this New York flood has insisted on coming
in by private car, that other vast portent of change. Once again, no one
foresaw what would be the effect of launching on the world's cities the
inundation of motorcars, which, with cheap fuel, became first in
America, then in Europe and Japan—and who knows how soon in Russia?—the most prized personal possession of the modern citizen. The
effect of the car on the city has been unconserving in the profoundest
sense. Quite apart from its predominant contribution to urban air pollution, it has added to the outward spread and the shuttle of movement, it
has helped to engulf more and more of once rural lands in indeterminate
suburbia, and its competition has begun to force public transport into financial breakdown. There can come a moment—as in such cities as
Dallas and Los Angeles—when over half the city the car is supposed to
visit is given over to roads, garages, and parking lots.

Another unfortunate development in cities has been the postwar experiment of putting usually the poorest tax-supported tenants into high-
rise blocks of unexampled anonymity and ugliness and surrounding
them with "open space" (which quickly became the muggers' and the
vandals' areas of operation). These dwellings proved in some ways
even more antisocial and antihuman than the little dank streets of back-
to-back houses they frequently replaced. Better sanitation did not entirely make up for the lack of human scale. Neighborliness did not seem
to flourish among apartments grouped too oppressively close for ac-
quaintance to be risked. Fear began to stalk the elevators and passage-
ways where twelve thousand people might be living in a single complex. From Bjilmerer in Holland to the *Grands Rassemblements* in Paris
to Ronan Point, which blew itself apart in London, to Pruitt-Igoe, which
had to be partially blown up as a social casualty in St. Louis, the high
rise as the answer to state-subsidized shelter proved on the whole a
major urban disaster. It did not even fulfill its original purpose—of
rehousing all those in substandard dwellings. Repeatedly, the "clear
felling" of sites for high rises led to the destruction of more dwellings—and small businesses—than the new mammoths could provide.

The remaining poor moved on, to double up where they could and spread the blight. Meanwhile, openings for work drained away.

These incoherences might be deemed enough for one century. But in the last decade, another sudden, unexpected change has swept over the unconserving city. Manufacturing and commerce, big and small, and the physical services they require in power or transport first launched the city. From the start, the process required other kinds of services—provided by clerks, accountants, bankers, brokers, government officials. Certain centers, particularly capital cities, grew as much by these tertiary activities as by the industry they served. But after 1950, there was an unforeseen explosion of these more immaterial forms of work. The electronic age, with the computer and the space satellite, vastly increased the sheer flow of information within the system—now more than ever a world-wide system—and as computerization and automation began to diminish employment in the traditional manufacturing and service sectors, there was a sudden explosion in what came to be known as the "knowledge industry"—including the software specialists who could program and use the new computer systems so that, say, at a flick of a switch every inventory in a corporation's warehouse round the world could flash on the screen. The combined effect of these changes can be seen in such centers as New York, where in a single decade, manufacturing and construction jobs fell by a quarter while service jobs increased by over 20 percent and government jobs by over 30 percent.

It has not proved a self-balancing change. The people who can do the service jobs tend to live in the suburbs. The manual workers from whom manufacturing activity has faded away cannot, because of poverty and exclusion, move from the city. Without exception in the developed world the worst centers of deprivation are precisely those areas, usually in the centers of older cities or along abandoned waterfronts, where the poor remain but the work has gone. Clydeside in Scotland can be taken as typical of a thousand other tragedies. In the Glasgow conurbation, industries such as shipbuilding and shipping itself have declined in the last forty years. Over 20 percent of its people live in deplorable slums. The level of unemployment has tended to remain at that same tragic percentage.

One other effect of the shift to tertiary activities must be mentioned, since it has shown a specially unfortunate mixture of good intentions

and invidious results. Since the Second World War, the British have led
the world in the effort to lessen the strains on large metropolitan centers,
by setting up on their fringes New Towns, built and administered by
special development corporations, with public control over land pro-
curement and use (and hence of the gains from any unearned increment). These, it was argued, would remove excess population from the
overcrowded centers, attract new industry and services, and become
self-supporting, self-employing communities, thereby cutting down the
daily commuting avalanche. The experiment, which began round London, was extended to other older, larger cities, such as Liverpool,
Glasgow, and Newcastle. In twenty-five years some thirty-one New
Towns left the drawing boards. No one denies that most of them have
become reasonably prosperous nor that people have left the old cities to
live in them. What could not be foreseen was the profound shift in types
of employment to the new tertiary and "knowledge" sector. Nor could
it have been foreseen that population would begin to grow more slowly.
The young and the educated left for the New Towns. Old decaying industries and people with outmoded skills were left behind in the city
centers.

One should not pick on city planning as the villain of this whole
drama. After all, New York City has lost as many industries and lively
citizens to indistinguishable suburbs as have English cities to New
Towns. But after two or three decades of experiment, it is becoming
clear that concentration of too much attention and capital on the fringes
and on the new communities can leave the center in dangerous decay.
The whole effort of metropolitan reorganization, it is now argued,
might have been conducted in a more comprehensive and systematic
fashion if old and new had been given equal claim to thought and funds.

Particular policies already discussed in these chapters—the control
of environmental degradations, a more sane and conserving use of energy, greater emphasis on smaller-scale enterprises and upon the more
direct participation of citizens—can all be taken as preliminary but essential steps to urban renewal. The point about pollution control need
not be much stressed. Wherever pollution is abated—in the air, in
water, in rubbish tips or landfills—the urban and suburban citizens gain
most directly, since they tend to receive the severest insults. One can
still dip into a stream in the Catskills, but neither the Rhine nor the Hudson is recommended for health.

Cities, too, obviously suffer most severely from the concentrated air pollution of automobiles, and it must be conceded that, in addition, they are the prime wasters of energy. It is no use beginning any discussion of possible mitigations and improvements, merits and demerits, of motorcars as such. The automobile is as embedded in developed life as the home itself. The motorcar, its life-span lengthened, one may hope, to twenty years, must be accepted as part of our inheritance. Changes to less polluting, less wasteful use can only come from another direction— an actual examination of what most people want in their towns and cities and the extent to which the car impedes or helps them to achieve these goals. Such an examination makes clear that what most people want most of the time is to get to and from work and to provide their homes with needed goods, services, and conveniences. The paradoxical character of the unintended city is that its scattered, incoherent layout means that for these purposes the car often seems the most convenient mechanism. But except on holidays or days off, the citizen's aim is not usually to get into the car. It is to go somewhere and do something. If that something could be made accessible and convenient by more conserving and economic means, a start could be made in weakening the car's limpet-like hold on urban society.

We can perhaps take it for granted that government pressure will, after however many postponements, produce a steadily more economical and more or less pollution-free vehicle. New types of engines and fuel are already far enough advanced for regulations to become not only necessary but successful. The bigger task is to change the patterns of use. Minibuses, big buses, and trains are, as we have seen, less wasteful of fuel, and there can be no doubt that less-polluted cities, less-congested streets, and less wasted fuel will all be chiefly promoted by a greater use of public transport. This is, in one sense, a recognized fact. In such cities as New York, London, Paris, and Tokyo, 70 to 80 percent of the commuting is done by public transport; and new subway systems have been or are being built (at considerable cost) in Washington, Munich, Rotterdam, Milan and a few cities in the Third World. Subway systems are supplemented by local commuter use of longer-distance railway and in many cities, separate bus lanes allow a more rapid and efficient bus service.

With all this so clear and established, why the malaise? The systems seem to cope. Why badger the private motorist when commuting after all appears to get itself done? The basic reason is, of course, cost. However blind American citizens may be at present to the energy crisis, $45 billion a year spent on importing oil—for, among others, the single motorist in the "gas-guzzling" private car—is devaluing the dollar and sending shudders of uncertainty through the entire international financial community. It is a ludicrous calculus to ride "my car to my job" and help precipitate a world slump that takes the job away.

A second reason is the rising cost of public transport, the result of wage increases and inflation, which has some tendency to send travelers back to their cars, thus reducing the number of public riders and setting in motion the vicious circle of ever fewer users and ever higher costs. Moreover, many people cannot revert to cars as public-transport prices rise. They cannot drive, or cannot afford a car. To these people—children, the elderly, poorer families, the housebound parent—public transport is as vital a service as electricity or sewage disposal. Are they to be left with simply no alternative? There is, in fact, only one fully conserving strategy, drastic as it may seem. It is to make the private car, by Draconian tolls, pay a cost which keeps it out of center cities, and to use the power of the purse to restore the sagging primacy of public modes of movement. San Francisco already charges higher tolls for automobiles with fewer passengers. Different communities will use different expedients, but the basic fact is the same. City centers are not the suitable domain of the private car. Buses, including jitney buses for intermediate journeys, better liaison between commuting stations and local bus routes, taxis with multiple use encouraged, company bus transport from public pick-up points—these are the workable means of movement within the city center, together with the bicycle and the leg. That such patterns are not a mirage can be illustrated from the experience in France. The town of Besançon, for example, achieved a 35 percent rise in the number of passengers using public transport after banning through traffic and introducing more regular buses, together with new kinds of public transport such as minibuses and collective taxis.

Much can be done to make the prospect more attractive. A reviving transport system can afford, like Paris, to have string quartets in its Metro stations. Streets can be redesigned, like the beautiful old Italian centers, with covered arcades for the pedestrian or, in commercial areas, with walkways crossing roads on imaginatively designed flyovers. In some areas, "people movers" such as are now used in airports might be introduced; they are after all much less remarkable than putting a man on the moon. The popularity all over Europe of pedestrian precincts, with all traffic excluded—one thinks of the space and strolling ease of the Piazza Navona in Rome—shows that the human leg is not yet obsolete. The car came cataclysmically. It must be controlled systematically, with other modes and conveniences substituted, and with total bans imposed in certain centers.

Indeed, this approach to more conserving modes of transport can be applied in the wider field of national policy. In the community at large, as in the cities, patterns of transport have evolved which no one particularly intended and which have turned out to be inordinately costly and unconserving. Road users never pay their full costs. Railways have to finance the whole cost of track, signals, vehicles, and depots; but gasoline taxes, car license fees and taxes, and parking fees nowhere approach the tax money spent on road building, traffic-control systems, and the many environmental costs that range from air and noise pollution to deaths and injuries on the roads. Taxpayers with or without cars can find themselves helping to pay for the enormous medical costs and for the police and other officials needed for traffic regulation and control. In addition, they can find themselves inadvertently financing car depots, such as parking places and factory bays, which are provided "free" by municipalities out of local taxes, by commerce out of sales, or by unconsulted homeowners on residential roads—a most unpopular gift when engines roar into life at five in the morning. Citizens using company cars usually get substantial tax benefits, while the more conserving citizens who walk or bicycle to work or use public transport get no advantage at all. The costing bias toward road transport is universal in developed societies. It reflects, of course, a viewpoint based on dirt-cheap oil, and one of the chief instruments of redress will be to compel motorcar users to cover their total bill, with rebates perhaps for poorer families, or possibly some form of actual rationing of gasoline—at least, the optimists suggest, until the cassava or hydrogen revolution solves the fuel equation. But even with assured, nonpulluting fuels, the private car is still an unconserving mode of movement in built-up areas, wasting patience, amenity, time, and the chance for less captive, mind-wasting activities. Nor are its land-gobbling propensities to be forgotten as we look forward to a period when farms may be among the nation's most basic assets.

A sane return to a wider use of railways—already occurring in France with the new high-speed trains—would have the added advantage of uncluttering airports by eliminating short-haul flights, particularly in regions of uncertain weather, and freeing planes for their most rational use, intercontinental air travel at the cheapest cost in capital and fuel. Provided not a sliver is cut from safety regulations, the jumbo-sized air bus with a twenty-year life-span (one recalls the long life and service of the old Dakotas) may continue to provide citizens with the vistas of sun-baked holidays and instant business deals which are yet another heritage of the cheap-oil years.

The changing calculus of rising cost should in no way be thought to rule out the car or the truck—the car because of its manifest pleasures and conveniences outside congested areas, the truck because roads, commanding many times more "lines of track" and "stations" than railways, give far more flexible access to homes and businesses, particularly for perishable goods. Furthermore, the railways, by abolishing marshaling yards, failing to put together small, fast freight trains, and all but missing out on the "roll-on-roll-off" container revolution have often been the source of their own uncompetitiveness. They have played their part in allowing mammoth, overfast haulage trucks to endanger citizens—and even their buildings and homes—on multiplying roads. But with the day of cheap energy over, a rebalancing of the books should be possible, to give the motor vehicle its share, but only its rational share, of a nation's transport.

But it is, of course, quite irrational to make the motorcar the villain of the piece. Quite apart from its hold on peoples' desires, its use reflects, again and again, the lack of alternatives. As we have noted, in most conurbations, the distribution of services and work—even basic services such as shops, laundromats, and garages and other repair facilities—is so incoherent that they do not lend themselves to regular bus routes. The users are too dispersed, the destinations too indeterminate. And very often stretches of derelict or abandoned land add to the general spatial unworkability of the areas. It is Dickens's London all over again save that the giant boots seem to have taken their brick and mortar steps not simply outward but round and round as well. How, out of these peripheries, all too often surrounding decaying centers, can more conserving communities be built?

The lessons of Britain's New Towns are not all negative. Starting from green-field sites, many of them have become functioning, concentrated communities with all the customary work, amenities, and services of a large town or small city. It is significant that there is little commuting to the center from London's belt of New Towns, since they have established themselves as centers of work in their own right. Their experience suggests two possible strategies for the largest conurbations. The first is to permit no more growth in the over-all area and even to remove some "spillover" to other places. This is France's aim in rivaling Paris with eight *métropoles d'équilibre,* located throughout the country, with comparable national and international services and prestige. The second is to pick a number of nodal points—sometimes in suburbia, sometimes in more open country—which would then be built up to city density, with all the attendant houses, work, services, and amenities. This is the aim of the five new towns in the Paris region. Neither strategy is inherently impossible, provided time and choice and opportunities for adjustment are ample and renewed; provided, too, there is, as in France, a central sense of national dedication to the undertaking.

The approach has the advantage of fitting conveniently with other conserving policies. We can begin with transport since the strategy directly reinforces the reforms proposed for the inner city. The creation of concentrated communities makes interconnecting bus or train routes practicable, thereby cutting down the inter-suburban private driving that unclustered settlements virtually impose.

Concentrated urban "nodes" can also be more easily served by some of the less-wasteful energy systems. No district-heating scheme or combined heat and power station can provide hot water and space heating cheaply and efficiently for commercial buildings and private homes if they are simply too scattered for a coherent pipe system to be laid. But new urban developments—and redevelopments—can take advantage of these energy systems to maximize the efficiency with which fuel is used, and thereby reduce fuel bills. They can also drastically cut air pollution, since one boiler serves hundreds of buildings. A large portion of the Soviet Union's rapidly expanding electricity capacity comes from power stations whose waste heat is used for district heating. This kind of power station is also being introduced on a growing scale in Eastern Europe. Most new housing in West Germany and the Scandinavian countries is linked to a district-heating scheme, and as we saw in chapter 7, city garbage is increasingly used as fuel in such schemes, once the valuable metals have been separated out.

As the urban "nodes" develop and people are lured into them by work (especially in small firms and services), by convenience, and by amenities, it may become possible, using youth conservation corps and other sponsored groups, to begin the much-needed clearing and renewing of derelict interurban land. In larger areas, the policy can be to encourage mixed farms, possibly linked with neighboring food co-operatives and farmers' markets. Allotments for the amateurs and market gardens for the professionals are another answer, with the promise of fresher produce and a sharp fall in haulage costs. Parks and open recreation areas and fish-stocked streams can be added, and as in some suburban regions in Britain, it will be found that the planting of tree belts and copses helps to rescue the landscape from dismal vistas of broken fences and derelict barns and, at the same time, defines boundaries between districts and provides open wandering space within reach of the city family.

The resourceful Chinese have tried out one version of this "cleanup" by ringing Shanghai's central area with a zone of vegetable farms and orchards. There is something of the same feeling in the British concept of "green belts" round major centers. Unhappily, these have sometimes proved green halters, strangling growth within yet encouraging the developer to leap to the outer rim to begin again. Dickens soundly denounced the unskillful sowing of mean (and not so mean) houses. The better concept is one not of concentric belts, but of an orderly network with lateral and central communication and, wherever possible, the green areas running right into the city's core, as does Rock Creek Park in Washington, D.C., or (if the plans mature) the Lea Valley down to London's Thames.

But the real test of this strategy of re-creating concentrated urban centers and giving them the means of becoming true and creative communities lies, unhappily, precisely where the obstacles to the policy seem most acute. The French have given special thought to the balance of housing, industrial work, amenities for leisure, and tertiary employment in their urban-development plans. They have tried to revivify stagnant provincial towns and restore humane and urbane living at the very core of the "metropolises," old and new. Yet they have found, as have the British, the Americans and the Dutch, that the old cores of center cities present the most formidable obstacles to creative action. Too many neighborhoods have been blitzed away to make way for slablike, high-rise public housing—and, with the houses, the small businesses have vanished as well. (In one British housing development, ninety-six establishments were destroyed and only six shops built to take their place). Again—one thinks of London's Rachman scandals—rack renters have moved in on restorable old properties, stuffed them with the homeless and the defenseless, and left the buildings to become decaying slums while themselves living high off the not inconsiderable rent bills. In some countries injudicious rent-control legislation, instead of giving rational defense to both responsible landlord and inoffensive tenant, has made repairs virtually unaffordable and the houses have simply been abandoned—to vandals, to junkies, to arsonists. In just four years, ninety thousand houses were thus left derelict in New York City alone.

A rather subtler disturbance can come in marginal areas where rich and poor still live in the old townlike atmosphere of the mixed community. Here property dealers may come in, buy up old but still handsome houses, terrify their poor, often elderly tenants out of them, and then resell the refurbished home to some wealthier folk, tired of commuting. The effect of all these changes, coupled with the decline in shops and businesses, and the vanishing of jobs in public transport or on the docks is to produce inner cities so desolate and downcast—not to speak of whole cities like New York on the verge of bankruptcy—that it would seem to demand pie-eyed optimism to assume that violence, vandalism, and desperation can be conquered and the random areas set back on the road to becoming socially mixed, economically functioning communities with a fuller measure of civic health.

But the outlook is not so despairing. We can start at the very nadir of misery. Here is a description of the A. Henry Moore high-rise housing development in the battered heart of Jersey City as it looked in 1973:

When the present Housing Authority took over in 1973, management and maintenance operations had all but ceased. Windows in communal areas were replaced with welded steel. Light bulbs were no longer replaced. Nor were entrance doors. No elevator worked. Garbage chutes were continually out of order and stairways were all but impassable because of rubbish. Tenants on higher floors threw their garbage out of the window. All the outside areas were full of rubbish. The project was a well known haven of hard drugs abuse; junkies slept in the courtyard. The crime rate was so high that police set up a mini-station on the estate—the crime rate rose even higher! People were ashamed to say they lived at A. Henry Moore and were victimized for it.*

But in one of the constituent high rises a new housing authority recruited responsible tenants to form a first management committee—voted into office by all the tenants. Among the members' first responsibilities was to install a reception committee in the entrance hall every

*Anne Power, *Tenant Co-ops or Tenant Management Corporation in the USA.*

evening to interview all comers and to explain to less interested tenants
the plans for improvement for which they and the housing authority
were prepared to take responsibility. Floor captains were appointed to
keep order in the corridors and elevator entrances. Nor was there any
suggestion that protection and safety were the sole concern. For instance, all tenants were consulted on the kind of color schemes they
would prefer once repainting began. All this started in one building in
the complex. Windows were reglazed with virtually unbreakable plastic
glass; all-but-irremovable ceiling lights were installed, elevators
mended, rubbish chutes cleared and repaired, and everything within
sight was repainted. Not entirely surprisingly, the idea spread. Other
buildings in the A. Henry Moore complex set up their management
committees and set in motion external repairs. Internal rehabilitation
followed—kitchens, floors, bathrooms. Outside, the dingy asphalt
alleys were lit with overhead lights, and, a daring step, grass began to
be planted and the first flowers to appear. They remained unplucked.

It was not only in the immediate housing that marked improvements
and a way forward were seen. Various managerial and service jobs
emerged in the process of cleaning up; they were allotted to tenants and
made some dent in high local unemployment. New relations were established with the neighboring school; a parent-teacher association was
set up, and by bringing parents in to discuss the children's report cards,
the teachers began to reverse the truancy, indiscipline, and indifference
fostered by childish rebellion and parental neglect.

One should not think of this Jersey City transformation as a freak
success. In 1977, a tenant-management demonstration brought together
thirty other housing authorities, two-thirds of them with similar suc-
cesses to chronicle. Nor is tenant management the end of the story. In
New York City, tenants threatened with eviction after a rent strike in a
totally exploited and unserviced building received city support in taking
over the freehold as a tenants' co-operative, contributed "sweat equity"
in the work they themselves did in rehabilitation, and ended as co-
operative owners of a decent, viable apartment block.

Another variation on the theme comes from London's North Isling-
ton, where the local council was persuaded to stop the "winkling out"
of poor, long-established, and often elderly tenants, to rehabilitate the
once fine old houses with public money, and then to transfer ownership
to a co-operative society, which in five years grew to include 160 tenant
owners. At this point, the management committee decided that new

units should be started to prevent the co-operative from outgrowing itself. And this, of course, is the key to all these schemes. Neighbors first get to know each other. Then they begin to be prepared to take decisions about their own and the community's future. There grow up among them feelings opposite to dereliction, apathy and neglect. They are no longer the despised recipients of poverty housing. They are controllers in their own right. Self-respect and responsibility—for their own families and for their neighbors—turn back the evil tide of crime and destruction.

Municipal or housing authorities who have started in this way with their most underprivileged citizens can find myriad ways of encouraging the trend. In the older city, where beautiful old houses, running to decay, survive—a Pimlico, a Brooklyn—the policy of restoring some for poor tenants and allowing developers to renew neighboring squares helps to re-establish the mix of dwellings and incomes that is perfectly normal in a small country town or in a Chelsea or a Montparnasse. Although it is tempting to pull down the more spectacularly horrible super high rises, there has probably been too much destruction in the last quarter of a century to let a new generation grow up with the sound of demolition in their ears. A measure of regeneration short of destruction is possible. Some municipalities have converted these monoliths from family accommodation to apartments run by and for young single people with communal responsibility.

Inside the monsters, whole floors can be set aside for playschools or old peoples' clubs. Between the ziggurats, across the aching, empty parking lots, new streets of small houses with groceries and candy stores and workshops can be built to restore not only human scale but human employment as well. This is also accomplished by "group factories," where a wide range of small enterprises can share telephones, restaurants, receptionists, energy systems, and cleaning and maintenance costs within a single building. Such a group factory in London's Covent Garden is working successfully and helping small businesses to return to the city center. Some 350 people are employed in a group factory in London's Chiswick, which incidentally receives no public support but pays its way.

Playgrounds, and the staff to run them, are a means of ensuring that the energy and search for adventure in children are not turned into petty vandalism and shoplifting while parents on the thirtieth floor are literally incapable of even the barest supervision, let alone any form of discipline and control. London has perhaps gone furthest in its commitment to no more high rises for low-income families and to a large extension of rehabilitation instead. Since, as we have seen, this is by far the most labor-intensive method of construction, it combines the hopes of a better environment with the certainty of more jobs.

In fact, the sheer variety of advantages of the new approach prompts a wider question. Should one go further and combine the creation and rehabilitation of urban "nodes" or communities with a more ambitious plan on a national scale? Why not devote a given percentage of GNP to the process and continue the expenditure until there are no substandard houses left and all communities have at least reasonable sources of work and basic amenities? Housing accounts for up to half the nation's fixed capital investment. It also, especially in rehabilitation, calls for a very wide variety of skilled workers—from plumbers to carpenters to bricklayers, to site foremen. But as an industry, construction tends to be afflicted with feast and famine, since much of it depends upon government spending—which can rise and fall with inflationary trends—and upon property builders and speculators who help to unleash the inflation. Possibly few strategies would more underpin the concept of a "social compact," stabilize employment, and respond to a really basic need than a sustained, undeviating strategy for national housing and community building. Like an arms budget, it would regularly set aside 5 or 6 percent of GNP for the construction sector, and it would systematically build up both the decaying center cities and any other established communities falling behind in the means of maintaining their population and replenishing their life.

Such a program could, admittedly, be afforded only if all unearned increment attached to the improvements remained with the community. This does *not* imply the nationalization of land, simply the transfer to the state (rather on the lines of mineral rights) of what one might call "development rights." After all, the whole justification of the free market is that rising prices are the signal for the need and production of increased supplies. But nobody can increase the supply of land—save, perhaps, the thrifty Dutch. Least of all can anyone do much to stretch Manhattan. Rising prices with fixed supplies spell fortunes for the few and inflation for the many. A national building program would require control over the returns on the benefits it created and over the use of the land in which its communities, old and new, were being brought to life.

There is a further economic argument for such a program. It is rooted in the universal desire among citizens to own their own homes. The plan could be accompanied by a national savings and mortage scheme which would further reduce inflationary risks and could be afforded even by poorer families if we assume, as we must, that a guaranteed national minimum income is one of the basic reforms of the conserving state.

If at this point, readers put down the page with a satirical eye and begin to murmer to themselves about "utopian fantasies," it should be noted that nothing proposed here for communities has not in one way or another been tried out. After the appalling devastations of the war, for instance, the Soviet Union raised its commitment to housing so that, in three decades, population doubled but the housing supply multiplied three times over. West Germany, starting from an abysmal prewar record of neglect and the repeated blitzes of the war, contrived by 1970 to build ten million new houses and managed to achieve the often proposed ideal of one room for each citizen. The Dutch, too, have all but moved into housing surplus, and in both countries the vast building programs did not restrain but stimulated other sectors of the economy.

High-rise building for housing the poor is mercifully on the decline. Rehabilitating older housing is beginning to take its place, and even if it is too late in some places—one thinks of the City of London—for the kind of restoration of history achieved in Warsaw or Leningrad, the bulldozing of old sites is losing favor. Clapham will keep its church precincts, Covent Garden its theatrical suppliers and wig shops, Paris's Left Bank its restaurants and art dealers and that precious social value—continuity and a sense of place—will no longer be put so casually at risk as it has been in the last quarter century.

The financial proposals underlying a broad national strategy for settlements are no more revolutionary. Gothenburg and Stockholm have secured land in advance of urban needs since the end of the last century. All Britain's New Towns—as we have noted—absorb the unearned increment, and many of them actually make a profit. France may be a little less successful since its zones where prices are controlled for future communities tend to attract land speculators to the fringes. But the principle is admitted. Even in America, it is argued that capital-gains taxes in part recover the speculative gains of developers for the community. The scale may be insufficient but, once again, the principle is accepted.

Nor are the wider schemes of urban management simply plucked from the air. Poland and Romania have each managed to decentralize industry and services sufficiently for the capital city to account now for a smaller proportion of the total population than it did thirty years ago. Paris, which once threatened to swallow France, is, as we have noted, balanced by eight distant *métropoles d'équilibre*. These have been developed to offer services, infrastructure, and attractions comparable to those of the capital city. They can thus divert growth from the Paris region while stimulating the development of their own region. Eight towns within 110 to 220 kilometers of Paris have also been developed as countermagnets. In each of these urban communities, road and rail services have been improved. And the community's growth has been stimulated by such measures as new towns close by (as at Lyons, Marseilles, and Rouen) or new universities (as at Reims, Orléans, Tours, and Nantes) or a new international airport (as at Lyons). And precisely in the suburbanizing Seine basin, the concept of separate urban "nodes" is being built into the regional plan, with new towns at Cergy-Pontoise, St. Quentin-en-Yvelines, Évry, Melun-Sénart, and Marne La Vallée. Nor should we forget the resourceful Swiss, with their high mountains, long lakes, and fiercely democratic tradition, who have managed to keep two-thirds of themselves out of cities with more than 200,000 inhabitants even though 80 percent of them are engaged in industrial and service occupations. No, a more urbane, conserving, decentralized urbanism is not just a dream. It is hard fact in many areas. It could be so everywhere, given the political will.

Unhappily, political will is a very doubtful commodity. In many developed countries, citizens are expressly excluded from matters of state, which have become the monopoly of the public bureaucracy. In open societies, the trouble all too often is not prohibition but indifference. Citizens can become interested in particular possibilities or threats, such as stopping the Spadina freeway from chopping into Toronto or fending off the Winchester bypass. But the longer-term effect of local interest and action is not always encouraging. Once an immediate objective is achieved, the coalition of interests that was successful tends all too often simply to fall apart.

However, there may be a not-fully-understood sequence of causes and effects here. Shorter hours, "flexitime," sabbaticals, adult education, a greater sharing of domestic responsibilities, and more part-time opportunities all play an essential part in breeding citizens not only able but anxious to participate and see for themselves. To design a more or less passive way of life and then expect men and women simply to emerge from it on their own initiative is asking too much of the often isolated citizen. This is simply another way of saying that we are unlikely to secure conserving politics in an unconserving, uncaring society.

From what force, then, can a more active citizen interest be derived? We can probably forget ideology. The passionate monetarist advocates of the free market have still not explained how massive unemployment and a totally skewed profile of rewards can be prevented from undermining this system. When Georges Marchais explains that only a tenth of the French own a third of France's disposable income, and waves jewelry sales manuals advertising diamond watches at $500,000, he scandalizes a wider group than the "outraged proletariat." Equally, Communism is no longer a vision, but the working system of a series of developed states run without a trace of citizen initiative and with rewards for the privileged bureaucracy—the *nomenklatura*—more steeply graded than in many Western societies. In fact, no democracy has gone so far as to establish shops which officially debar the ordinary citizen and serve only the elite. Moreover, this particular piece of patronage is a reminder of the degree to which on both sides of the ideological divide, high material consumption still dominates economic thought— in the West, to maintain expectations and revive employment, in the East to catch up with the West and possibly make up for the lack of other opportunities.

Perhaps we can equally leave out a more modern and perhaps more relevant debate between those who argue that further economic growth can be painlessly achieved and the bonanza of the fifties and sixties restored by moving massively toward the "hard" technologies—breeder reactors, mining the moon, orbiting vast solar stations—with their infinite supplies and energies, and those who believe that at the end of this route lies nuclear destruction and total chemical disruption of living organisms. Thus, they argue, only an end to compulsive economic growth will preserve a viable biosphere.

However, the whole argument of these pages is that there are a thousand policies and technologies between these extremes which mankind can accomplish and which simply do not entail catastrophic risks. Science can be used to enhance, not disrupt, our knowledge of natural systems. Growth can be true growth if it preserves the renewable resources upon which sustained and reasonable expansion depends. Science and growth working creatively together will vary in the patterns of their use according to local resources and needs. The sunbelt does not include Manchester. The pattern of needs and opportunities can and should be as varied as nature itself. But to dismiss science as a usable tool is to ensure planetary destruction by another route.

And perhaps it is in this growing sense of intermediate possibilities—of output, thought, and work which are not extreme in their politics or their technology—that the best hope lies for a more lively and enlightened public opinion. Looking back over the last century, we have no reason to despair of the force of ideas and the possibilities of steady, uncataclysmic reform. The guaranteed annual income may not yet be achieved, but it has been seriously discussed by a not notoriously liberal American president, and the welfare state is an established if not always a welcome fact. Restraint on income explosions may still be chancy. Yet some form of control over wage bargains is far from exceptional. Participation in the work process is still only patchy, but clearly it is an idea whose time has come—the number of practitioners attests this fact—and it was not a Fabian Socialist, but the chairman of a large automobile company who recently urged his workers to participate in schemes to care for the elderly and retired workers and carry on the solidarity of past partnership. The need to break away from the contradictory concept of a "productivity" which reduces jobs while keeping wages as the main determinants of purchasing power may still be obscured by traditionalist thinking. Yet it is not the late E. F. Schumacher but the British president of the Institute of Civil Engineers who recently appealed for a better match between factors of production and their availability, advocating in fact the leaner use of capital.

Energy conservation may not yet be at the center of public attention, but most Western nations now include it as an essential element in energy policy, private firms have given a lead in cutting use by as much as a fifth of traditional practice, and thousands of private citizens, from thrift as much as duty, are insulating their houses. We should not forget the pocketbook. Today it works toward many of the critical elements of conservation. In any case, who can doubt that the environmental movement itself is a largely spontaneous expression of citizen concern sparked not only by popular revulsion at the evidence of growing waste and pollution but also by eloquent individual leaders and by new "shaping ideas"? And it is already enough of a force to exercise direct influence on American politics, to determine a Swedish change of government, and to have upset the whole internal political balance in a couple of recent German elections. There clearly *is* some fallout from the new mood. The governor of California loses no popularity by refusing the ornate splendors of his predecessor and living in his bachelor's pad. Hundreds of young people seek to ''live poor with style.'' Figures like the late Aristotle Onassis are far from commanding universal respect, and the whole reaction to the scale of rewards paid to the heads of multinational banks—or teamsters-union officials—has in it not only envy but some measure of distaste.

Are there, however, any signs of a deeper transformation? It demands something more than strain on family finances or a vogue of simpler living to meet the fundamental challenge of conservation, to use both things and people with less greed and exploitation, to see fellow human beings as ''other selves'' and the natural environment as a sacred inheritance to be passed on, in viable condition and good heart, to the generations to come. In one sense, the times are unpropitious for such deeper explorations of the human spirit. An obvious point must be repeated. It is only in this century that the majority of developed people have had even a first impression of the economic elbow room and social choice formerly available only to the wealthy. It may have made them not much happier in the deepest sense than their predecessors in the Trianon or in Caligula's Rome. But it is a vast improvement on serfdom or early industrialism, or the long depression or the rationed years of war. Must the cup be dashed to the ground after only the first sip?

There is a profound psychological obstacle to be overcome here, and continued stagnation with inflation will raise it higher still. But once again, the debate must be withdrawn from such extreme forms. Massive impoverishment is not proposed, nor a return to the Stone Age. At the most, the aim is an abandoning of the perpetual pursuit of ''more'' which is the root of inflation, the core of boredom, the rungs of a meaningless treadmill. Here perhaps our century is not entirely fixed in its materialist fantasies. It is precisely among younger people that the philosophy of ''enough'' is making headway. It is they who head off to work in communes on the land and who often take the lead in urban renewal. It is among them that interest is growing in all the world's great ethical traditions, with their universal witness to the need for generosity and self-control. Above all, the young seem more alive to one of the primordial facts of the late twentieth century, the fact that merely to be born into the developed world is already to be a privileged member of a small, inconceivably endowed (and wasteful) elite. Indeed, it may be that it is through the growing, aching contrast between the fortune of the developed few and the misery of the vast mass of humanity that a stronger political and ethical commitment to world conservation and generosity can still be found.

This is the hopeful vision. But there is another. Given the openess of planetary communications, the established contacts between extremists on a world-wide basis, the proven impatience and violence of potential despair, it may be that if the underpinning of greater solidarity is not found through compassion and responsibility, we cannot rule out more cataclysmic possibilities. The vastly outnumbered quarter of humanity who live in reasonable affluence are, on the whole, inward-looking in both their interests and their aims. But so were the courtiers of Versailles and the bureaucratic elite of czarist Russia. If wisdom, good will, and vision are insufficient to awaken the sense of need for new directions, there are more violent and ominous routes. As the twentieth century moves to its last decades, its day-to-day experience—from Belfast to Mogadishu, from Amsterdam to Bulawayo—is very far from suggesting that violence, terrorism, even a sort of fusing of local and planetary civil war are lethal possibilities that can be comfortably ruled out. A billion earthlings now live in unspeakable misery. Another billion are on the way. Can their passivity and patience be made the safe foundation for greedy minorities either at home or in the planet itself? This is not what history has to teach. Nor is there much time in which to learn.

Part Two: Priorities for Development

16 A TIME FOR CHOICE?

ENOUGH HAS NOW been said of the changes in techniques and perspective experienced by the industrialized nations in the last decade to indicate that, added together, they tend toward something not much short of a new concept of the technological society. This possibility is proving confusing enough for the already developed nations. But what effect is it likely to have on the three-quarters of mankind whose processes of modernization are not complete or hardly begun? If developed societies are in a period of uncertainty, how much more marked must it be among the others, for whom, for a quarter century, the motto has simply tended to be, Hurry up and follow on.

The reactions, naturally, cannot be uniform. The "Third World" includes "low-income" countries with almost a billion people with average annual incomes of $250 or less and almost a billion and a half more in "middle-income" countries with an average annual income of less than $1,000.* (People in the industrialized market economies enjoy an average annual income of more than $6,000.)

How, too, can one make plans or predictions without taking into account the vast differences in size or potential wealth among the nations of the Third World? To include them all in a single category of "developing countries," without proper distinctions between a country, say, like Mali with 5.8 million inhabitants in 1976 and a per capita income of

* Appendix B lists the 125 nations of the world with populations exceeding one million in 1976, with selected statistics for each, such as population and life expectancy. The nations are grouped within such categories as "low-income" and "middle-income." China belongs in the "middle-income" category for this statistic, although it is listed in the Appendix under "centrally planned economies." It qualifies for both categories.

$100, and a country like Brazil with 110 million citizens and an average annual income of over $1,000, does not do much to advance understanding of how the new trends in development will—or should—affect the modernizing states. The nearest one can come to generalization is to say that virtually all of them have been European colonies. The emancipation of Latin America did precede that of the rest of the world by about a century, but in 1945 it still tended to conform to colonial patterns of trade—the export of primary products to the Atlantic center, the import in return of Western manufactures.

This condition in its turn explains another valid generalization—that the developing countries exhibit a universal determination to "catch up" with the old imperial powers and round off the end of political dependence with an equal social and economic emancipation. This is the political ambition behind the whole discussion of a "new international economic order." It is also the cement of a loose alliance—the so-called Group of 77 (now with more than 110 members)—between developing peoples as remote in their particular interests as, precisely, Mali and Brazil.

It can also greatly complicate the catching-up process. The developed world has been changing its structures, technologies, and scientific insights for nearly two centuries, and is in the midst of changing them again. It does not therefore necessarily follow that the strategies the developed nations are pursuing now are the ones best suited to countries at totally different levels of skills and resources. So much of the drive for development in the last quarter century, and so much of the advice given about it, has been based, almost unconsciously, on twentieth-century experience that the totally different stages of development, endowment, and opportunity in various nations have been too often overlooked. And now there is an extra reason for caution and reconsideration. The present discontents in the *developed* world suggest that all has not been well with its policies of growth and technology, even in the most highly endowed and sophisticated societies. Possibly, therefore, the path of wisdom in the Third World is not only to consider the new opportunities and techniques but to look back as well and see what history has to say about critical turning points where right or wrong decisions were taken. If all had been well along the way, the present doubts would not have come to the surface. Are there then critical phases through which developed nations have passed—for good and evil—and which can now, with hindsight, be better understood and mastered? The Third World has lost forever what advantages there were in being pioneers—and for a time that meant world domination. But this does not mean these nations cannot gain the advantage of followers— that of picking out and avoiding the first comers' mistakes. This means, in the first place, looking at developed countries in their own early stages of modernization and trying to discern the decisive steps—or mistakes—by which the process flourished or floundered. The forms they took at earlier times may often seem unrecognizably different. But perhaps they offer a number of vital clues, and possibly those clues have been overlooked or understressed.

The clearest lie in agriculture. If we go back to the earliest "modernizer," Britain, we tend to think of Newcomen building his steam engine and the Darbys of Coalbrookdale inventing coking coal in the nick of time to prevent the exhaustion of all forest reserves for charcoal needed in the iron industry. But we can easily forget "Turnip" Townshend, the Irish peer who introduced the fourfold rotation of crops and the turnip's use as a winter feed for cattle, or Coke of Holkham, an early and influential promoter of the "New Husbandry," who revolutionized farm productivity by new forms of crop rotation and "marling" (a primitive form of fertilizing the fields). Such technical advances in productivity (the "more for less") when applied to farms consolidated through the enclosure acts—and helped by a phenomenal mid-eighteenth century span of good harvests—provided a surplus of food and rural wealth which country bankers and country entrepreneurs helped to tap and, to give only the most obvious example, utilized to turn rural Lancashire into the base for the new cotton industry.

This first example of agricultural priority and productivity has, however, its dark shadow—one which is present in some areas we can see again today. In the creation of the types of farm that could use the new techniques of crop rotation and animal husbandry, many of the landless workers—the cotters of the Highlands, a mass of the villagers in southern England—lost their right to glean and to keep their animals on the old communal lands. They were part of the growing proletariat thrust into the unspeakable miseries of the new industrial cities or forced to distant exile in the New World. The effects were in some ways comparable to the dispossession of the rural poor being brought about in the developing world by today's "Green Revolution"—with big machines, new seeds, artificial fertilizers, and increasing output for the well-to-do farmers, but a steady shedding of manpower in the process. Britain's

sufferings were probably less than today's evils. The work force was
growing on average by only about 0.5 percent per year, not the 2 or
more percent per year common in the Third World. The current industrial techniques were highly labor-intensive, and work could be found in
the cities. Migration was an important safety valve. In Britain, too,
there was a strong tenant-farmer yeoman class and a responsible
squirearchy that mitigated some of the social evils. Even William Cobbett, the most vivid critic of the enclosures and dispossessions, spoke
with respect of a "resident native gentry, attached to the soil, known to
every farmer and labourer from their childhood, frequently mixing with
them in those pursuits where all artificial distinctions were lost." These
men cared for tenants and laborers and were contrasted with the evil absentee landlords who were seeing land "as a mere object of speculation
and relying for influence not upon the good will of their vicinage but
upon the dread of their power." In all too many areas of the Third
World the latter words apply today, and just as Britain had to endure
several decades of rural disaffection and urban discontent in the wake of
radical changes on the farms, the result today will be infinitely more violent in countries where a mistimed introduction of capital-intensive
technologies causes employment to fall away even as the number of
people multiplies.

Almost a century after Cobbett, at the other side of the world in a totally different culture, another island offered similar proof of the primacy of agriculture but avoided a number of the social disadvantages.
Japan's Meiji Revolution in the 1870s marked the beginning of rapid
modernization. But careful as the Japanese had been to keep themselves
in touch with industrializing trends elsewhere, the most fundamental act
of the Meiji change was to transform the rural sector. All feudal inter-
mediaries were abolished. With this act went the freeing of the peasant
farmer from arbitrary payments and compulsory work. The farm tax
still to be paid to the state represented not much more than a third of the
old feudal dues. At the same time, direct encouragement was given to
improved agricultural practices—new seeds, fertilizer, better implements, water control. Research stations, established at the level of the
prefectures, carried the new possibilities to the farmers. Between the
Meiji upheaval and the Second World War, Japanese rice production
grew from 2.5 tons to 4 tons per hectare. (One should add that a further
round of reform—introduced, of all things by the American forces of
occupation—redistributed the land, strengthened co-operatives, and in-

creased extension and credit services. As a result, rice yields grew to 6 tons per hectare.)

Two aspects of this Japanese experience can be seen, with hindsight, to have played particularly significant roles. One was the provision of a full array of supporting services for the newly enfranchised farmer. The second was the abolition of feudal forms of tenure. This latter point, not surprisingly, follows the slightly earlier European experience. Taking the French Revolution as a starting point, we can almost see the modernizing impetus moving eastward across the Continent as the old feudal institutions were modified or abolished. Denmark, by abolishing the old tenures before the end of the eighteenth century and introducing a co-operative framework for farming, and high schools for general literacy, turned a spit of sand into Europe's most productive farming system in less than a century.

But the primacy of successful agriculture in the early stages of modernization was overlaid in peoples' more recent thinking by two profound impressions, both historical, which blurred the image of early modernization. The first, almost universally held in the postcolonial world, was the vision of industry as the instrument of freedom from continued "neocolonial" economic control. It was widely believed— and not without cause—that colonial powers had either actually impeded or at least not encouraged local industrial processes that would compete with their own. The Indians compared their struggles against Lancashire—which insisted on countervailing duties on Indian textiles—with the genuine "giant leap forward" of independent Japan's textile industry at the turn of the last century. The successful effort of the irrepressible Tata family—in the numbing atmosphere of official disapproval—to create an independent iron and steel industry on the basis of India's own resources led one ironical commentator to compare the attitude of the British colonial officials with the well-known Victorian revision of the ten commandments:

> Thou shalt not kill; but need'st not strive
> Officiously to keep alive.

Once again the contrast was with Japan's bounding, government-supported progress. Given this background, it was almost an unconditioned reflex to assume that the first task in the postcolonial order would be to achieve the most rapid possible rate of industrialization and an end to the overwhelming dependence on the old metropolitan suppliers of manufactured goods. Agriculture would be made a source of saving—by requiring the farmers to subsidize the town workers with forced food deliveries and low prices—and a reservoir of labor. The tendency was to forget that for both, some agricultural surplus would first be necessary.

And this folk myth of development was reinforced by a second which, by historical accident, gave a quite distorted view of how easily surpluses could emerge. North America entered the industrial era with a unique advantage—the sheer scale of cultivable land compared with the number of farmers available to farm it. There were barely 5 million Americans in 1780. Yet by then, both India and China already had more than 100 million inhabitants. Moreover, the American settlers were descendants of a Europe in which the New Husbandry had been going on for more than a century and in which, in the wider context of human hope and confidence, the Baconian dream of improving and mastering nature was an underlying energy of most of the leading minds.

Fired with such energies and opportunities, the North American agricultural revolution made up for its shortage of manpower by a steadily greater elaboration of machines. Farm boys invented automatic drillers in their fathers' stables; Eli Whitney (who revolutionized the textile industry) was a farmer's son. So was the inventor of the combine harvester. So, incidentally, was Henry Ford. A great surge of cheap grain, increasingly produced by mechanical means, overlaid other farming systems—the British, for instance—and virtually pushed agriculture into the techno-industrial sector before its own independent origins and needs had established themselves in development theory. At the same time, the unparalleled plenty helped, almost unremarked, to spark and feed the urban sector, to buy its goods, to encourage consumer variety, to launch, in short, the modern technical order. As the farmers went west, the cities and industry went with them in a mutually reinforcing process.

In fact, in only one part of North America was there a strong institutional obstacle to modernizing and mechanizing agriculture. In the American South, slavery repeated the feudal pattern of binding the propertyless worker to the land and directing all the gains to a small class of proprietors. The consequences were observed in the 1850s by one of America's most remarkable innovators, Frederick Olmsted (who went on to persuade the unwilling city fathers of New York to establish Central Park—"the rich do not need it, the poor will abuse it," they argued—and then, moving onward again, launched the great national parks in the American West). Olmsted wrote in *The Cotton Kingdom* an analysis of the effects of slavery and concentrated plantation ownership on the entire Southern economy. Since the mass of the people had virtually no purchasing power, local industry and production and services could not much develop. The plantation owners were little interested in trade and left all middleman services to the Northern and British entrepreneurs. Cotton was grown and exported and the primary income of the owners secured. But little or no stimulus and diversification was passed on to the rest of the cotton kingdom. As the Civil War approached, slavery was becoming not so much a source of secure wealth as a debilitating institutional trap. Thus North America's only experience with a "colonial" type of agriculture bore out the vital link between feudal emancipation and technological advance. Even in abundant America, the older system could not work.

But however much the picture of great farming machines effortlessly moving over the land and pouring out a limitless bounty of agricultural surplus may have touched the human imagination for a time—it certainly influenced the Russians in the 1930s—the chief and obvious need in the developing world today is to recover the sense of the earlier Japanese model of rural priority and accept the need to make agriculture not the Cinderella of national development, but the lead sector in the most sustained and rigorous sense. The reason is simple, if the prime aim of society is to conserve people. Three-quarters of the people in the developing world (more than two billion) live in rural areas. Even in the middle-income states, where growth rates of over 5 percent were maintained in the fifties and sixties, the growing wealth all too often failed to reach the countryside. It is there, among the farm people—sometimes in pockets and regions of greater wealth, sometimes, as in the poorest countries, in the whole community—that is to be found 80 percent of the world's "absolute poverty," with malnutrition, high mortality, crippling disease, illiteracy, and lack of work.

And this list of lack and grief, however horrifying, does not give the final dimension of misery—its dynamic character. It is among the poorest peoples that birth rates are highest—the percentage can be as high as 50 percent above the national average. As a result, over 40 percent of the people in the world's rural areas are less than fifteen years old. They will have to find work in communities already underemployed. They will grow up to double the number of families living in misery. The pressure of their migrations will bring further insecurity to cities where 30 to 40 percent of the people may already be short of work and contriving to exist on totally inadequate incomes. If the first goal of a conserving planet is some minimum standard of hope and decency for the totally deprived, there can be no argument about priorities. They lie in the rural areas of the developing world among the poorest farmers and the landless families. Allow their fate to be another twenty years of stagnation in all but numbers, and the human catastrophe will reach an irreparable scale.

Is there in fact any other possible outcome? Are not numbers, needs, supplies, availabilities, already so hopelessly skewed that the rich had better resign themselves to watching disasters forever unfolding on their television screens? To this the answer can be a tentative no. Just because the rural sector has suffered such relative neglect, it has reserves to mobilize which can begin to reverse the downward spiral. And a number of countries—typically the most successful of the modernizing societies—have made experiments in new forms of rural organization and output which give at least the possibility of checking the run down to disaster. So far, on average, only 20 percent of the investment of most developing nations has gone to the 70 to 80 percent of the people who are in the rural areas. To rebalance such a distortion opens up a whole range of new possibilities. And of some of them at least we can say that they have been tried out, modified, adapted, redesigned, and put successfully to work.

17 "THE LAND TO THE TILLER"

WE CAN START with a country with some of the highest agricultural returns per hectare in the world. As we have seen, Japan's launching of modernization, with root-and-branch land reform, offers two lessons above all. The first is the critical importance of transferring "the land to the tiller"—in other words, ending absentee landlordism and exploitative tenancy while enlisting the full energies of the small farmer in the productivity of his land. The Meiji Revolution was only the start. Japan's 1947 Acts expropriated all absentee landlords' farmland and limited the amount of land resident landlords could rent to one hectare; ownership of the rest was transferred to the tenant. Tenanted land, which had made up nearly half of all farmland in 1945, fell to 10 percent of the total farmed area by 1950. Then in 1952, a three-hectare limit was set on all farms (with the exception of the island of Hokkaido). The second lesson is the degree to which all the small farmers are organized in co-operative structures for marketing and purchasing, and their efforts supported by continued extension services and sustained research and innovation.

This pattern, with local modifications, has been followed in Taiwan and in South Korea. In both countries, the small farmer in a co-operative structure of credit, extension services, and conserving practices is now the dominant figure in agriculture. In Taiwan, soon after the last war, a Sino-American Joint Commission on Rural Reconstruction concentrated on getting land to the working farmer and introducing more productive methods—new hybrid seeds, more fertilizer, new agricultural technology—a process which then continued under indigenous leadership. Fertilizer use, for instance, went up by 40 percent between

1953 and 1960. The over-all effect was a rapid and sustained increase in farm income and output, and this brought with it something like a 10-percent increase in rural employment.

Land reform in South Korea had the same political base—the extension of ownership to tenant farmers. The Korean war caused some disruption to the unfolding of the scheme and to the parallel policy of increasing investment in the rural sector. But by the sixties, government policy had brought increased irrigation and heightened farm productivity. However, these were years of overwhelming concentration on a rapid growth in industry, where the bulk of the nation's capital was invested. Rural incomes fell sharply in relation to urban levels, and there began a big drift to the cities, above all to Seoul, following the typical Third World pattern of massive migration to overcrowded and underemployed urban sectors.

Happily, the strains were heeded. To redress the deepening imbalance, South Korea's Third Five Year plan, for 1972 to 1976, proposed a two-billion-dollar investment in rural development, a government-supported New Community Movement in the countryside, and an emphasis within the Movement on village activities such as irrigation, reafforestation, road and bridge building, the formation of credit unions, and the expansion of health and literacy services. Moreover, the Movement had a strong element of decentralized industrialism. Nearly four hundred factories sponsored by the Movement had been built by 1975, and a hundred more were planned for 1976. The official claim is that all these moves have not only redressed the balance between urban and rural incomes but started an observable movement back to the countryside.

Naturally, efforts at land reform have not been confined to the Far East. An end or a lessening of feudal patterns of landholding has taken place in some Indian states, in Egypt and Iraq, in Bolivia, Peru, and Chile. In Venezuela, state land has been set aside for settlers and oil wealth for rural investment. By 1971, 120,000 peasant families had received about 4.6 million hectares of land, grouped together in some thousand *asentamientos,* or rural settlements, in which training for better productivity and conservation began to be given in agricultural schools, while extension services were set to work to increase the understanding of food production, irrigation, health, and diet. Many of the settlements are served by irrigation schemes, and most of them are on farm-to-market roads. A special agricultural bank provides rural credit, and the government claims that at least a third of all farm families are now much better off. These settlements also helped to sustain a very rapid growth rate in agricultural production throughout the sixties and early seventies and to make the country self-sufficient in a number of important foodstuffs.

The Venezuelan reform was, of course, eased by the wide user of public lands and the extent of its financing with "black gold"—the country's oil income. This is a critical factor, since simply to change the forms of ownership without the necessary credit, extension and social services, roads, settlements, and water—in short, the needed range of rural investment—can reduce the whole effort to a directionless muddle in which, as often as not, the new peasant proprietors cannot cope with their supposed opportunities and sell out to the old owners, the village merchant, the moneylender, or anyone with the margin of resources and experience they lack. This has been the type of "slippage" experienced in a number of Indian states, and it is, of course, encouraged wherever pressure on the land is so great that the peasants' new holdings are in any case barely economic.

The chance in many developing countries is unhappily that this will be the case, and here we reach the fundamental problem of effective rural development in the Third World. In fifty-two of the eighty poorest developing lands, there is less than 1 hectare of arable land available for each rural inhabitant (Canada has 25 hectares, the United States 23). Take India, Pakistan, and Bangladesh. The minimum economic holding for Indians and Pakistanis is held to be between 3 and 5 hectares. In Bangladesh it is about 2 hectares. But the land available for each peasant in India is less than 0.5 hectare. In Bangladesh it is as little as 0.2. Even if land were redistributed on the basis of minimum-sized viable holdings, there could remain over 25 million landless families. How can any reform based upon the small family farm on, say, Japanese lines deal with this flood, this deluge, of landless people? However effective the supporting services, however large the rise in productivity, will not the inexorable growth of people beyond available and viable land simply become steadily more catastrophic?

But the Japanese, Taiwanese, and Korean experiences are still relevant. Part of the answer lies in their higher level of investment and hence of employment within each small farm. A survey in the late sixties found that in spite of, or rather because of, far higher levels of mechanization, Japan and Taiwan employed *twice* as many agricultural workers per hectare as did India or Pakistan. The machines were on a small scale. Far from removing labor, they encouraged its greater use by allowing the quick turnaround and replanting which make double- and triple-cropping possible. And investment was not confined to machines. As we have seen, new seeds, agricultural research, fertilizer, credit and extension services, were available to each farmer. And as a result, the value of the produce of each agricultural worker in Japan was four times that in India and Pakistan. Far higher and better-distributed agricultural incomes and hence wider effective purchasing power were thus possible. If countries such as India and Pakistan—or indeed Bangladesh and the Philippines—could attain Japan's level of labor intensity in agriculture, a very large number of today's underemployed would be absorbed into farming and there would also be room for many of the new entrants to the labor market. Indeed, the United Nations Food and Agriculture Organization estimates that overall, investment in rural needs has the chance of increasing jobs by as much as three to five fold.

Another part of the answer lies in much higher levels of investment in nonfarm activities in the countryside, such as those already mentioned in connection with South Korea's New Community Movement—rural industries, afforestation, woodcrafts, fish farming. The critical importance of full and diversified investment is borne out in what is by all odds the world's greatest rural-development movement—the transformation of China's agriculture since 1949. It has been through a number of phases. At first, as in Japan or South Korea, it was a question of getting rid of the large, usually absentee landlords, distributing the land of the wealthier peasants, and guaranteeing the small man's tenure. But even if it had been the final aim, China, like the whole Indian subcontinent, does not have enough fertile land to make viable farm units simply through small-scale individual redistribution. The solution of the fifties was to draw on a very old Chinese tradition, which R. H. Tawney has called ''village communism''—the unstinted mutual help poor peasants traditionally gave each other. All land, implements, and supplies were pooled in a single commune. For a time there were even no private plots. Everybody worked. All were paid on a daily basis, and in the euphoric time before the ''great leap forward,'' the communes were much enlarged in size—an echo here perhaps of Soviet advice, harking back to the vision of the big virgin lands and the big machines.

But the experiment did not work too well. Food production failed to increase. The typical vast migrations from the countryside were set in motion. As the sixties began, the Chinese thoroughly rethought their agricultural policy, in terms of both structure and investment. The size of the communes was sharply diminished by tripling the number on the same land, and private plots were allowed once again. Although the timing and the structure of these changes varied considerably from province to province, it can be argued that the final pattern bore some resemblance to China's millennial tradition of co-operative village farming. The basic unit, the production team or brigade, was about village size. The production could mobilize several villages for the kinds of rural work—river-basin management, irrigation, reafforestation, terracing and building, the setting up of small-scale industries—which single units could hardly organize separately. Finally, the over-all authority, the commune, to which very wide powers of planning, co-ordinating, and using its own resources were handed down by the central and provincial governments, tended to correspond in scale to the old market town with its catchment area of villages. China had learned to mix old and new; and what was poured into the structure has proved to be one of the world's most comprehensive ventures in rural investment and renewal.

This point cannot be too strongly underlined. The "big industry first" of Soviet planning was put aside. The key elements we have mentioned—more direct investment in the farm sector, more investment in nonfarm activities in the countryside—became the accepted policy of the sixties. Chinese farming has always been incredibly intensive. Traditionally, a peasant could just manage to feed a family of five on a fraction of a hectare. This he achieved by heavy manuring, using all wastes and excrements he could secure, by double-cropping, and often by growing two crops simultaneously. Now this pattern was reinforced by new investment and new technology in the shape of new seeds, some new fertilizer, new emphasis on fisheries and animal husbandry, and small-scale mechanization, with tools often manufactured in village workshops. These local advances were combined with systematic reafforestation, a very large extension of flood-control works, and irrigation, with hydroelectricity generated at every suitable site—not necessarily the big sites but even convenient points along the rivers' fall which could accommodate small generators. One effect of increasing energy supplies should be particularly underlined—the diversification of the rural economy. This was done at all levels, from the production team or brigade running an orchard, a dairy herd, or some small agro-industrial enterprise to the commune undertaking larger industrial enterprises. On an average, as the sixties advanced, 10 to 15 percent of the available work force could be engaged in forestry, fisheries, animal husbandry, and small-scale industry, while the income derived from these diversified activities amounted to 30 to 40 percent of the commune's total income.

The activities were social as well as economic. Schooling was increased to give almost complete literacy, and a simple basic health service was extended to reach all the people. In a one-time land of famine, food increased to provide for 250 million more people, farm incomes appear to have trebled, and the combination of better health and opportunity not only lengthened life but brought the population's annual growth rate sharply down—to 1.7 percent now, with an ultimate (and strongly advocated) two-child family for the future.

There is perhaps a greater gap in rhetoric than in fact between such fully collective systems as those of China or Cuba and the combination of very small private ownership within a strong co-operative structure which we find in, say, Taiwan or South Korea. It is difficult to work out the exact trade off between the extreme economic productivity of the small family farmer and the political attractions of an egalitarian society. The calculus becomes specially complicated when a measure of private production and trading survives among the collectives, as it does in China since the restoration of small private plots, and when dissent is not precisely encouraged on either side. But what is absolutely clear is the difference between the effects of making agriculture a lead sector, with a foundation of basic investment and broad popular participation, and the effects of leaving the old feudal farms and privileges to control the countryside. Outside of Africa, where traditional communal systems of land tenure are still the dominant form, the degree of inequality in land distribution and the neglect of rural investment can make it inevitable that the majority of the people, still largely living in the rural sector, remain on the very margins of opportunity and survival.

In India, in spite of many much-passed and much-evaded land-reform acts in individual states, half the arable land is still in the hands of only 7 percent of the landholders. Over a quarter of the rural households (over a hundred million people) have no land at all. In Bangladesh, probably a fifth of the rural families are in the same plight. Latin America has, as we have seen, some record of land reform. Yet the present estimate is that over half the agricultural land—and, at vast speculative gains, most of the urban land—belongs to less than 5 percent of the people. One estimate gives the feudal landowner an income fifty to a hundred times larger than that of a typical *minifundista*—a peasant barely making a living on his hectare or so of land. The contrasts are pervasive. In one of the smallest states, Guatemala, about 2 percent of the farmers own 62.5 percent of the arable land. In Brazil, the giant of the continent, two-fifths of the agricultural land (and probably the most fertile) is accounted for by only 1 percent of the farms. As for investment, it is broadly true that until the Green Revolution of the late sixties—with mechanization, more fertilizer, and hybrid seeds— savings tended to go the other way, from farms to cities, and the increased opportunities of the Green Revolution were largely engrossed by the big farmers with their own land and savings to mobilize. Even today, it can still be the rule that no more than 20 percent of a nation's investment is devoted to the 60 to 90 percent of the population who make up the rural poor.

This vast maldistribution contradicts the basic aim of a conserving society in a variety of ways. In the first place it does not even make economic sense. The small farmer is, again and again, more productive than his large neighbor. He feeds himself and his family. With a rather less restricted margin he could, as in Taiwan and China, feed the rest of the country as well. To give only a few instances, in Colombia, where the small farmer works only a quarter of the cropland, he produces two-thirds of all the output in agriculture. A recent World Bank study shows that the value of the output from small farms in Argentina, Brazil, Chile, Colombia, Ecuador, and Guatemala can be anything from three to fourteen times higher per hectare than from the big establishments. Similarly, in India, estimates make the value of output per hectare of small farms one-third higher than the level of larger ones.

The reason for the higher productivity is, of course, much harder, intenser work, crops planted more closely than by machine, every inch of land employed, and multiple- and double-cropping practiced wherever soil and water make it possible. Unbacked by modern seeds, fertilizers, extension services, and credits, this combination can represent the old, incredible productivity of, say, traditional Chinese farming. Backed by the needed scale of rural investment, it can become the key to the most basic form of national strength, self-reliance in food. The big estates are, on the whole, more extensively and carelessly cultivated for the very simple reason that the pressure is very much less and the landlord often an absentee. In Central America, the richer valley bot-

toms are often given over to extensive cattle ranching, while tiny, profoundly worked mini-farms are shoved up the less productive and
dangerously eroding mountain slopes. The same extensive-intensive
contrast ensures that in northeastern Brazil the one-hectare farms tend to
be fourteen times more productive per hectare than the thousand-hectare
estancias. And this contrast occurs in spite of the lack of basic and essential investment in the rural poor.

Now, some weighty arguments are made on the other side—that
larger estates are required for a number of indirect objectives which, in
the longer term, will increase the whole country's wealth so decisively
that the standards of the poor will be raised by the prosperity of other
sectors. This, it is argued, has occurred in developed countries—Britain, for instance, buying cheap food from America after 1870, bringing
manufacturing costs down, and thus boosting its exports even at the expense of some neglect of British farming. Today, in the Third World, it
is argued, large farms can introduce such indirect benefits through the
whole range of productive improvements summed up in the Green Revolution. India doubled its wheat crop in just seven years. Average wheat
yields in Mexico tripled in just two decades. And even if new rice varieties have not matched these spectacular improvements, some Southeast
Asian countries can meet their own needs and may even join in the export trade.

Exports are another argument for scale. Much of the meat produced
on the extensive valley-bottom ranches of Central America is exported,
and in the words not of a Marxist critic but of the Brookings Institution
of Washington, D.C., the meat ends up "not in Latin American stom-
achs but in franchised restaurant hamburgers in the U.S.A." Brazil's
large ranches receive subsidies for beef exports. In Mexico, estates send
early vegetables and fruit to North America. Latin America as a whole
has a flourishing trade in exporting produce—including flowers—from
land which once grew corn, wheat, and sunflower seeds for consumption at home. It is not only local owners who join in the trade. Such
multinational corporations as America's canning giant, Del Monte,
have farms, fisheries, and canneries in two dozen countries—the inducement being, in addition to climate, the rock-bottom price of labor
and, in many developing lands, tax grants, subsidies—and loopholes—
to lure foreign investors in.

Yet if the basic aims of a conserving society are decent standards
now and the passing of the national patrimony intact to future genera-

tions, these arguments for scale have a dubious ring. No one doubts the potential advantages of the Green Revolution's new breakthroughs in more highly productive plants and more sophisticated uses of fertilizer and controlled water supply. But these can be used on big farms and small, provided irrigation and credit and the needed supporting co-operative structures are provided. And as we have already noted, the Chinese and Japanese have also demonstrated a range of suitable farm machines on a relatively small scale—pumps, small tractors, rice planters, crop dryers—that can make double- and triple-cropping a more widespread possibility. It is not agricultural investment as such that is the problem. On the contrary, it is an essential part of the solution. The problem lies in the social and political issue: who benefits from a renewed rural sector? Where large farms are dominant, they tend to engross whatever aid is available for rural development—credit, extension services, subsidies for tractors, concessionary irrigation, farm-to-market roads. They tend to be the chief or sole beneficiaries of such investments as electrification for the villages. In India, in those villages with electricity supplies, it is normal for only a fifth of the households to be connected to the grid. The increased use of power and mechanization has usually sharply cut the amount of employment available for landless workers and "advantages of scale" have frequently encouraged owners to dismiss tenant farmers and take over the land themselves, working it with the big machines. The factor that is most abundant, labor, is set aside. The scarcest, capital, is employed to give higher returns to the smallest but most powerful rural group.

This skew in agriculture is one reason why, in such countries as Brazil, virtually all the gains of over a decade of rapid growth have, as we shall see, been engrossed by the top 10 percent of the people. "Wealth accumulates and men decay."

Arguments based on the scale of export effort need an equally critical scrutiny. No one denies comparative advantage in the sense that cocoa, coffee, tea, and palm oil simply do not grow in the Atlantic or Soviet regions. The question is, how much should be grown and at whose expense? At one point in the nineteenth century, the Dutch so stressed export agriculture in their East Indian colonies that lack of land for food produced local famine. In this century, there are African and Latin American countries in which 40 percent of the children are malnourished, yet in the rural sector, export crops chiefly engross the soil, investment, research, and government concern and support.

There are multiple distortions here. Some of them concern the unfavorable terms of trade and the instability of prices earned by the exports—a point to which we must return. In addition, the earnings from cash crops tend not to return to the countryside. They are in varying degrees spent upon industrial plans or consumer demands or, too often, land speculation in the more affluent cities. In some countries, the final paradox is that food imports are sharply growing, and all that those exports of beef and soybeans—and spring flowers—are procuring is wheat and maize which could have been grown locally at less expense and with direct advantage to the rural people.

And this is not simply a rural issue. If the mass of the people on the land have little or no purchasing power, not all the industrial plans in the development minister's dispatch case will produce goods that can be sold and the gains reinvested. The massive poverty of 70 percent of the people becomes the leading constraint on lively industrial development.

This is not to argue against the value of a cash-crop sector. On the contrary, properly managed, it can become a means of sharply increasing the returns of the small farmer, provided wider agencies protect him against the flagrant instabilities of world prices. There is, for instance, the Gezira model, in the Sudan, in which small farmers work their individual cotton holdings, but the over-all irrigation, servicing, and marketing are carried on by a central body. In East Africa, nucleus tea plantations have been set up, each with its own processing plant. Then peasants cultivate plots grouped around it, producing the same crop, working the same machinery, and, over time, using a part of their earnings to secure a co-operative stake in the whole venture. Another example can be found in the many small farmers in India who grow sugar cane on part of their land since it brings higher returns and hence income per hectare than food crops and can also better withstand the vagaries of weather.

One can only repeat the point. Successful agricultural development is not finally determined by questions of scale or types of cultivation or even particular crops. It turns on a fundamental question: Is the small man involved? Are the mass of rural people gaining ground? Is the rural sector dynamic in the full sense of giving all its people some hope of a livelihood and literacy and health care? If the answer is no, then the immediate disruptions are forced idleness and malnutrition and massive departures for the cities. The longer-term disasters are more ominous still. It is precisely in countries of violently skewed wealth and rural hopelessness that the annual population growth rate does not fall much below 3.5 percent a year. The outlook is thus a dynamic and growing misery. And as the land grows ever more crowded, the hillsides clear-felled, wood and crop residues burnt for fuel, and water sources befouled by an ever greater press of disease-ridden people, it is not simply this unhappy generation that must suffer and die. What is vanishing is the chance of providing even the shell of life for the generations still to come.

18 FUEL FOR BASIC NEEDS

AT THE CENTER of the Third World's need for greater investment in the rural sector stands, inevitably, the basic need for energy. For the poorest peasant, the chief source of energy—to till the fields, to fetch the water, to collect the wood—is human labor. It is perfectly rational, in such a context, to try to ensure that there is enough of such labor. Children perform a multitude of farm duties, they take care of little brothers and sisters, and the farmer expects at least some of them to survive and care for him in his old age. This is the basic reason for high birth rates in poor societies—not irresponsibility, irrationality, or even ignorance, but sheer grinding economic necessity. It follows that one of the most direct routes to smaller families is the provision of alternatives to human labor, and this indeed has proved to be the case. Not only in advanced energy-rich countries are populations becoming stable. In the Third World, falling birth rates everywhere coincide with the diversification and increasing sophistication of resources, including energy, in the rural scene.

At the same time, the pressure of population, left to follow its primitive rationale, makes it steadily more difficult to secure the productivity of agriculture, and with it better surpluses and greater opportunities. Each peasant family has its few basic needs. It must cook its food. In high places or cool winters, it must try to keep warm at night. It must find water, even if the nearest stream or spring or well is from four to ten kilometers away. As numbers increase, the pressure on wood supplies grows in the same measure. Over half the world's people use wood as their basic fuel. In some countries, 90 percent of all nonhuman energy is in the form of wood. It is cut, it is carried, it is used—all too often in primitive and inefficient cooking stoves. And since a peasant can consume as much as a ton of wood a year, it is no surprise that, in area after area, the trees are not being replaced. The worst areas of decimation are on the desert fringes of the Sahara, in parts of the Andes, in extensive areas of Central America and along the Caribbean, and perhaps above all in the Himalayas, where the 1978 floods downstream are an appalling reminder of the growing risk of denuded hillsides and uncontrollable monsoon rains.

Nor is this the end of the devastation. As the search for wood becomes more prolonged and weary, peasants turn to using up crop wastes and dried-out excrement for their cooking and heating. Thus essential nutrients are no longer returned to the soil. The two processes together—the retreat of the forests and the increasing depletion of the soil—leave farmland more and more liable to instability, with topsoil blown away by the winds, and washed away, especially down cascading slopes, by the very water that should have helped it retain its productivity. Once forests are cut down, the waters they used to retain turn to uncontrollable flooding. The forests were virtually the equivalent of reservoirs. As they vanish, the hills turn into waterfalls. It is the Himalayan story, repeatable in every fragile mountain area.

As drought and flood begin to alternate, scrub, brush and tough grasslands spread inexorably, taking the place of productive land. In arid areas, the deserts and sands can encroach on neighboring land, piling hummocks round trees and bushes and spreading a film of sand over fertile soil. Millions of hectares of fertile farmland are being lost or degraded each year. Add a period of drought and you have the tragedy of the Sahel, where on the fringes of the southern Sahara perhaps a quarter of a million people have died since 1975 and with them uncounted numbers of the herds of their livelihood. Unless this most vicious of all progressions—the permanent destruction of fertile land—can be checked, the Sahel may well be the first signal, in the Third World, of recurrent cycles of starvation.

The fundamental means of reversing this cycle of disaster is, clearly, to increase the supplies of nonhuman energy and the reliable flow of nutrients and water. To begin at the smallest level, the village itself, the direct use of crop wastes and dung for cooking and heating can be transformed by the construction of the "biogas" plant,* which, after extracting biogas from waste matter, for domestic use, leaves behind a safe and dependable fertilizer for the village fields. The plant should be

---

* Biogas is mostly methane—i.e. it is similar to natural gas—but with some carbon dioxide and traces of other gases.

large enough to serve the whole village community. Smaller ones tend to be too expensive and to have too many maintenance problems for a single family. In general the number of biogas plants is rising. There are more than sixty thousand in India, where much of the research into more reliable and manageable plants is being conducted. South Korea is reported to have thirty thousand, China more than four million.

An added advantage of these machines is their ability to follow the pattern of energy demand. Manure and crop wastes can be stored in times of low activity and provide a steady source of fuel when nights are cold or the irrigation pumps are hard at work. By fueling small walking tractors, they can also reduce human strain and the amount of cropland used up in feeding draft animals.

Nor need they depend only on by-products and wastes. In areas of rich, rapid tropical growth, fuel crops can be specially grown for such gas plants, or indeed for local power stations. Indian estimates suggest that 3.5 hectares of such crops could fuel a power station delivering 500 kilowatts of electricity per day at a quarter of the present cost of kerosene and half the cost of most rural-electrification schemes. Rough crops grown on marginal land can be used, and the small farmer, selling this fuel crop, buying a small tractor and releasing land no longer needed to feed his oxen, can make a useful addition both to his efficiency and to his income. Thus mechanization need not depend upon nonrenewable and steadily more expensive fuels. They can be renewable, cheap, and locally grown.

In fact, the value of biogas for mechanical power—for transport and for pumping—is such that it may well be the course of wisdom to provide for such domestic needs as cooking and heating very largely by the old route, the supply of firewood, but to do so by making the wood easily accessible and putting it on the conserving basis of sustained yield. Some of this wood could come from trees planted in the village itself and along its approach roads. Windbreaks round village fields are another source which does not compete with land for food. Then some land can be set aside as a permanent investment in forestry—a hectare of woodland can provide enough wood for forty to fifty people. Depending on their local geography, villagers may be able to plant slopes threatened by denudation and not very suitable for food cultivation. Many trees are themselves suppliers of human food. Or in some areas, the proper choice may allow food crops to be grown in the shade of the trees as they mature. Suitable trees can also be grown on cleared land during fallowing periods, and can both enrich the soil and provide firewood. Since, according to some estimates, twelve million hectares of tropical forest are lost each year, village schemes linked to a more general reafforestation—joining self-interest and sane conservation—may be the main answer to the risk that over wide areas first the forests, then the soil, and then reliable water supplies may all be on the way to being lost to human use.

As in the industrial world, more energy-efficient appliances can play an important role in reducing energy demand and, in the Third World villages, in reducing pressure on supplies of firewood. Traditional stoves are, as we have mentioned, inefficient. Adding a chimney and an extra air inlet to a typical design can cut fuel consumption by 25 percent or more. Improved cooking utensils, or even as simple a procedure as stones placed on top of covered pots to create a rudimentary pressure cooker, can also reduce the demand for fuel.

Happily, experiments in linking afforestation with fuel supply are beginning to show some success. For instance, in the Zinder district of Niger, seventy villages are being provided with woodlots. The hardy neem tree appears the most suitable species on the land planted so far. A workable model could be the first step in reafforesting some 100,000 rain-fed hectares where domestic cutting and also the need for wood for pottery kilns and for construction have eaten the forests away. In a wholly different terrain—the uplands of Bolivia—more than half the nation's rural population scrapes a living from generally denuded slopes. There work is well advanced in determining what type of tree and what methods of afforestation can, on a sustained-yield basis, protect the land, provide for the villagers' own needs, increase the country's supply of timber for reconstruction, and establish a profitable and labor-intensive exchange with the area's mines, hungry for charcoal and pit props.

In Peru, as well, similar schemes are being considered. The central and southern regions—Huarás, Huancayo, Cuzco—are poor and ravaged. Here the aim is to establish at least 100,000 hectares of forest in each zone, probably of pine and eucalyptus, to provide logs for the mines, pulp for chemicals, wood for local fuel, and income for all the communities.

One should notice the emphasis on recovering degraded or denuded land. This is not simply a question of such rational and straightforward aims as ending soil erosion, protecting watersheds, and reviving rural life. There is a further reason, which has only started to become appar-

ent in the last decade. On the face of it, the vast tropical moist forests—
of Amazonia, of West Africa, of the Congo—would seem to be simply
waiting for exploitation on the basis of sustained yield. But it is beginning to be realized that we know too little about these immensely complex ecosystems to be able to say, with certainty, how sustained yields
and lasting exploitation are to be secured. Apparently they do not have
the power to regenerate naturally once their exploitation begins. Nor
have a wide range of experiments in different forms of rehabilitation
been encouraging. Nowhere is this more apparent than in Amazonia,
where more than eleven million hectares were cleared between 1966
and 1975. Once the loggers secured the timber, the peasant settlers who
were supposed to turn the cleared land into productive farms were generally unsuccessful, since neither they nor their advisers had any pre-
knowledge of the fragility of the resulting soils.

There has been a similar experience in tropical moist forests in West
Africa and Asia. Logs of such valued woods as mahogany are massively
exported. But even selective clearing in these dense, interwoven ecosystems can damage or destroy the trees the loggers have no use for.
The end result can be forests too degraded for natural regeneration or
any useful rehabilitation. So long as such ignorance prevails, the course
of wisdom, whatever the loggers' protests, is to confine activity in the
tropical moist forests to the most careful experiment, and to concentrate
on what is already safely practiced and well understood, the replanting
of denuded or marginal lands with the types and varieties of trees which
have been shown to give the highest and most stable yields.

Then the uses are truly vast. Tree plantations can do more than provide basic energy and halt soil erosion. Different species of tree can provide fruit, protein-rich food for humans and for livestock. The species
chosen should be adapted to local conditions and local needs. In arid
areas, quick-growing trees, above all eucalyptus and neem, planted in
carefully designed shelter belts, could accomplish the vital task of halt-
ing the creeping deadly advance of the deserts. In Rajasthan, desert
encroachments are resisted by plantations of algaroba, which also
give fodder for cattle and goats. The obliging carob positively thrives
on poor and rocky soil and is a prime crop all around the eastern
Mediterranean. (St. John the Baptist probably survived in the desert on
carob and wild honey, "locust" being a biblical mistranslation.) Mul-
berries and acorns go to the pigs. Walnuts and chestnuts are widely used
in East Asia. The Chinese, who have probably planted more trees in the

last thirty years than in all their history (twenty-four million in Nanking alone) have a particular use for persimmons, which dry well and make excellent fodder.

There are obvious dangers to be avoided. As we have noted, the moist forests in the humid tropics rely on enormous ecological diversity for their stability. Research has shown that tree species not native to a local area should be introduced with very great care. Large plantations of single species should be avoided. But the warnings do not alter the basic fact of the fundamental importance of forests in sustained and renewable development. If one adds to energy and food supplies a whole range of further uses—for construction, drugs, dyes, industrial raw materials, indeed eventually feedstock for the chemical industry to offset escalating prices of petroleum feedstocks—one can see the recovery and expansion of the forests as one of the great and realizable sagas of conserving enterprise for the whole Third World, indeed for the planet itself.

Before we leave this beautiful and life-giving resource to discuss the use of water—which it so essentially conserves and recycles—there are a couple of footnotes to be added concerning energy use for developing lands. Wood is, as we have underlined, a basic, irreplaceable reserve of renewable energy. But there may be similar opportunities in other forms of plant life. We have spoken of farmers growing fuel crops. We should therefore surely mention the largest of all such experiments. So far, Brazil is the only nation to have embarked on a national program to "grow its own fuel." Already, ethyl alcohol derived from sugar cane and cassava (also known as manioc and tapioca) is added to the gasoline sold commercially. More than a hundred industrial distilleries are now built or being constructed as part of a billion-dollar program designed to replace by the year 2000 most of the oil-derived fuel now needed in the transport sector. This could drastically reduce Brazil's massive spending on imported oil. It would leave the country's oil reserves for more valuable products, such as chemical feedstocks, and cut down polluting emissions from automobiles—a major source of air pollution.

Most of the needed alcohol will come initially from sugar cane, since its conversion to ethyl alcohol is quite simple. But the Brazilians also hope to convert massive volumes of cassava into alcohol, using a special enzyme to break its complex starches into fermentable sugar products. Cassava has the advantage of thriving on poor land and being easily stored for year-round alcohol production. Modified internal-combustion engines (whether in cars, tractors, or farm machinery) can run on 100-percent alcohol, and Brazil may well be giving the world's car owners the answer they anxiously await before the end of the century. One should add, however, that in Brazil itself, the social and economic effect will depend overwhelmingly on the structure of the new crop "industry." Cassava could be a most valuable extra cash crop for the small man, and could add to rural employment and to the use of marginal land. But if only the large farmers gain from the scheme, with the peasant majority as usual excluded, the year 2000 may see an elite in Brazil driving round in cassava-powered automobiles while the poor still lack enough to eat.

Forests and fuel crops depend for their energy on the sun. We should not forget that most of the Third World lies in the planet's sunbelt, and the flood of radiance can also be used without mediation through trees and plants. Mexico is already planning to use thousands of solar-powered pumps for water in isolated communities, and over fifty solar pumps are already operating in twelve nations. In the Sahel, communities more than a hundred kilometers from electricity supplies—and one can easily imagine how many there are of them—are more cheaply supplied with energy from a 50-kilowatt solar pump (and this at 1976 prices; for solar pumps, costs are likely to be very much lower as the technology develops and the production runs increase). Solar water-desalination units are already no more expensive than conventional fossil-fueled ones for villages and farms and are already in use in the Soviet Union and in parts of Australia and the Caribbean. Solar-heated air, provided by simple, locally made panels, can be fed into crop-drying sheds, eliminating all the risks of pests, birds, and weather which wait to pounce on farm produce drying in the open air.

Simple solar water heaters can also supply domestic needs, or the needs of local artisans or a health-care center. A workshop conducted by the U.S. National Academy of Sciences and the Tanzanian National Scientific Research Council compared the cost for Tanzanian villages of electricity derived from diesel generators and from the national grid with five renewable energy resources—wind power, small-scale hydro, biogas, solar refrigeration, and photovoltaic cells. Although comparative costs depend on such imponderables as the amount of energy needed or the remoteness of the village, three of the renewable resources proved economically competitive with conventional sources under all circumstances and all five had economic advantages for certain purposes.

The least competitive renewable resource proved to be the photovoltaic cells. But as their costs continue to decline and storage problems are overcome, these cells are expected to be cheaper than both diesel generators and the national grid for most villages by the early 1980s. Already, they are competitive in some areas for powering small pumps and educational television. It is thus not entirely fanciful to begin to dream of towns and villages in the sunbelt richly powered by various fuels derived locally and cheaply from solar radiance—their safest, most abundant, and entirely renewable resource.

But these dreams may have to wait for the next century for widespread application. There are some sharp realities to be faced at once. And the most fundamental one is almost certainly that the building of energy resources for village improvement, the restoration of humus-producing wastes to the soil, the recovery of woods and forest, and beyond that the essential control and use of water are all virtually impossible on the needed scale if the community itself is not profoundly involved in the projects and committed to them with a sense of genuine personal and communal interest.

No woodlot can grow if any villager feels able to put his goat to forage on the young plants. Reafforestation cannot take place if marauding woodcutters and their beasts continue in the old ways. Dung and field wastes will still be used for cooking unless the biogas plant serves the whole village and is not the preserve of a few better-provided families. Wells will not be maintained, sanitary disciplines observed at standpipes, manure safely and economically handled, or irrigation ditches dug, cleaned, and maintained if the local background is largely one of exclusion, ignorance, and apathy. Parts of the developing world are positively strewn with well-meant governmental or international efforts to upgrade settlements, to bring in power and water and set going an upward spiral of achievement. But nobody remembered to consult or involve the people. As a result, all the evidence of effort may be a broken pump or a contaminated well. The most basic of all basic needs turns out to be the right to participate in the adventure of change and to see the advantage of the work. Without this, the old ways, heading to new disasters, remain the tragic background of village life.

19 WATER AND FOOD SUPPLIES

THERE MAY EASILY come a point when well-meaning discussion of manure and wastes, woodlots and even massive reafforestation, will come to stir in Third World minds an irritated sense that there is to be a sort of "Upstairs, Downstairs" pattern for development in the planet, with the upstairs of high energy, high industry, high processing, and high standards remaining inexorably with the early developers, while the rest of humanity scratches along behind, planting trees and preserving manure. It may be, as a developing nation's critic could argue, that the South lacks the massive coal supplies—and the shrinking oil reserves—of the North. But the OPEC countries are at least honorary "Southerners"; China, Mexico, and Bolivia have important oil reserves; coal is already being exploited in Brazil and India. Above all, nearly 70 percent of the world's most useful source of renewable energy—hydropower, the power of falling water—lies in the South, and so far, there has been no very large development of this resource. But think of the scale possible when the effort has been made—the 16,000 megawatts already obtainable in Brazil, with 12,600 more to come from the nine billion dollar Itaipu Dam. Remember Venezuela, with nearly three billion dollars allocated to hydroelectric installations on the Caroní River; Egypt relying on the Aswan Dam for more than half its electricity; India's high dams built in the fifties and sixties; the damming of the Volta, the Zambesi, and the Nile's exit from Lake Victoria. Such vast installations do not only light the cities and provide for a full range of developed services. They can make possible speedy forward leaps into energy-intensive industry, into the processing of local minerals, into the break from the old North/South dependence in manufacturing. They seem to promise modernization achieved not at a snail's pace but with the dynamism of genuine and transforming innovation—and with the steady growth rate of 5 percent per year in fact achieved by many developing lands in the fifties and sixties.

But this is to misunderstand the argument for priority for basic needs and the primacy of agriculture. Neither precludes industrialization. They both entail it and can lead to its greater, safer, and more conserving expansion. The argument is rather that the quick, single-minded jump for modernity, *via* whatever big fuel resources are available, risks leaving the bulk of the population behind, and risks also the discovery at a certain point that the most basic of economic needs, the food supply, is in critical condition. Take hydropower, for example. Most of the big dam schemes in the developing world have been built with what one might call an urban-industrial bias. They often flood fertile valleys and displace large rural populations. The Aswan High Dam flooded out 120,000 people, the Koussou Dam 100,000. There are examples of dams where construction is finished, turbines are turning, power is being transmitted, and yet the local farmers still lack power. Irrigation channels have not been built. There are not even plans to ensure that the steady flow of water demanded for continuous electricity generation does not dangerously disrupt the local farmers' pattern of water needs. Most large dams constructed recently in the Third World have also had unforeseen effects on environment and health. The Aswan High Dam disrupted the flow of sediment-laden water that used to enrich the farmlands on the flood plain and also fisheries established where the Nile's waters reach the sea. Both forms of food production have suffered. And, in general, too little thought has been given to the spread of waterborne disease. To give only one example, the newly irrigated farmlands and the reservoirs provide ideal habitats for the snails that are the host to the parasite carrying schistosomiasis.

One reason why rural needs are ignored is, of course, cost. Long transmission lines are extremely expensive, costing up to $5,000 a kilometer. If a village is thirty kilometers from the grid, it must be already wealthy or socially well connected for the needed $90,000 to $150,000 in investment to be made available. India has many examples of what happens where such costs are met. The electricity is simply too expensive for all but the wealthiest farmers. Up to ten billion dollars had been spent by 1971 on rural electrification, with at least as much again planned for 1975–1985. But thirty years of experience suggests that the number of electricity users tends to stop increasing when one-fifth of the families have been connected. Whether among the cooking pots at home or the pumps for irrigated farming, investment in electrification can—like so many other forms of rural investment—actually increase the gap between the rich villagers and the poor.

These drawbacks do not in any way undermine the promise of properly balanced development in hydropower. They simply underline two wider issues—the need to include all the rural people in the planning of water resources, and the need for a proper attention to ecological effects. It is not necessary to think only on a giant scale. Rivers, streams, or even canals can have their water flow harnessed for power without dams by the use of smaller installations, such as axial-flow turbines. Massive human disruption and environmental damage can be avoided and the small farmers' interests are more easily protected. This strategy has played a major role in China in bringing electricity to remote areas, and some sixty thousand small hydropower installations are now in operation. The Indonesian government is also expanding its "microhydro" program after a number of successful demonstration projects, and the Pakistani government has begun to introduce such units in order to electrify isolated villages in the northwestern frontier provinces.

The importance of keeping industrial and agricultural use and investment in equal balance in the planning of water-resource development has its ultimate justification in a simple fact. In many parts of the world, the only hope of keeping food supplies growing to match the increase in population lies in success with double- and triple-cropping on all suitable land. And this, virtually everywhere, implies two essential preconditions. One is sufficient investment in all needed new technical supports for farming. The second is reliable irrigation. This point is underlined with extreme clarity in the definitive report on rice growing in South Asia prepared by the Trilateral Food Task Force. Given the extreme pressure of population on the land in Asia and the likelihood of an extra billion inhabitants in the region by the next century, the Task Force sees little contribution from farming new land. Virtually all land worth farming is under cultivation already. But it does see the possibility of at least doubling production of the basic staple crop, rice, provided one critical step above all is taken—that of bringing under permanent and reliable irrigation all areas which are now inadequately served.

Using figures assembled by Dr. Saburo Okita and Dr. K. Takase, the report shows an almost exact correlation between the reliability and quality of irrigation and the amount of paddy produced for each irrigated hectare. (One and a half tons of paddy equals about a ton of rice.) Where, as in Japan, 98 percent of the rice lands are fully irrigated, the output of rice is 6 tons a hectare. In a second group, which includes South Korea and Taiwan, 75 percent of the rice areas are securely irrigated, and the output is, on average, 4 tons a hectare. (Although China's figures are not mentioned in the report, in the early 1970s, production there had reached 3 tons a hectare, an increase of about a third in total production, closely following the amount of land brought under permanent and reliable irrigation.) Nations in a further group, including Thailand, Indonesia, the Philippines, and—in commanding scale and importance, India—have reached or are approaching 2 tons of paddy for a 35 percent level of secure irrigation. The lesson is clear. Improved seed, more fertilizer, suitable pesticides, can be part of the farmer's new battery of productive equipment, but none of these will serve him fully unless his water supply is ample and assured. It follows that the only certain method of improvement for the basic food crop, rice, is the upgrading of the irrigated fields, if not to Japanese standards, then at least to those of South Korea and Taiwan. The first resource for careful conservation is thus water.

There are three elements here, in no order of priority. One is inevitably water itself and its full availability for rural use. Another is the reworking of the land; a third, the social structure which permits the needed changes to be carried out. They can be illustrated, each one of them, from different areas, cultures, and ideologies. First, then, we can take what is virtually a snapshot of a particular experimental plot and examine in some detail the changes in land management that turn inadequate irrigation into a more sustained and reliable pattern. The example is 140 hectares at Angat, in the Philippines. In 1968, the decision was taken to see how the land could be upgraded. It had on the average about 16 meters of irrigation channel for each hectare. A single drainage channel at the edge of the plot amounted to only 9 meters per hectare, and with relatively small supplies of water and only one external drain, the water for the crop simply slopped about, leaving some areas underwatered, drowning others, in an ensemble of unregulated and haphazard distribution. The output of paddy was low, only 2.3 tons per hectare.

Then came the reworking of the land. In one year, full irrigation channels were extended to 62 meters per hectare. Drainage canals not only surrounded the area but drained it internally, increasing in the process to 23 meters for each hectare. As a result, water was evenly distributed over the whole experimental area and the yield of paddy rose 40 percent. This is the sort of transformation which, as Japan and Taiwan have shown, lies within the reach of the small rice farmer.

This experiment in Angat exemplifies the kind of transformation that has been carried out on a massive scale in China. The national program announced for agriculture in 1956 had three aims to be achieved by 1968—to increase irrigated areas from 26 million to 60 million hectares (the actual figure for 1975 was 50 million), to increase the capacity to store water for existing and newly irrigated fields so that they could withstand a thirty- to fifty-day drought, and, in the areas most suitable for double-cropping, to extend the period of safety up to seventy days. The precondition of so vast a scheme was, of course, to secure control of the needed water, and given the violent and turbulent nature of China's vast rivers, very large scale measures to control flooding—dams in mountain gorges, dams and reservoirs in upstream tributaries—had to be undertaken by the central authorities.

But the main work lay in mobilizing the millions of peasant workers in the communes to undertake, on a nationwide scale, the sort of work we have looked at in the Angat model. Channels were dug or improved, drainage was extended, paddy fields were terraced and leveled, small barrages and reservoirs were constructed to give the necessary days of secure flow during dry weather. At first, the water was supplied in the main by gravity irrigation. But in the 1960s, the surpluses generated by rising yields helped to finance new energy technologies. These years saw the introduction of microhydro units and of the pumping stations and irrigation pumps that allowed for a more secure control of water resources. The Chinese claim that in 1949, only 0.25 million hectares had any access to mechanical irrigation. By 1975, the land so served had increased to 7.3 million hectares. In this transformation, the number of water pumps rose from 100,000 in 1965 to 1.5 million ten years later. One Chinese estimate has particular interest in the light of the discussion about policies designed to maintain balance between big and small hydro works. The Chinese estimate that irrigating land through small barrages, pumps, and ponds costs five to six times less, per hectare, than irrigating through the construction of large dams and storage lakes—quite apart form the possible ecological and social disruptions of very large schemes. But, of course, this does not lessen the need for larger-scale works upstream to control large-scale turbulence. It is, as usual, a question of balance.

To give only one striking instance of the degree to which, on the basis of a mass mobilization of peasant labor, water and power have been utilized for food production, we can take Linhsien County in Honan Province, where, in the 1960s, a work force varying from ten thousand to thirty thousand built the Red Flag Canal. With little help from higher authorities, save for some of the machinery and dynamite, the local people diverted water from a nearby river through mountain tunnels, across valley aqueducts, and down into their 2,000 square kilometers of land, where before the project—in 1949—barely 1,000 hectares had any irrigation at all. Today, 40,000 hectares are securely watered through main canals and subsidiary channels whose length totals 1,500 kilometers. At the same time, microhydro units have been installed to take advantage of each large channel's drop in elevation to power a water turbine. For example, microhydro units, twenty-six in all, have been placed wherever there is a 5 meter drop in elevation along one of the channels of the Number 1 branch canal. The whole scheme has something like seven hundred pumping stations and sixty-five electricity-generating stations totaling 10,000 kilowatts.

Before we leave Linhsien County and its fifteen communes, there are two further points to stress. One we shall come back to. There is absolutely no contradiction between a strong emphasis on agricultural development and the expansion of industry. The cheap hydroelectricity used in part for powering irrigation pumps is also available for local industries and workshops, and as we have seen, a rising percentage of the income of the communes comes from these establishments. The other point to be underlined and repeated is that all the people shared in both the work and the gain. We return here to the earlier point of ending patterns of privilege. That this critical theme entirely transcends any ideological preconceptions can be seen from a quotation from the Trilateral Food Task Force, a body drawn from what would no doubt be called "establishment experts" and serving the unofficial but influential Tripartite Commission of the not wholly collectivist or radical national groupings of North America, Western Europe, and Japan. After discussing precisely the point of greatly increasing the extension and intensity of irrigation as a precondition of meeting Asia's coming need for food, the Task Force comments:

> It has been reported that community work programs are difficult to organize for irrigation projects that primarily benefit larger farmers and landlords. A recent study at the International Rice Research Institute suggests that the participation of community members in communal irrigation projects is greater and more uniform in a village where villagers are more homogeneous in terms of tenure and farm size. If this is the case, redistributive land reform is critical not only for equity considerations, but also for the mobilization of local resources for the sustained increase in food output under the severe constraint of limited land resources.*

Linhsien County is not alone in bearing out this lesson. So do the largely literate rural communities of Japan and Taiwan and the increasingly diversified communities of South Korea. Even in an area as plagued with high unemployment as Kerala, in India, an inheritance of land reform from the past and the efforts of reforming governments since independence have given the local people higher literacy and lower birth rates than in other, better endowed Indian states.

But Linhsien County deserves a little further description. The canals, the rice paddies, the generating stations, the rural industries, are not the end of it. The 700,000 inhabitants now have 16 senior high schools, 230 junior high schools, and 690 primary schools, and although their instruction may have been retarded and disrupted during the Cultural Revolution, with a resulting lack of special skills, there can be little doubt that literacy and health have advanced dramatically. Each commune has a hospital, each brigade a clinic with fully trained doctors aided by the medical assistants who have come to be known as "barefoot doctors." Moreover, the Chinese claim, the degree of increasing involvement and literacy at all levels makes it easier to deal with one of the risks of increased water use that we have already mentioned—the spread of water-borne disease, particularly of schistosomiasis. By careful instruction and by making the farmers themselves clean the disease-carrying snails from their habitat—the channels where earth and water meet—the hideous wasting disease can be kept in check. So, too, through safer wells and clean water supplies, can the gastric complaints spawned by contaminated water. It is certainly no idyll for thirty thousand workers to dig 1,500 kilometers of canals, blast out 134 tunnels,

*Rice Production in South and South East Asia, Report of the Trilateral Food Task Force, p. 42.

and move sixteen million cubic meters of earth and stone. But if the whole community thereafter derives the benefit of secure food, increasing literacy, and better health, there would seem to be little doubt about where the balance of advantage lies.

Works on a comparable scale are both possible and necessary in neighboring India, where the growth of population is still at least a percentage point higher than in China and the need for more food (not only rice but wheat and maize and other staples) correspondingly more urgent. It is fortunate for the subcontinent that basic resources of water and land are available for the task. But the problems of mobilizing them are fully as daunting as for anything undertaken by the Chinese. We encounter the familiar four basic elements—water, forests, power, and participation. There is, of course no absolute shortage of water. Fed by the annual melting of Himalayan snows and by the heavy monsoon rains of the summer months, the average annual runoff of the Ganges is nearly 500 cubic kilometers (80 percent of which now simply flows into the sea). On average, the Brahmaputra provides over 500 cubic kilometers each year. In fact, only the Amazon and the Congo boast larger discharges of water than the Ganges-Brahmaputra system. The trouble lies in the enormous irregularity of the water's flow and the long months—after the monsoon and before the spring melting in the mountains—when the rivers' reliable supplies can fall to the danger point. With a failed monsoon, disaster is certain.

To give only the most striking example of the irregularity, the Ganges, which flows on into Bangladesh (to become the Padma River), has an average discharge of more than 2,800 cumecs* of water for eight or nine months of the year. During the monsoon, the flow rises to an incredible 56,000 cumecs or more, but at the tail end of the "water year," in late April and early May, the flow falls to less than 1,700 cumecs, and this lean allowance must be shared, India requiring enough down the Bhagirathi tributary to keep Calcutta's port flushed from silt, Bangladesh needing every drop it can get for irrigation. It says much for the statesmanship of both countries that when India put up the Farakka Barrage to secure at least a minimum flow from the Ganges down to Calcutta, both countries in 1977 negotiated for a minimum of five years a division of the much-needed waters during the lean period, 37.5 percent going to India and 62.5 to Bangladesh. But of course, the whole

---

* A cumec is a cubic meter per second.

need to negotiate illustrates the folly of minutely dividing a 1,540-cumec flow when, with upstream management of both great rivers, a minimum 2,800-cumec flow could be perennial and the whole problem vanish in the face of ample supplies.

But what can be done? One of the keys is clearly storage, simply because the monsoon rains fall so massively and in so short a time. Their sheer scale makes upstream reservoirs only a very small part of the answer. You cannot entirely drown Nepal's and Bhutan's valleys, even though, with care, both can become massive exporters of hydro-electricity. (In Nepal's case, official estimates for economically feasible hydropower capacity go as high as 40,000 megawatts, and little more than 1 percent of this has been tapped to date.)

Besides, all the Himalayan hills offer special risks of denudation. They are geologically new and disintegrate easily. Unhappily, a combination of unwise exploitation by logging concerns and the peasants' usual desperate search for firewood has already brought dangerous denudation and soil erosion in many areas. With melting snows and pounding monsoons pouring down valleys stripped of forest, soil and silt go along to be lost in such floods as those of 1978 or to fill up reservoirs that can see their expected useful life cut by two-thirds. Massive reafforestation is thus an essential part of the Himalayan story, and there are perhaps grounds for hope in the fact that in some areas this notion has spread down to the tree roots. In Uttar Pradesh, for instance, the Chipko Andolan ("embrace a tree") movement has sent the villagers out in their hundreds, literally to clasp the trees in their arms when the news spreads of logging companies on the way. Ominously, some of the embracers seem to be ending up in jail, instead of the loggers.

Even with all the care in the world in the upper-river reaches, not more than 10 percent of the monumental rains can be stored there in traditional reservoirs. And for this reason officials and experts are considering downstream alternatives. One of the most promising possibilities is to turn the vast network of underground aquifers into storage areas. A sustained-pumping program over a number of years would lower the water levels in these aquifers and enable them to receive an increasing portion of the monsoon flood. During the lean season, this water would be pumped up by tube well for normal irrigation, and the aquifers would then be ready to receive the next surge of water. Something like a sustained-yield basis could be secured. As in China, small microhydro units could be installed along the fall of the rivers and their tributaries, and contribute to the power needed for the pumps.

No one denies the difficulties and doubts. Would there be widespread subsidence of the soil? Could contamination of the aquifers be securely avoided? Experimental pumping as soon as possible in some of the tributary valleys could begin to answer the questions, and the scheme could be extended as its engineering and conserving opportunities and difficulties became clear. But the basic facts remain. There is no way in which upstream reservoirs, however well reafforested and protected, can provide all the needed storage space. Alternative systems must be developed if steady water supplies are to permit double- and sometimes triple-cropping right across the catchment areas of the Brahmaputra and the Ganges, with possibly even some water to spare for India's south. And given the prospect of perhaps a billion Indians by the next century, where but in the intensification of cropping can any hope be seen to feed the multitudes?

And this brings in the last and essential point—that the whole scheme recognizes the absolute primacy of the small farmer. The Green Revolution—of hybrid seeds, fertilizer, pesticides, water, and mechanization—has come to India, and while securing self-sufficiency in wheat in a good year, it has given the gains to the big men with the tractors; even more landless laborers are off on the trek from the countryside to underemployed urban slums. If the same bias appears in the extended-cropping programs, the social disintegration both of country and town will only accelerate. Nor will the food be grown. Take, for instance, the Kosi canal system, built to stabilize the river's course in the late fifties and planned to irrigate 570,000 hectares. Today little more than 160,000 hectares are usable. A fifth of all the canals are silted up and derelict, for there was no land reform to mobilize the small men to do the kind of ditching, clearing, draining, and reafforesting that is at the root of China's advance. Least of all has there been the progress in health and literacy that would have helped depressed castes and landless people to get to work themselves. This is the lesson of all that is progressive in the Third World—from a Taiwanese village to a Chinese commune to a Venezuelan *asentamiento*. Technical change without social transformation cannot renew the rural economy. And as we shall see, it is a shaky basis for industrialization as well.

20 "WALKING ON TWO LEGS"

THE EMPHASIS GIVEN to agriculture in these early chapters on the developing world needs to be strongly repeated as we approach more directly the problems of accelerated industrialization. This does not, in some obscure or sinister way, represent a plot to delay or prevent effective Third World modernization. On the contrary, strengthening agriculture is the safest route, proven not only by the historical experience of the early developers but inescapably by the logic of facts and numbers. Since of the three billion people who live in the developing world, over two-thirds live either on the land or in villages, a stagnant, languishing agriculture—or a farming system which virtually excludes their interests—simply means there will not be sufficient resources or skills or markets for anything else.

The need for resources is obvious. From Lanchashire's first mill to the latest cellulose factory, forest and field have fed industry. Exported cash crops from the tropical belts have been a chief means of earning foreign exchange to import industrial goods and to encourage local investment. Even today more than a third of Brazil's exports, after a quarter century of forced-draft industrialization, come from the land. But what is equally true though perhaps more easily forgotten is that the skills and the markets too, required for expanding modernization also lie, to a critical degree, in developing, prosperous countrysides.

If one begins at the simplest level—in those parts of the Third World, largely in Africa but also in the mountains of Latin America and Southeast Asia, where the scattered cultivators subsist virtually without a local village—little change in the inhabitants' hopes and possibilities for better diets, health, or skills is conceivable in their present condition. Where, too, their farming is based, as it often is, on "slash and burn" (clearing parts of the forest, planting crops for a time, then moving on and leaving the land fallow to allow it to regain its fertility), the method becomes more and more precarious as fallowing periods are diminished, the forest recedes, shade trees are cut down, and a deadly loss of fertile soil sets in. Then the whole community suffers permanent damage from the neglect of a single but vital sector.

It is to obtain units of habitation large enough for a measure of modernization to begin that a number of countries have set in motion the process of simply creating villages. This is part of Venezuela's land reform and an indirect effect of the reforms introduced into Bolivia in 1953. For a time, Israel's kibbutzim, the communal farm communities, helped to underpin an earlier stage of modernization, but they can hardly now be called typical, in a developing land where 84 percent of the people live in urban areas. The best-known example is perhaps the program of villagization in Tanzania. Over the last decade, more than ten million people have been drawn, sometimes toughly, into permanent village life for the first time. In return, they are receiving the first elements necessary for conserving people—primary schools for the children, adult education, in part by way of radio, schools giving special training in farming and technical skills (these schools incidentally grow their own food), health workers and simple clinics (with more education, this time for health), and a steady extension of clean water and safe latrines. These village communities are compact enough to provide a new basis for modernizing agriculture with the support it needs in machines, extension and marketing services, and agricultural supplies. The ultimate aim is to encourage more completely communal villages through the Ujamaa program.

Another principle in Tanzania's program is to try to decentralize the widest range of decision-making, returning it to the people who will both in their work and in the results of their work be directly affected by the decisions. The remote official in his air-conditioned office at Dar es Salaam, looking despondently at an "in" tray full of proposals for places whose names and localities he has hardly heard of, is not perhaps the most effective instigator of local dynamism and self-confidence. Mainland Tanzania has been divided into seventy-two separate districts with specific powers and responsibilities, reinforced by twenty intermediate regional headquarters for needs and services which are more nearly national in scale—an essential step in effective, decentralized ur-

banization. In this process, a new capital, Dodoma, is being built to
prevent the sheer inertia of tradition from bringing everything back to
those air-conditioned offices in Dar es Salaam.

This political decentralization recognizes squarely one of the most
frustrating and insidious of the problems of early development—how to
encourage truly local talent for management and entrepreneurial drive.
Throughout the developing world, the question reappears. If the old
feudal or bureaucratic or simply traditional leadership is weakened, will
new forces and new talents be found to take their place? Luck, culture,
past history, all play a part in the answer. But one factor is universally
true. The new leadership must be sought and must be encouraged. This
required commitment and purpose, with all the new schools and training
institutions and adult education the modernizing state can provide. But
there are worse ways of learning to swim than by being thrown in at the
deep end. The rural people must believe in their new powers. Then the
possibilities of leadership are almost certainly greater than public fears,
development theory—and those comfortable offices in the capital city—
tend to suggest.

In the Tanzanian experiment, there is, undoubtedly, a good deal of
healthy "deep endism." The schemes cover more than village regrouping and services and transformed agriculture. Since 1973, the attempts
have been expanded to produce more diversified patterns of work and
life. These are based, in addition to intensified agriculture, on an effort
to discover whether the simple village crafts of cobbler and weaver and
blacksmith can become the nucleus of rather more sophisticated activities. In 1973, the Small Industries Development Organization was set
up, with the task of promoting the growth of small-scale industry and
technical change in food processing, leather goods, textiles, and building materials—this last a vital factor for such essential village improvements as reliable crop storage and unleaking drains. It is organizing
small industrial estates in several towns—with a sharing of such services as infrastructure, repair shops, and testing facilities. It is running
training courses in sheet-metal work, woodworking, blacksmith's
skills, and handloom weaving. The aim of SIDO is also to help small
enterprises by providing loans, technical assistance, and marketing out-
lets. And it ensures that a certain portion of the central government's
purchases come from small producers.

However, the Tanzanians are not romanticizing the benefits of local
action. They are also giving quite undoctrinal help to traditional entre-

preneurs in the towns, many of them Asian, in such matters as bank credit for businessmen or a new welcome to foreign capital. Local efforts at decentralized industrialization are clearly being matched by action at the national level to secure more sophisticated types of industry.

Tanzania's attempt to create and vivify local communities is part of a growing world movement. Examples come from all round the Third World. In historical perspective, we should perhaps begin with the Japanese, since one of the most marked features of their early pattern of modernization was not simply the primacy given to agriculture but the decision to exercise strict control over imports of technology and types of foreign investment. Local skills and development were preferred, imported technology was adapted to suit the local market, and a specific effort was made to keep a balance between large and small enterprise. To this day, Japan has followed the route of linking large and small enterprises with the technologies suitable to each. Even now, 60 percent of all small and medium-sized manufacturing firms are connected with larger corporate customers.

Nor need the policy be one of governments only. An interesting variant of the pattern has been evolved by one of the large multinational corporations—Philips of the Netherlands. Its research center at Utrecht was first established to help it solve some of the problems, of communication, of legislation, of custom, involved in dealing with other developed countries. (One tends to forget that nearly 80 percent of multinational enterprise takes place in the industrial countries.) But the Philips Unit also investigated the particular difficulties of Third World enterprises. A balance must be held between employing local people and finding people with needed skills. The possibilities of using labor-intensive and simplified technologies have to be recognized, yet at the same time, international standards of performance must be achieved. The lack of local suppliers has to be balanced against the expense and tying up of working capital entailed by too much reliance on imported parts. None of these dilemmas is escapable in early development. For instance, a major preoccupation in the minds of Chinese planners today is clearly the problem of balancing the vitality of local production against the essential uniformity of standards and interchangeability of spare parts required in modern machines. The skill lies in securing the best working compromise.

Since the Philips Unit was established in 1961, it has been used as a center of research and guidance for a widening range of Third World activities. Significantly, the usefulness first demonstrated by Japan of building up related producers within groups of larger and smaller members as a means of achieving greater dynamism and spreading the gains—and risks—seems to be borne out by the Philips experience. In India, for instance, for the manufacture of all types of electrical and electronic equipment, Philips has set up 560 small-scale suppliers—all labor-intensive, some with turnovers of less than $200,000 a year, and all designed to encourage their own dynamism and direction, and to rely on Philips directly for no more than 30 to 40 percent of their orders. But the big company gives active assistance in management problems and in methods of improving and diversifying the goods produced. In a sense, Philips is behaving like a mini Small Business Administration, and its stimulus has probably helped to provide at least 25,000 jobs, in different parts of India. Thus by support and stimulus—but not by total control—it is giving the small-scale sector of industry a useful boost. China's newly established organs of central economic supervision could do worse than consult the Philips record.

Every continent has its examples of this growing interest in the viability of small, decentralized, labor-intensive industrialization. Sri Lanka strongly encouraged small-scale rural industries during the five-year plan which began in 1972. Light-engineering industrial co-operatives were set up all over the country to organize the supply of raw materials and the marketing of finished products for their members. These were usually traditional village craftsmen, but they were encouraged to adopt new technologies and widen their range of products. For example, the village smithy's operation could be improved by introducing more efficient hearths and blowers. Later, mechanical equipment such as grinding wheels and drills could be added to increase the smithy's productivity further and to improve the reliability of the products. Industrial co-operatives were also set up at the regional level to encourage and to organize co-operative projects on a rather larger scale for machine shops and repair garages. It was the plan's intention to assist other traditional village craftsmen—potters, woodworkers. However, a change in government has postponed these developments and indeed seems to entail some risk of change in the general direction of the plan.

One of the driving forces behind the Sri Lankan government's earlier strategy constantly recurs in recent development plans. It is the recognition that modernized agriculture, even though it is labor-intensive and small-scale, requires mechanical help if the essential aim of moving

Building up the rice crops

Better irrigation channels

Inhuman dwellings—which is worse?

A good catch for Chinese fish farmers

Peter Fraenkel

Fuel for the home, desert for the land

The beginnings of the answer

More efficient cooking stoves

Using organic wastes more efficiently... a methane digester in K...

Peter Fraenkel

Harnessing natural energies

Experimental solar water pump in Dakar

Windmill for irrigation in Ethiopia

on to double- and triple-cropping is to be achieved. An outstanding center of innovation designed to respond to this new insight is the Agricultural Engineering Department of the International Rice Research Institute (IRRI). Its staff members have already developed designs for low-cost and reliable agricultural machinery, including two kinds of threshers (one for the small farmer, one for larger operations), a walking tractor, a power weeder, a batch dryer, and a stove that burns the waste product of rice milling—rice hulls—for both cooking and water heating. All the designs aim at simple construction. They use commonly available materials and components so that they can be easily manufactured and maintained. The IRRI encourages local production of these machines wherever there is a market, provides the designs free of charge, and assists prospective manufacturers in setting up their operations. Over 100,000 IRRI-designed machines have been produced in thirteen nations. In addition, many small manufacturers have indirectly copied IRRI designs, adapting and modifying them to suit their local markets.

But perhaps developments in India offer some of the most significant examples of the new trend. We have already noticed various efforts in another part of the world, the Andes, to combine reafforestation with the local production of construction materials and of supplies for the neighboring mining industries. In a similar combined scheme under development in Mysore, an iron and ferrosilicon plant is being supplied with forty thousand tons of charcoal a year by foresters working in the state forests who clear selected areas, prepare the charcoal (and some timber on the side), and replant on a sustained-yield basis during the rainy season, when there is a labor surplus. Over five thousand people are employed in the operation, quite apart from work in the plant itself, and profits from the operation more than cover the costs for the forestry department.

From India, too, comes a widely extendable technique for combining agricultural productivity and industrial development. We have mentioned the added income small farmers can gain from growing sugarcane. There is a significant story behind it. The main bulk of India's sugar comes from over two hundred large modern mills, employing 200,000 people. But the great mass of small farmers have had neither the means nor the roads to get their small cash crop of cane into the big league. They had to be content to use traditional measures of sugar refining with a low yield and poor financial returns. Now, however, a mini-plant has been devised which, although it achieves only one-twentieth of the output of the big factories, costs only one-fiftieth as much. It provides workplaces at one-tenth of the cost of the larger plants, and the ultimate price of sugar is about the same. Scattered round the countryside, these small mills now produce a fifth of India's sugar, increase seasonal basic income for over 100,000 workers and give the very small farmer an extra return. The mills are already being exported to Pakistan, Nepal, and Sri Lanka. Ghana and other developing countries are considering the investment.

This whole development may well be part of a wholly new emphasis in India's development. In a sense, it repeats the Tanzanian objective of balanced, decentralized growth, but from the other end. It does not build up from the villages. Half a million of them exist, and most rural people rely on them for part or all of their income. It tries to build down from the vast urban-industrial concentrations which, after twenty-five years of an all-out strategy of massive modern industrialization, are now increasingly seen to have left the villages and indeed intermediate centers and markets dangerously out of the mainstream of growth. The large industrial bias in India—or anywhere else in the postcolonial world—has been understandable. Colonialism seemed, as we have noted, to be expressly designed to keep its peoples as dependent primary producers. It took a giant of prescience like Mahatma Gandhi to see an opposite danger in hyper-mechanization: ''Men go on 'saving labour' until thousands are out of work and thrown on the open streets to die of starvation. . . . Today machinery merely helps a few to ride on the backs of the millions.''

But apart from some obeisance to village industries and community development, India's earlier plans have all plunged on in the direction of industrial priority. In a skilled and cultured nation, the result has understandably been a vast increase in technical competence and industrial capacity. The country can manufacture anything from nuclear power plants to the most elaborate chemical complexes. Its exports circle the world, and it also has thousands of trained engineers to export—particularly to the now skill-hungry oil exporters. In fact, the scale of this ''brain drain'' is becoming a matter of increasing concern.

But with the perspective of a quarter century of modernization, it is instructive to see that the latest draft five year plan admits that new directions are essential. If one adds together those who are completely unemployed and those who find only part-time work, on which their families can barely live, the figure for March 1978 gives the equivalent of 20.6 million people unemployed—16.5 million in the countryside, over 4 million in the cities. Six million more workers enter the labor force every year, but the public sector and the "formal" private sector organized on present lines can absorb less than 600,000 per year. There has to be a massive turnabout toward regional development, higher labor intensity in decentralized small-scale activities in the rural sector, and an equal emphasis on the small-business sector in the cities themselves.

Overall, the plan aims to create 50 million new jobs—23 million through more intensive agriculture, forestry, fish farming, and rural services; 17 million through power, road construction, and social services, above all in rural areas; over 9 million in mining and manufacturing (most of these, again, in village and small-scale industries). The minister for industry particularly emphasizes the decentralized nature of the new approach. For example, he has pointed out that only three firms provide all the nation's soap. Yet five hundred small companies spread over the whole country would satisfy the same market at a vastly smaller capital cost for each workplace and a correspondingly greater intake of labor.

Matches are another example. The minister points out that a single, largely foreign company provides 30 percent of the output and employs only fifteen thousand people. The small-scale plants providing the balance give jobs to five million. The key lies, in India as elsewhere, in the costs of the workplace. In the small or "informal" sector, the capital per worker needed in a blacksmith's shop growing into a repair center en route to becoming a small engineering firm may be no more than $300 to $500. In an imported machine-tool factory, the sum is perhaps $7,500. By the time you reach petrochemicals, each place can cost over $100,000. These facts do not mean a radical or doctrinaire reversion from large to small is necessary. They reflect an acceptance of the fact that both must go together. Indeed, the point can perhaps best be illustrated by looking at two giants, enormously endowed, plunged into the middle of the transition to modernity and about as far from each other on the ideological spectrum as it is possible to go. One is China. The other is Brazil. Both in their quite different ways—positive and negative—illustrate the intimate link between flourishing broadly based agriculture and successful industrialization. Both, in the changes and redirections of their policies, show the emergence of common problems in coming to grips with the modernizing process—problems involving food supplies, capital accumulation, the availability of jobs and skills, the rural-urban balance, the scale of an effective market. If we find common dilemmas in lands politically so far apart, we can guess that they have a wider validity.

Take first the Chinese experience. So far, we have underlined the degree to which farm investment, local conservation, and decentralized decision-making and development have underpinned a rapidly modernizing society on a strong basis of shared resources and equality. But China had to get from 1949 to the late 1970s, and as we have noted, in the fifties and sixties, changes, upsets, deroutings, and restarts occurred which illustrate the basic links between flourishing and diversified agricultural growth and rapid modernization in the other sectors. We are, of course, handicapped in making exact estimates since official statistics have not been available for two decades, but the evidence suggests that the primary aim of the 1950s was to follow the Soviet route toward a maximum degree of national independence through heavy industrialization. Ninety percent of the state's industrial investment was devoted to iron and steel, cement, electric power, petroleum, and the chemical and engineering industries. And for a poor country the share of investment in GNP was high—up to 20 percent in the mid-fifties.

The resources for this expansion had, inevitably, to come in the main from the agricultural sector, largely through the government's fixed-price purchase of grain and cotton. Urban population grew by 30 percent during the period, rural population by only 9 percent, although peasants still made up 70 percent of all the people. Progress fluctuated with the ups and downs of harvests, but by 1958, Chinese leaders felt confident enough to launch a massive mobilization of investment and work on both the farming and the industrial front. In this "great leap forward" agriculture was to provide the basic raw materials of much of consumer industry to permit heavy industry to go forward on its tremendous momentum.

Only this is not how it worked out. As we have seen, pressure was too great, the new collective-farm units were too large, the transfers from the country too heavy, the mass of the people bewildered and even discouraged. Farm production fell off. By 1960, there was near-crisis, with all agricultural supplies falling and their failure in turn hitting at the country's industrial and indeed its exporting base. Poor harvests accentuated the problems. So did the sudden withdrawal of Soviet aid. But the lesson was learned. The approaches that have been previously described—smaller communes, peasant plots, the decentralization of small and modern industry to the countryside, widespread works of water management and rural hydroelectricity and conservation—these became "lead sectors" for the sixties, and while the course of heavier industrialization continued, urban growth was held back and much more stress laid on small-scale and traditional technologies developed by the villages and communes. Agricultural needs such as fertilizers and farm machinery, and rural needs for cement, iron and steel, machinery, and light consumer goods, began to be met from enterprises at the county or commune level. Indeed, their co-existence is proudly proclaimed as a basic principle of economic management—"walking on two legs." One leg represents all that can be gained from modern science and technology, the other all that can be usefully revivified in traditional techniques. Clearly, in the post-Mao phase, under Teng Hsiao-p'ing's guidance, the "leg" of Western-style modernization is receiving quite new emphasis. But it can be successful precisely because the other leg has been allowed to stride ahead.

When we turn to Brazil, there can be no doubt again about the scale and speed of growth and change. In 1940, it had the usual developing-country pattern of a predominantly rural population, with only 30 percent of the people living in urban areas. First a strong effort of import substitution in the fifties and early sixties laid the basis for industrial growth. Then in the sixties and early seventies, while industrial growth continued at an average 7 percent a year, a very large export effort was mounted which gave a tenfold increase—to $25 billion a year—in fifteen years. Average national income per capita rose above the thousand-dollar-a-year level, and the country emerged as the competitive growing giant of the Southern Hemisphere.

Yet, thanks to the frank publication of Brazilian statistics, one of the best-known facts about this notable phase of industrial expansion is that, at the end of it, the rewards of society, the opportunities, even perhaps the means of esteem and self-respect, are more unequally divided than they were at the beginning of the process. If the first aim of a truly conserving society is the advancement of all its people, what does one say when the charts show that after thirty years of consistent economic growth, the richest 10 percent of the people take nearly half the national income, while the share enjoyed by 90 percent of the Brazilians actually fell between 1960 and 1970?

There are a number of reasons for the phenomenon. One is the degree of foreign ownership of industry, with the high exemplary salary structures and the capital-intensive "labor-saving" technologies foreign companies have introduced. We should add domestic reasons—the linking of wages to an inflation index which always underestimated the degree of inflation, the weakness in any case of organized labor under a military government. But one of the basic roots of imbalance lies without question in the vast rural sector.

We return to an earlier point—the need for feudal forms of land control to be modified as, for instance, in Meiji Japan before modernization can be securely established. Brazil's supply of land is not the problem. Of its cultivable land, only 20 percent is fully farmed. Even so, with nearly one full-cropped hectare of land for each citizen, the ratio is close to North America's. But the land is still almost wholly owned by large landowners (the *latifundistas*) or equally large, often foreign, business enterprises. One tentative effort has been made in the last fifteen years to propose a land reform by which the "big" men should be encouraged to give up land they did not actually cultivate. But their opposition canceled the plan. Deprived of better land, the government also announced a large scheme in the seventies to establish peasant holdings round rural centers in the empty Amazon region. But the soil was too poor, the follow-up—extension services, co-operatives, access roads—insufficient, and the schemes petered out. All that continued were the large timber and ranching concessions made to big firms, many foreign, with as yet unsure but disturbing risks for the areas ecological stability—and with, incidentally, an accelerating destruction of local Indian reserves and cultures.

Meanwhile, on land once meagerly sharecropped, the sudden explosion of the soybean as a prime export earner has led to the arrival of the big tractors, the expulsion of the "marginal" men, and even, in some areas, the disappearance of the humble nutritious bean from the local diet. In all this there is the strong and all but irresistible weight of past tradition. In the eighteenth century, sugar barons grew the crop in the northeast, exported it to Europe, and turned the area into a near-desert. First coffee and later industrialization have since concentrated the growth of wealth in the south, and the agricultural resources that go out as exports come back to serve and expand the fortunate groups and cities. São Paulo, above all, with 80 percent of the new growth, is the hub of a wheel in which wealth is gathered in and but meagerly redistributed—either to the provinces, to the rural millions, or the underemployed migrants to the southern cities.

To their plight we must return on a later page. Here a last general question must be raised. In the longer run, can ever expanding industrialism be maintained if internal purchasing power is too cramped? A growing middle class and a small but increasingly skilled and expanding working class in the cities are served by the present patterns. So are a range of foreign enterprises, while Brazil attempts to manage a $24 billion foreign debt. But an "export-led" expansion is a tricky affair in a depressed world economy in which oil prices have quintupled. Might not a more productive, better-endowed, and expanding mass market *within* the country, based upon more decentralized growth and healthier, better-distributed gains from agriculture, provide a more secure basis for future expansion? This question is at least being asked for the first time by the Brazilian government, with proposals for modest tax increases and even for a small attack on the extraordinary profits from urban land speculation. The scale may not be large, but it does raise the central issue—a wider and more balanced distribution of the gains from the whole process of modernization.

21 TAMING THE CITIES

JUST AS historical misunderstandings over the role of agriculture and traditional land tenures have, to a degree, distorted the patterns of latter-day development, so do we come upon comparable paradoxes in the burgeoning industrial-urban sector. On the one hand, one can argue that developing societies today have the immense advantage of not having to go through the whole process of inventing the methods of industrialization. Even at the peak of nineteenth-century industrial expansion, in Britain, in imperial Germany, in the United States, the over-all growth of the economy (the sum of goods and services, or GNP) did not average much more than 3.5 percent per year. But in the sixties and early seventies of this century, the economies of the fifty-eight middle-income countries grew on average by an annual 6 percent, with their industrial sectors growing on average by 8 percent per year. No such speed of expansion—with all the increasing experience and diversification it represents—would have been conceivable if the established manufactureres of the developed world had not made available for sale every need, from complete plants down to the smallest spare parts.

True, the process launched the developing lands rapidly on all the waste and pollution of industrialization—not much different in Detroit or in Seoul. But, in time, they will be diminished by the means already discussed in earlier chapters. And here again, the developing nations may secure some advantages from the fact of being latecomers on the industrial scene. It is not simply that with still relatively light pollution in some areas they feel they can afford to import polluting industries—smelters, pulp mills—from older saturated producers and carry on without too much danger to themselves. A few such exchanges have occurred between Japan and its neighbors, but this clearly is an "advantage" with very strict limits both in space and time. The true advantage lies in the sea change in the developed world's own attitude toward pollution and the growing realization that industrial processes can be designed to eliminate residues or that the residues can be resources, not wastes. Even two decades ago, there was no fluidized-bed combustor able to use trash and low-grade fuel to provide steam for electric power and for process heating with minimal pollution. There were no paper mills like the one described in chapter 6 which reclaims and recycles process water and chemicals. The Soviet Union had not developed its new conserving processes for making ammonia. No food-processing factories were turning their biological wastes into cattle feed. Nor, at a humbler level, were cheese makers recycling their whey as pig food. In fact, the whole concept of seeing wastes as potentially valuable materials had only just begun to bring new techniques from the planners' drawing boards. But the new insights imply as we have seen, that a nonpolluting technology, far from being more expensive and beyond the reach of "beginners," can be the opposite—cheaper, more sparing of materials, more conserving of the environment, more compatible with a clean and decent industrial order. It is no bad thing to be a late-starter in a process if it means that some of its messiest and most disagreeable phases need not be experienced at all.

Even in the critical field of energy—where hydropower potential hardly balances a lack of widespread coal reserves and the nuclear option threatens to swallow up much of the capital needed to develop the sectors it is supposed to serve—it is not impossible that the developing nations, largely to be found in the sunbelt, with its vast availability of direct radiance and quickly growing "biomass," may be on the verge of a breakthrough as momentous as the turning of coal into steam in the cloudy North. As we have seen, even for the temperate, changeable, winter-ridden United States, the President's Council on Environmental Quality believes that, given research and resources deployed as they are for nuclear power, solar power could provide at least a quarter of the needed energy for a society which already, on a per capita basis, uses twice as much as Western Europe and a thousand times more than the poorest nations in the sunbelt. Their equivalent of coal—solar power—may be on the point of reaching economic use, and without a trace of pollution or a single wasting asset to pay for it.

But little in history comes without a price tag, and today after more than two decades of unprecedented success in rapid industrialization, we are beginning to see the costs more clearly. Most of them have been

mentioned—the developing nations' concentration on "modern" technology, which by neglecting the one abundant resource, labor, has
created in many countries the vast degree of underemployment foreseen
by Gandhi. Then the concentration on industrialization and economic
growth as *the* means of modernization has too often meant a lack of adequate social and educational services, the bypassing of the countryside,
no check to rural misery, higher birth rates, and a hemorrhage of depressed people to the cities. In fact, it is in the cities of the Third World
that the evils become cumulative and we see the effect of more than a
century of faulty strategy beginning to add up to what could, within
twenty years, become a crisis or urban explosion or collapse.

The tendency to imbalance was to a certain extent built into the old
colonial system. Trade in the nineteenth century, stimulating the production of raw materials overseas for export to Europe and North
America, ringed the world with cities designed to serve international
commerce, not the local hinterlands. It is astonishing to recall that early
in this century, Latin America, with less than a tenth of its work force in
manufacturing, was more urbanized than Europe, where over a quarter
of the work force was in manufacturing. But there the cities were, whatever the backwardness of their hinterlands. There stood the beacons and
symbols of "modernity." It was to them, inevitably, in the period of
rapid postwar growth, that the new industries tended to gravitate—for
convenience, for infrastructure, for a market and a labor force. Thus
from countrysides where agricultural change was not reaching the poor
family (and the number of families was growing prodigiously), an unprecedented migration began to take place to cities in which the major
distortions of our century were concentrated—industries too capital-intensive to provide more than a minority of jobs, a failure of urban services such as water, sewage disposal, health care, and education to meet
the needs of more than a minority, and round virtually all big Third
World centers, growing rings of squatter settlements where the migrants
arrived in hope of advancement and stayed on simply to survive.

Some of the figures are mentioned in an earlier chapter, but they are
worth repeating. There were only 11 cities of over a million people in
1900, 6 of them in Europe. By 1950, there were 75, with 24 in the developing world. By 1985 there may be 273, and 147 of them will be in
the poorer lands. And these statistics of cataclysmic growth leave un-
mentioned the cities of ten million people—4 of them in 1970, perhaps
17 by 1985, 10 of them in the developing world. When one recalls that

in 1820, only one city in the world—London—had a million inhabitants, the scale and speed of the migrations, uprootings, upheavals, and urban cataclysms of the last half century are almost beyond our capacity to grasp. Yet by the end of the century, about half the world will be urban, more than half will be living in the developing lands—and perhaps nearly half of that half will be either unemployed or unable to earn enough to live on.

Drift alone will not reverse these fatalities. Self-interest, skillful salesmanship, the high hopes of the long boom, postcolonial aspirations, pride of observable achievement—all helped to build on the earlier urban patterns of colonization and in the last quarter century have created a formidable body of people and interests committed to continuing on the same route. Perhaps the most remarkable result of the world's recent upheavals—in fuel and food prices, in inflation, in prolonged recession—has been, since 1973, to begin to crack a little the superconfidence of the fifties and sixties and to compel governments to face with more sober judgment the gathering consequences of the old systems. But they will not drift out of the way. In central fields of policy, it is time for a new start. Where should it lie?

Very few generalizations can be valid for all the world's cities. Simply to give an extreme example, how can one compare the opportunities and dilemmas of oil-exporting states able to think of towing icebergs from Antarctica to the Persian Gulf with those of the sand-besieged settlements of the Sahel? Yet there are possibly one or two points of policy which have general validity. The first concerns sheer size. Happily for the developing world, at least half the settlements it will need by the next century are not yet built. The decision is therefore physically possible to build no more monster sprawls and to concentrate policy, physical planning, and resources on the creation of communities built to a decent and rational human scale.

If the Mexican and Indian governments, following in this some of the most creative examples of the developed world, decided to have a dozen cities of a million or twenty of half a million, then neither Mexico City nor Calcutta will need to double or treble in size in the next two decades. Simply because there has been little or no land-use planning in the Third World does not mean that it is ruled out as a future expedient. Such countries as Poland and Romania have shown how rapid industrialization can be combined with dispersed urbanism. Proportionately, there are fewer citizens in Bucharest today than there were twenty years ago. France, as we have seen, is staking its urban future on an entirely new comprehensive decentralized model. It is significant that some of the clearest recommendations for national action put forward at Habitat, the United Nations Conference on Human Settlements, in 1976, concerned the dispersion of population throughout a nation's regions, the "development of a system of intermediate centers having sufficient dynamism to counteract the attraction of the big metropolises," and a policy for transport and communications which would discourage the convergence of everything on the overblown cities.

What would such a strategy entail? One critical aspect of it we have looked at already—the restoration of some primacy of interest and investment to the rural sector. Another, carried out so far by very few nations, would be a careful land-use survey, pinpointing natural resources, water-supply systems, areas of natural beauty—and potential disaster—and picking out a number of settlements which already have an air of life about them. These can become either larger cities or what the Habitat resolutions call "medium-size towns as service centres for the rural hinterland." Since, as we have seen, a lively labor-intensive rural sector can support three or more times the number of jobs available in a stagnant rural sector, it is in these market and service centers that commerce, transport, storage, and credit begin to grow, that the processing of local products starts up and traditional trades—as in Sri Lanka—begin to turn into extended workshops and small factories. If, in addition, government policy—as in China in the sixties or perhaps in India in the eighties—encourages these trends by a purposive strategy of decentralizing larger industrial units, the growth of the kind of urban centers that can both serve and be stimulated by a lively rural hinterland will give some promise of more balanced regional development, a wider spread of wealth, and hence a check to massive and destabilizing movements of population.

When we turn to actual patterns and strategies for new cities—or the expansion of lively existing towns—once again, generalizations are precarious. Cities like Singapore and Hong Kong simply lack a range of choice—good or bad—because they are small island sites. Yet one or two principles recur sufficiently to have a measure of general validity. If the experience of the developed world's cities is to be drawn upon, there can be little doubt—as the governments agreed at Habitat—that urban communities can be more truly human and "urbane" if they can secure the incremental land values which their own growth creates. The supply of land with easy access to the city's industries and services is obviously limited, and as the city grows and develops, the value of this land increases rapidly. If such city sites are simply put up to the highest bidder, costs rise astronomically, high-rise building takes over to recoup costs, no shelter for the poor is affordable near center-city jobs. Indeed, the majority cannot afford even to be housed at all. The land speculator does very nicely for himself in return for absolutely nothing. The city administration on the contrary loses a large potential source of capital for its needed basic investment—in water, in sanitation, in transport. This lack is made doubly serious by the frequent unwillingness of the central government to contribute to city expenses. As the mayor of São Paulo remarked, ''I have only enough money for a city half this size''—a view perhaps not unshared by the mayor of New York.

The developed world's settlements have demonstrated many ways of securing for the community the value which its existence and growth alone have created—national land ownership, municipal land banks, purchase by public development corporations, zones of controlled prices, even stiff capital-gains taxes on land transactions. But it is no use supposing that in mixed economies, the decision is not a highly charged political issue. Nor is it one which, so far, Third World governments have shown much willingness to confront. Yet in city after city, land prices can make up more than 50 percent of the cost of housing and must be counted, like the skewed tenure of feudalism in the countryside, as one of the main institutional reasons for the continuing destitution of the poorest citizens. Certainly the result has been that large-scale housing projects—in Argentina, in Mexico, in Brazil—even when successfully financed by levies on industry, and in part specifically designated for the use of poorer citizens, end up as the homes of the new urban middle classes, since the unskilled and underemployed have no way of paying even a nominal rent where governments are unwilling or unable to face the cost of subsidized housing.

Lack of municipal resources often means that other basic needs, like power, water, and sanitation, may be provided only to the citizens able to afford them. The paradox can then emerge, as in Karachi, that the very poor pay twenty times more for their water (from itinerant water carriers) than the well-to-do who receive piped water. (Sprayers can be playing on lawns and golf courses while children die of gastroenteritis within a couple of miles.) Even roads—a fundamental means of access to jobs, clinics, and schools (not to speak of their importance in manageable waste disposal)—are sometimes based upon the valorization of houses along the proposed routes, and once more, the homeless poor are cut out. Add the appeal of private cars to the well-to-do and one can end with such distortions as occur in Bangkok, where 12 percent of the nation's population choke its streets with nearly three-quarters of its cars, or in São Paulo, which is approaching New York City in the number of automobiles per head—the whole process inevitably increasing the bias in transport against the poorest citizens.

However, one should not think of this as the universal picture. Quite apart from official bus lines and subways, jitneys which carry anywhere from 100 to 150 people a day and minibuses carrying twice this number—compared with the private cars which at best serve an average of ten—are coming into increasing use. Jitneys serve half a million people a day in Caracas. There are two thousand of them in Teheran. Cars with less than four people entering the central district of Singapore during the morning rush hour have to buy a three-dollar ticket and face high parking charges. A similar scheme is under consideration for Kuala Lumpur. In Dodoma, the new capital of Tanzania, the underlying city plan is based upon a structure of neighborhoods in which essential services can be reached on foot or by bicycle, while bus lanes link the different neighborhoods into a single city.

This example of Dodoma brings us to another strategy of urban construction which is sufficiently widespread to warrant some claim to general interest. Once the decision is taken to expand some promising intermediate center or develop a specially suitable original site, planners will discover that one concept keeps recurring, in practice or in theory, right round the world, almost as though differences in ideology or culture or geography itself could be accommodated within it. This is the idea of seeing a basic urban unit—either on its own or clustered together with others—as a single community containing not only shelter and services but commerce and work as well. Those master builders the Russians, who have constructed nearly a thousand new towns in the last half century, saw the unit at a level of about 50,000 to 80,000 inhabitants, with movement and work served by public transport, and schools and shops largely accessible on foot. As cities grew under the impulsion of accelerating industrialism, full new units were to be added. There was even a ratio worked out of how many service workers would be needed to uphold the efforts of a steelworker or an engineer, and thus to determine the balance between economic and urban expansion. The most frequent criticism of the concept inside Russia—once a titanic effort had begun to make up the postwar housing deficit—was that the promised services did not always keep pace with the building of the new communities. Nor have we much idea of the long-term effect of Russia's permitting a still undetermined scale of use for the private car. But the concept of what one might almost call the "self-serving" urban unit has been a key to Soviet expansion.

There were elements of the same pattern in China's determination in the sixties to push industrialization and urban growth out to the provincial centers (once again, the 50,000-to-80,000 scale seems to have been the choice for basic urban units) and to depend entirely upon public transport and the universal bicycle. But for those who see in this pattern a common dedication to collectivist principles, one should remember that Singapore's massive public-housing program has included the development of eight integrated settlements with housing, factories, and community facilities, each several miles from the city center. Queenstown, for example, aims to bring together a population of 150,000 and is divided into seven separate neighborhoods, each with an extensive pedestrian town center and enough factories close to the housing area to provide 25 percent of the work force with jobs.

Attempts at this type of urban planning can be found also in the developed market economies. Many of Britain's New Towns have a similar (although rather smaller) approach to "neighborhoods," with a careful balance between housing, services, and employment. In the United States, the well-intentioned but ill-fated idea of building new "cities within cities" had a comparable concern for easy communication and access, and the approach is being successfully tried out in such experimental communities as Columbia, Maryland. The French, as we have noted, have adopted it in their rather larger plans for producing recognizable centers in the suburban belt of Paris and preserving in a number of provincial towns the basic concept of "urban villages" (the Chelseas, the Trasteveres, the Greenwich Villages), where mixed communities of work and leisure, reachable by foot or bus and providing some of the basic services of life, often allow a vitality and an attractiveness which the world's concrete suburban deserts, slurbs, and sprawls so demonstratively lack.

Another reasonably valid generalization can be applied to the types of urban services which should receive priority in the Third World. It is, inevitably, tempting to adopt what are felt to be the most modern and prestigious technologies. ("Developed" experts frequently urge the same practice.) But there are two overriding reasons for caution. The first has already been outlined. It is the degree to which developed countries themselves are changing their policies toward urban wastes, services, and needs. The second reason is even more compelling. If standards—of water supply and sanitation, of housing, of transport, of health and education—are fixed at too high a level of sophistication, the bulk of the citizens will simply secure no part of the services. This does *not* mean the acceptance of permanent inferiority and penury. It implies the concept of incremental change. The beginnings should be modest. But upon them, as wealth increases, more ambitious structures and services can be built.

We can begin with a primary need—shelter. In preparing their plans and layouts for the new or extended settlements, the authorities have to recognize that 60 to 80 percent of the citizens will not be able to afford anything that corresponds to developed standards of housing and services. If annual income is about a hundred dollars, most of it has to be spent on food. The margin left for rent or water rates or transportation is pitifully small. As this fact has become steadily more evident in the explosive urban expansions of the last decades, more and more official housing bodies (and also more and more international lending agencies, with the World Bank at their head) have come to realize that the course of wisdom is to encourage most citizens to continue to do what they have done for millennia—to build their own shelter on land provided with minimal services and underpinned with reliable tenure. In spite of all their variety of scale, of siting, and of culture, the "sites-and-services" schemes of recent development plans all have at their base these two elements—self-help building by the citizen, coupled with the security and the minimum infrastructure which only the community can provide.

This does not mean that large-scale government-backed housing has no part to play. One thinks of Brazil's experience beginning in the sixties. A million houses were built by its National Housing Bank in the first decade, and two million more were constructed privately, partly as a result of the Bank's stimulus. As a result of this type of program, employment expands in the labor-intensive construction industries; savings are encouraged by access to mortgages; the house, like the motorcar a much-wanted "consumer durable," stimulates both savings and market demand in a wide range of other industries. But housing of this sort does not reach the mass of the people. As we have noted, even when percentages of the units in public projects are set aside for them, poor tenants often rent their quota to wealthier neighbors, or simply leave it unoccupied. This is especially true where the projects have been built at too great a distance from possible places of work, and fares for transport eat still further into the narrow margins of income. The neighborhood concept of accessible work, habitation, and services is not an agreeable afterthought in urban plans. It determines the whole quality of urban life. When, in monster cities, the worker can find himself two to three hours from any employment, survival itself is at stake. Systematic plans for encouraging small-scale enterprise, expanding workshops, and helping to finance a full range of services are as critical to urban regeneration as to the revival of the countryside.

Once the basic "sites-and-services" concept is accepted, clearly a very large choice among styles and layouts is possible. There can be different types to meet different levels of income. To give a representative example, in three towns chosen for expansion in South Korea—Gwangju, Mogpo, and Yeosu—the World Bank is assisting a project to give two thousand plots basic services; a harbor with a fishery, and other processing industries, are being developed to provide employment in two of these towns. The plots vary in size, and in one project, 30 percent of the larger areas have been auctioned off to cover service costs and subsidize the smaller plot owners. The Bank has also started the development of over eight thousand new serviced plots in Tanzania. In Malaysia it now has a Sites and Services Unit which not only prepares plots but is undertaking a feasibility study for a new urban center. One risk it has to watch: areas designated for sites and services attract a vulture group of land speculators wanting to secure control of neighboring sites. But given reasonable equity and security, in every continent one factor does seem to recur—the readiness of urban dwellers to put their "sweat equity" into more solid construction as their jobs and incomes become more secure.

Urban dwellers are almost invariably on the lookout for possibilities of self-improvement, and with a little elbow room and enough confidence, extra rooms will be built and let, another floor will be added, a tailor shop will open up in front. In any case, in the great sunbelt of the world, shelter does not need too much elaboration. For instance, the traditional Indian preference for a courtyard and a covered room gives a very flexible basic design, either for improving existing housing or on new sites. Nor need one think only in terms of self-building. The man who has built a house—perhaps with the help of friends—may decide to specialize in the trade and set up his own little enterprise to build for others who are fully employed. Since in all these activities the scale is small and the turnover rapid, the return on capital may well be higher than in more ambitious schemes, and in every aspect, the work is highly labor-intensive. In fact, one of the most useful inducements public authorities can provide for the rapid expansion of such undertakings is not only credit for small entrepreneurs but encouragement to others to begin such supporting activities as brick- and tile- and pipe-making, to provide a growing building industry with basic supplies. The point must be underlined again. Businesses and services must be built into "sites-and-services" schemes from the very start.

There can be similar mixtures, with variations of scale and choice, in the provision of municipal services. The fundamental need is clearly safe water, and the aim should be to provide piped water with proper chlorination. But at first the delivery points can be conveniently placed standpipes. Then houses can be connected up and payments made according to the amount of water used. Similarly with latrines, the first step may be to establish hygienic public ones. Later, households can have their own, with the "nightsoil" removed—some central wards of Tokyo are still served in this way—or connected to communal cesspools. Where there is sufficient water, full-scale sewage systems can be introduced when the community has developed the needed resources.

Some ways of minimizing water waste in such systems have already been discussed—the dual water system, the minimum-flush toilet. But far more useful technologies can be introduced if the wastes are recognized for what they are—potential fertilizer. Nightsoil removal by truck needs very little water, and once the wastes have been composted and treated to kill such pathogens as worm eggs, they can be used directly on the land. In the new biogas plants, animal and crop wastes produce biogas and, again, fertilizer for fields or fishponds. The nightsoil collected from the city of Tainan, in Taiwan, enriches six thousand hectares of fishponds, providing nutrients for the bacteria which feed the algae which feed the fish. In China and India, a number of low-cost sewage-treatment schemes are being developed that integrate the treatment with aquaculture, algae production for animal feed, fertilizer production, or fuel supply. One such scheme represents a pleasing reversal of fortune. Until quite recently, quick-growing water hyacinths were regarded as a menace to tropical irrigation, since they clogged canals and ditches. Now it has been discovered that grown in sewage-stabilization ponds, they provide high-quality treatment far more cheaply than conventional systems. In addition, they can be harvested for use as an animal feed supplement, organic fertilizer, or feedstock for biogas plants.

And while these physical steps are being taken, the communities can make a similar advance in the training and expanding of peoples' minds and understanding. With the coming of water must come instruction in its use and misuse—not to leave taps running, not to leave the soil around them a watery mess inviting the nearest mosquito, not to forget to wash little faces and keep away trachoma nor to wash hands after using the latrines. All such instructions belong to that area of primary *preventive* health care which is a thousand times more beneficial than dealing with a trouble once it has taken hold. And here two lessons are clear. The first is that when, as early as 1918, the French in Senegal introduced the system of what they called *médecins africains*—people prepared by a few years of simple medical training to work directly through vaccinations, simple diagnosis, sanitary instructions, and so forth—they showed a basic understanding of what is at long last beginning to be seen as the basis of any really effective system of community health. The Chinese have probably carried the activities of their paramedical "barefoot doctors" (and workers and housewives) further than any other developing community, and no village or street is without its simply trained but effective health workers. (It is illuminating that this service, too, dates from the big revulsion of the sixties. Mao is reported to have discovered that three-quarters of the medical profession were in the big cities, and then did for health care what he was doing for economic development—sent it back to the land.)

China's village and street committees underline the second point— that no amount of careful para-medical training will work well unless it is part of a fully accepted pattern of community behavior and participation. The little trachoma-threatened eyes will not be dried unless mother has learned about the disease, and her chances of learning are meager indeed if the whole element of group instruction is left out of the pattern. Indeed, this principle is of universal application. Whether it is rehousing, upgrading existing housing, guarding latrines, learning about child care and family planning, installing standpipes, digging drains, building a communal house for the area's activities, or agitating for a needed bus service, not much more can go into a community than it is capable of generating itself—in interest, activity, commitment, and pressure. It is in this context that literacy—for the beginners in school and for the adults who got left behind—can become a basic instrument in the building of more responsible and human settlements. It is not that only literates are capable of culture. Millennia of folk worship, music, and dance refute the idea (so, unhappily, does much of the provender of modern literates). But in the modern world, citizens cut off by their inability to read a direction or decipher a seed package or make out a bill are deprived of one of the chief means of dignity and neighborly influence. In the village or the shantytown, they lack what is perhaps the most vital element of self-expression and self-defense.

But one should not think of the concept of the balanced urban community, with its sites, services, work, and enjoyments, as relevant only to the planning of new cities or the expansion of regional centers. Many of the same concepts are as critical—and usable—in the vast urban conglomerations which cast so dark a shadow over Third World urban development. One of the World Bank's largest schemes for assisting urban improvement is in Jakarta, where over five thousand hectares of run-down, filthy, disease-ridden *kampongs* (neighborhoods) are receiving roads, storm drains, clean water, sanitation, schools, and clinics.

Embedded within such vast conglomerations as, say, Calcutta with its 8.3 million inhabitants, there are in fact thousands of urban enclaves, large neighborhoods of the scale proposed in much modern urban planning, held together by intimate links of common ancestry and village association. (A study of jute workers in Calcutta in 1973 showed that 79 percent had houses in their native villages although they had never been engaged in any way in farming.) And it is precisely in such relatively closely knit communities that some of India's most successful upgrading of squatter settlements is taking place. The Calcutta Metropolitan Development Authority, for instance, has systematically upgraded fifteen hundred slum areas (*bustees*) over the last six years—replacing old latrines with sanitary ones and installing drainage, street paving, and piped water. In addition, the authorities have allotted the various latrines to specific family groups to ensure that the people themselves are involved in maintaining the standards which keep at bay cholera, typhus, gastroenteritis, and all the other scourges of unclean water. These community areas can be found in most giant metropolises, and with appropriate, sustained, and locally supported aid, with lively public backing for local business and expanded employment, can become communities which have a sense of coherence and common responsibility and are capable of development into hygienic, hard-working, and increasingly well-cared-for boroughs or "urban villages."

That the decisions and strategies required for upgrading the world's run-down shantytowns do not fundamentally differ from those needed in planning and building new settlements is, after all, not surprising. Vast as are the differences in wealth, culture, and geography among various countries and locations, there are fundamental human needs—shelter, work, access, services, amenities—that have much in common. Both in public thinking and in the programs of the aid agencies, there has been a remarkable growth in analysis and comprehension in the last decade. In fact, it is all but impossible to recall that as late as the 1960s, the policy for settlements practiced by most governments was still to send the bulldozers into the shantytowns and slam them down.

But if understanding of the kind of communities needed in the poor world's cities has advanced with unlooked-for speed, two vast obstacles confront the translation of the understanding into policy. The first is quite simply the weight of drift and inertia. By the year 2000, it may indeed have been proved to be infinitely more productive in human and in economic terms to, say, divert Mexico City's next fifteen million newcomers to a properly conceived ring of satellite towns and to build up such neglected and deserted regions as the parts of the Gulf coastline where a whole fishing industry—quite apart from promises of new oil—waits to give an economic basis to new settlements. But Mexico City is *there*. The set patterns of generations, links of kinship, traditional hopes and chances for jobs and self-improvement, must continue to exercise their habitual attraction unless heroic governmental decisions and countermeasures are taken to shake society from its migratory rut. The difficulty of making these measures fully effective can be illustrated from every continent, culture, and governmental system. Even Moscow has grown to nearly eight million inhabitants, after having its upper limit officially fixed first at three million and then at five.

The second obstacle is even more basic. A sustained, rational, well-planned urban strategy will, even if the authorities engross all the unearned increment they are creating, entail large new capital expenditures. Apart from the oil exporters, hardly a Third World government faces anything but severe constraints and obdurate difficulties of choice and priority in its capital programs. The need for an urban strategy was not even perceived until fairly recently. How can it now be added to so many already established needs? Where does it fit in? What gives way to it? As with every other problem in basic development, resources are both the key and the roadblock.

And here the questions and difficulties cease to be local. No one denies that the dedication, honesty, and sense of equity of local leadership are decisive. Nor can there be any doubt about the fundamental need to draw the citizens themselves into the plans and efforts that will determine their future. But if *world* policies remain unchanged, all the honesty and all the self-help conceivable will still leave three-quarters of the planet's peoples in control of only 20 percent of its resources. Global imbalance on such a scale remains a critical determinant of the extent and success of development—in the farms and forests, in the factories, in the cities, old and new. It is in fact the ultimate determinant of the central issues of scale, speed, and timing. No purely local effort can meet the onrush of the two billion more citizens born between 1976 and 2000.

Either it is the whole world's business. Or it will not be done in time.

Part Three: A Conserving Planet?

22 AN EMERGING WORLD COMMUNITY?

WE CAN SURELY say in theory at least that between today and the year 2000 the planetary community has the means to achieve more stable, conserving, and satisfying ways of life. In developed societies, if waste and pollution are overcome, there are few prospects of immediate stringency nor any doubt about the nations' vast accumulation of capital and skills. In the developing world, vigorous investment in the basic needs and infrastructure of the communities can provide the food, the water, the secure farmland, and the growing labor-intensive industry which are required to bring genuine productivity to the present billion "marginal" men and women, to raise them above absolute poverty and prepare decent living standards and more stable levels of population among the next two billion people, who will be born largely in developing lands in the coming two decades.

Technically, all this is possible. Neither the doomsters who tend to write off science as even a possible contributor to human well-being nor the techno-fixers who believe breeder reactors and hydrophonics will solve all our confusions can make more than half their case. Technology looks both ways—to weal and to woe. What determines the outcome is the human strategy that gives technology both its stimulus and its limits. And here, we must in honesty confess that our world in its present post-imperial upheavals, its wholly unprecedented growth in population, its changes and demands on life, its great switch from rural to urban living, still lacks the strategies of conservation in the broadest and yet the most critical area. The sense of equity and availability, of "compassion" and "frugality," are not yet to be found at the *planetary* level.

The fundamental reason for this rift, this virtual vacuum, was hinted at in the Prologue. Every society, global or local, is in part what it is because of the inner history of its own development, and as the twentieth century draws to a close, the global society built up by four centuries of colonialism, two centuries of industrialism, and a few decades of advanced communication and space technology is an extraordinary mixture of the traditional and the unprecedented. It is unprecedented, as we have seen, to abandon the idea of the legitimacy of empire. But it is totally traditional to lapse back into accepting the absolute sovereignty and inward-looking self-interest of individual states. It is unprecedented to set up a global system of institutions, from the Security Council to the latest, humblest recruit to the United Nations family. It is traditional to leave all large decisions to the greatest powers and most smaller ones to local states. It is unprecedented to spend a whole decade within the United Nations system discussing the fundamental issues of the planet's common life—environment, population, food, the role of women, employment, settlements, water, the deserts—as though joint strategies and agreed-upon policies offered the only hope of secure survival. It is traditional to leave the global system very much unchanged in the meantime, and in practice, if not in rhetoric, to give to virtually only one aspect of global unity the attention which realism commands—that aspect being the world-wide market system largely inherited from the colonial years.

The basic reason for this predominance of world-wide economic connections and interests is of course quite simple. The nations cannot escape from them. Centuries of mutual trade underpin them. The internationalization of investment grows more intense, and with it goes a steady adaptation of new types of production in one set of countries to developing patterns of demand in others. Cumulatively, in spite of political decolonization and bitter ideological disputes, all these threads of economic interdependence—in price, in supply, in services, financing, and management—have woven the continuous fabric of a single planetary economic system. No amount of political rhetoric or wish fulfillment or simple benign neglect can conjure away a bedrock economic reality. If the Soviet Union has to struggle with a seventeen billion dollar debt to Western producers, if Angola deals amicably with American petroleum giants, if Eastern Europe seeks joint enterprises with West German capitalism, the reasons are the same. The world's economic life has a genuinely and inescapable planetary element. Of virtually no other organized human activity is this even remotely true.

There is something of a paradox here, since no one consciously planned or even intended this degree of underlying economic interdependence. True, the desire to trade for the silks and damasks and spices of the more civilized and endowed Orient was what first drew Europeans across the world's oceans, to discovering the Americas, when they really wanted to reach "far Cathay." But the actual pattern of control was extremely haphazard. Wherever local power remained strong and coherent, the Europeans were content to go on trading, abiding by the stringent rules laid down by Indian moguls or Chinese emperors; in fact, they barely penetrated Japan at all. But where the local authorities were weak, divided, tribal or primitive, one or another trading nation—Portugal, Spain, the Netherlands, France, Britain—usually ended up in control of the territory, often after long intrigues and struggles to keep the others out. And where land was largely empty, the settlers followed the traders and made the Americas, Siberia, Australasia, and parts of Africa outposts for people of European stock.

While this formidable though unplanned global takeover was running its course, the launching of industrialism, first in Britain, then in Europe and North America, changed and reinforced the whole economic bias of the world system. Briefly to recall the historical background sketched in the Prologue, we should remember that earlier European traders had bought goods abroad and often had to pay for them in bullion. But now the textiles came not from Bengal or China, but from Manchester and Lille and Massachusetts. What the hungry new machines and mouths of the Atlantic nations wanted were raw materials, such as minerals, cotton, sugar, coffee, tea, and palm oil (industrialism's filth made soap a vital product). All round the dependent territories, old handicrafts vanished before the competition of the new technology—as they did in Europe. Mines and plantations were opened up. Roads and later railways served the new commercial exchanges, most of them leading to the coast for the dispatch of materials overseas and the receipt of Western manufactures. From Vladivostok to Valparaíso virtually all the dependent cities were seaports. By the end of the nineteenth century, the whole globe had become to a very considerable degree an interdependent market system.

It had also begun to demonstrate on a world scale some of the characteristics which all markets display, whatever the area they cover. No one denies the value of a market in providing a mechanism for exchanging all the infinitely diverse needs and desires of human customers. The ability to balance the cost of a haircut easily against the price of a new pair of shoes is a very real and time-saving convenience. In fact, the benefits are such that almost invariably, if markets are tightly controlled, as under total war or total planning, black markets or *marchés parallèles* grow up, nourished on private deals, overpayments, and corruption. But if normal markets are to function, three conditions at least seem to be basic. The first is that the power of buyer and seller should not be too skewed. The second is that the mass of buyers should not be too poor to enter the market and thus stimulate further production. The third—which has hit markets recently with unexpected force—is the opposite need, that purchasing power should not too far outgrow the means of satisfying it. These conditions are not guaranteed by the market alone. They form the social and political context within which it operates. And if they are too distorted, the market itself cannot fulfill its proper function of evening out demand and supply in a flexible and decentralized fashion. In fact, as we have seen, the modern industrial state has enmeshed its market in a whole series of social and political prescriptions and institutions which make it something closer to a community than to a raw confrontation of opposing interests. The process is still obviously and indeed often tragically incomplete. Nor can we be sure in what direction Western societies may be led by such "taxpayers' revolts" as California's reduction of property taxes by referendum. But we do know that moderating social and political institutions curb and influence at every level the bitter confrontations of pure economic power and interest. However, such moderating institutions are either stalled or nonexistent at the critical level of the *global* economy.

The formal ending of political imperialism has not been accompanied by any really systematic effort to remodel the colonial economy. Since, by definition, imperial control concentrates power, and since in addition the imperial powers were the industrial pioneers, it is hardly surprising that at the end of the Second World War, the overwhelming bulk of the world's wealth, trade, and skills still lay with the third of the population living in the industrialized states. What is more surprising is the relative stability of the relationship in the following quarter century of rapid world growth. As the 1970s opened, the developed nations' share of population was falling to little more than a quarter. Their share of wealth, trade, investment, industry, remained above 80 percent. The rich nations were, of course, considerably richer. Many developing economies had achieved high rates of growth—if not of distribution.

But a dead weight of a billion impoverished citizens lay at the bottom of the pyramid, and their numbers tended to increase most rapidly.

Above all, the fundamentally dependent relationship between North and South seemed to be changing not at all. Southern exports were still largely confined to raw materials. They tended to decline in value compared with manufactured imports, and much of the "value added" (the value gained by processing the materials) flowed off to the North. In 1974, the developing nations received $30 billion for the export of their twelve major raw materials (excluding oil), but by the time the goods derived from these materials were sold to the final customers, they cost $200 billion. The bulk of the difference, $170 billion, flowed off to the North.

Indeed, in some ways, the determination to modernize with all speed appeared to increase dependence. Much of the new manufacturing—eagerly invited in by governments determined to break the old preindustrial patterns—was now controlled by multinational corporations with headquarters in North America, Europe, or Japan, and it was by no means clear—what with tax concessions, capital grants, import advantages, and intercompany trading deals—that the local communities were securing a fair share of the resulting gains. Meanwhile their debts increased, and they had little confidence that organizations such as the International Monetary Fund or arrangements such as the General Agreement on Tariffs and Trade, set up by the developed nations in the 1940s to introduce more orderly procedures into world trade, did not in fact bypass the developing nations' interests. The reason once again had its roots in history. They inherited their colonial disadvantages. They had only a minority vote in the new institutions' decisions. They had no direct power to reorient policy. In the early 1970s, for instance, international reserves rose to $130 billion, but the developing nations (outside OPEC)—with nearly three-quarters of the world's population—received just a 4 percent share.

As independence came to state after state in the 1950s and 1960s, the contrast between the appearance of political sovereignty and the fact of economic dependence became inevitably, more felt and resented. A first manifestation was the formation of a group of Asian and African "nonaligned" states at Bandung in 1955, a movement which grew to embrace most of the Third World. To press their sense of delay and grievance over the unchanged character of world trade patterns and world economic balance, they persuaded the developed nations to join with them in the United Nations Conference on Trade and Development (UNCTAD), and then at the UNCTAD session of 1964, they set up their own bargaining partnership—the Group of 77—with the express purpose of redressing a little the balance of power in global trade negotiations.

By the early seventies, some of the main points of controversy were well established—the Third World's relative lack of control over its own local resources, the higher returns secured for Western manufactured exports compared with Southern primary products, multinational investment patterns too often bringing capital-intensive technology into low-wage, labor-intensive Southern communities, an element of protection inhibiting a range of potential Third World exports, rising Third World debt, the steady drain of payments for patents and services of all kinds, and all the while a comparative fall in the flow of concessionary finance from the rich lands to the postcolonial states.

The grievances increasingly stimulated counterproposals by the Southern states for what before long came to be called the "new international economic order." The Southern states sought acknowledged control over their own resources, with the right of nationalization to secure that control; a new search for the technologies appropriate to labor-rich economies; higher export earnings for primary products—to be attained possibly by indexing their prices to those of imported manufactures, possibly by establishment of a special fund for the financing of buffer stocks of essential but unstable commodities; a reconsideration in depth of Third World debt; an increase in Third World industry in the next two decades from 7 to 25 percent of the world total, and a "global compact" to guarantee some steadier flow of resources from rich to poor, in part at least on an automatic basis, thus introducing the key concept of taxation into the world system.

Like the early bargaining between incipient trade unions and unwilling yet anxious owners, the debate tended to drag on without coming to firm decisions or even agreements on definitions and analyses. And power remained in the North. It was not until 1973, when the oil embargo quadrupled oil prices and a disastrous Russian harvest helped to triple the price of grain in a single year, that an atmosphere of any urgency began to surround the talks. And the reason was straightforward. The North suddenly found its power diminished. Its essential oil supplies were no longer under its comfortable control. Grain shortages sent prices up 300 percent for rich and poor alike. And even though the Southern countries were as profoundly affected (the cost of India's imports of oil and petroleum products went up to a quarter of its import bill), they held together in the Group of 77—the "trade union" of the poor—and intensified their negotiations with the now slightly more flexible rich. Moreover, the profound disturbances of 1973 could not be quickly banished. Excessive purchasing power—both local and and international—continued to exercise inflationary pressures in domestic economies, and the skill of Western money markets was taxed by the need to recycle so sudden and volatile an increase as the new sixty billion dollars a year earned by the oil states, many of them too small to offset their gains by a quick increase in effective demand. In all this turmoil, investment was discouraged, stagflation prolonged. In these circumstances, new questions began to be raised, and all turned fundamentally on the question of whether a social and political context of mediation and material interest could be created—as in domestic society—to offset destructive confrontation.

Seen in this light of historical experience *within* states, could the "new international economic order" begin to look a little less like a radical dream? Could not a bargain be made, a compact of interest on all sides? The first rounds—again as in nineteenth-century history—had been adversary contests, with clashing interests and incompatible demands leading to recrimination and deadlock. Could the deepening of the dialogue since the oil and grain crises, the prolonged world recession, and the narrow but vital shift of power in the area of oil supplies change the tone and open up a new phase of negotiation? Could the debate be enlarged beyond the relatively narrow range of interests of those seeking trade, investment, and economic advantage? Could deeper dimensions be brought in—of common purposes in an interconnected human community, of conserving interests in a single biosphere, of survival itself in a troubled, divided, and finally interdependent world? After more than a decade of increasingly urgent yet frustrated debate, the time for a new round of common search and understanding may have come. And it could turn precisely on those issues which allowed earlier national communities to break out of evident deadlock— the issues which provide the social, political, and moral framework for economic debate and, by transcending the narrowest self-interest, create fundamental interests which all can share.

23 THE COST OF JUSTICE

In TRYING to envisage possible approaches to a co-operative global system, we really have only one model available to us—the *domestic* economy, which when functioning with reasonable harmony, does seek to promote and protect the interests of all its citizens. That such "domestic" economies can be as vast as China shows that sheer scale need not defeat the effort to attain a measure of planetary solidarity. What has been achieved for a fifth of the human race is at least not inconceivable for all of it.

A first principle in the modern domestic economy is that the community as a whole and not individual citizens should exercise a measure of control over the distribution of wealth. In any society, certain groups, by inheritance, by skill, by health, by luck, will tend to secure higher rewards than others. Virtually until this century, redistribution in favor of the less fortunate was largely at the discretion of the rich. At the planetary level, this is still the case. Eighty percent of the wealth may be concentrated among a quarter of the world's people. But any transfers they make in development assistance are voluntary—charity, not justice—and at present these transfers do not often exceed 0.5 percent of a nation's GNP. A first step toward the equivalent of the automatic transfers secured by domestic taxation might be a binding institutional convention which secures the acceptance of the developed states' often proposed target for official development assistance of a transfer of 0.7 percent of GNP from rich to poor nations, 84 percent or more of it in the form of grants, loans at minimum interest rates with long repayment terms, or other suitable concessions. Norway, Sweden, and the Netherlands have already exceeded the 0.7 percent target and propose to reach 1 percent by 1980.

It is ironic that in 1976, the three strongest Western economies—

West Germany, with aid at 0.31 percent of GNP, the United States, with aid at 0.25 percent, and Japan with aid at 0.2 percent—were proportionately among the smallest givers. On an even more niggardly scale, the centrally planned economies gave less than 0.1 percent. At the other extreme, Kuwait's percentage was 3.23, that of Saudi Arabia 5.77, that of OPEC donors as a group 2.14.

To this modest first exercise in direct taxation, the international community could add a variety of automatic transfers corresponding in some measure to the systems of indirect taxes within a nation. A small sales tax on materials entering widely into international commerce might be acceptable—provided the poorest states were assured of the compensating finance they would require. Tolls could be charged on international sea and air journeys. Once international authority is finally established over seabed resources lying beyond the proposed two hundred-mile exclusive economic zones, corporations given concessions there for mining minerals or for extracting oil could be taxed by the Seabed Authority for the benefit of poor and landlocked states. Alternatively, the Authority could carry on the exploitation itself and utilize the profits to satisfy the needs of the poorest states.

Another potential area for international control lies in the Southern oceans, where jurisdiction is shared by a consortium of twelve treaty powers and no decisions have yet been taken on the types of control over local resources that are acceptable. Yet these resources include among other valuable products the small shrimplike krill, a source of high-quality protein and so prolific that its annual catch could equal the whole of the world's present marine harvest. The protection of this resource against the kind of greedy overfishing which is already reducing regional fish stocks, and the transfer of a proportion of the sales revenue or profits to assist the protein-deprived children among the poor rather than simply to profit the rich through providing cheap feed for cattle and battery hens, could at one and the same time conserve the Antarctic commons and tax them for the good of the whole planetary economy.

A further possible extension of automaticity might be thought of for the international community's principal financial agencies. It was inevitable that at the time of their foundation—at Bretton Woods, in 1944—neither the World Bank nor the International Monetary Fund (IMF) could be designed to take into full account the interests of what were then in the main still dependent, colonial countries. Today, the

whole balance of needs and numbers underlines the advisability of a
new approach. The scale and renewal of appropriations made to the
World Bank for concessionary loans through its International Development Agency (IDA) might, for instance, cease to be a matter of decision
(and dissension) among individual governments, but be fixed by an international convention, stipulating, say, five-year renewals at agreed
rates of expansion. Similarly, it could become accepted practice at the
IMF that when the world economy requires stimulus, its own contribution—the issue of fresh capital in the form of what have come to be
called "Special Drawing Rights"—should be assigned in whole or in
part to the neediest economies.

This brings us to a second principle in domestic society—acceptance of the concept of the "general welfare." Can anything so indeterminate be more clearly defined in planetary terms? To what ends should
a much larger flow of automatically appropriated public funds be devoted? As in domestic society, there can be little doubt about the first
priority. It is to abolish absolute poverty by the end of the century. This
goal is conserving in a double sense. It can be defined in ways that are
directly conserving of the citizen's life, health, and human dignity. It
can also be conserving in the indirect yet vital sense of preserving the
patrimony of soil and water, of clean air and uncluttered oceans, upon
which everyone's survival ultimately depends. In fact, the two cannot
be separated. To repeat only one example, half the world's grain supplies are grown on lands which are environmentally fragile—from low
rainfall, from intensity of cultivation, from the salting and silting up of
irrigation systems. It is no use talking of balanced diets for all by the
year 2000 if meanwhile a critical part of the land needed for raising food
has been allowed to deteriorate beyond hope of restoration.

Satisfaction of basic human needs can cover a number of specific
physical targets in developing lands—a doubling of per capita incomes
in poorer nations, an adequate diet for all, access to safe water (in 1975
only one-quarter of the low-income and half the middle-income nations'
people had achieved this fundamental need). Life expectancy should be
advanced to sixty years or more (in several of the poorest African and
Asian nations, it is still below forty). Universal primary education and
adult education could raise literacy from the present level of 23 percent
in low-income countries and 63 percent in middle-income countries to
75 percent or more. As a cumulative effect of all these measures, infant
mortality could be brought down from 122 to 50 children for each

thousand, and national birth rates (which often exceed 40 or even 50 per thousand) lowered to 25 or less.

Clearly, a large part of the investment required to secure these targets will be mobilized by the developing nations themselves—just as they now generate some 80 percent of the capital for their own development. Indeed, as we have seen, some countries and regions which are very poor in terms of per capita income—Sri Lanka, Kerala, China—have already achieved remarkable progress toward some of these social objectives without either very rapid internal growth or large-scale foreign help. (The contrary case has also occurred, as we have seen—high growth and pitiable distribution of benefits.) But the sheer scale of world need for such basic factors as food, soil conservation, reafforestation, energy, water, and sanitation—all essential to any effective attack on basic poverty—and the need to speed up the whole momentum of the program as two billion more world citizens arrive to take their share, require that sustained international transfers of capital should be a central part of the strategy. Indeed, it can quite simply not succeed without them.

As a result, in part, of the series of United Nations consultations on substantive issues in the 1970s—from environment in 1972 to deserts in 1977—we have some guidelines to the scale of transfers that could be required. The World Food Conference in Rome in 1974 made three critical recommendations for the management of world food supplies. Two of them concerned distribution—the setting up of an immediate reserve of ten million tons of grain for sudden disasters, the long-term establishment of international buffer stocks on a scale to finance, maintain, and replenish grain supplies equal to sixty days' world consumption. For this whole structure of support, the recent and more abundant harvests could provide the needed surplus grain. It is not yet clear whether the opportunity may not have been missed.

The third and most vital recommendation—both for food supplies and for world conservation—underlined the need for a very large increase in investment in Third World agriculture and the building up all round the world of self-sustaining food systems securely protected by sound husbandry. In this context, success must be seen not simply in the more sensational increases made possible by new seeds and fertilizers and higher mechanization, but in the gains achieved by reafforestation and careful soil conservation, by waste recycling and small-scale local power generation—in short by the types of farming and technology, described in previous chapters, that are appropriate to small farms and large populations.

The needed scale of investment was estimated to be of the order of $30 billion a year, of which some five-sixths would be provided by the work and savings of the people themselves. The addition of $5 billion to $7 billion to the level of external assistance would round off the sum and would indeed be essential for such areas of pressure as imports of artificial fertilizer, paying for grain stores, and purchasing the equipment required for the local manufacture of necessary agricultural supplies. But it is probable that such sums represent a considerable underestimate. Neither rural energy needs nor the critical importance of improved forestry was stressed at Rome. These were more clearly underlined at the United Nations Environment Programme's Desertification Conference, where it was estimated that $500 million a year should be spent in the next twelve years to protect the most vulnerable farming areas, where low rainfall, the growing pressures of cultivation and animal husbandry, and unimproved irrigation are putting millions of hectares at risk.

Nor could the Rome calculus include the later insights of Habitat. There it became clear that the spread of industrial production to smaller decentralized communities would immeasurably strengthen and diversify the rural economy. Nor, for the same reasons, was much attention given to the catalytic effect of building intermediate agro-industrial settlements with "sites and services"—sites with water, sanitation, roads, communal buildings—designed to form the basis for construction of houses in traditional materials by the people themselves. A full program of rural renewal could thus well demand three to four times the Rome figure. Indeed, at least $10 billion a year would be required for safe water and sanitation alone, again with a strong external capital input to speed up the work and finance the more sophisticated treatment plants which could from the start ensure that the nutrients in municipal wastes were returned to the soil, that fuel was derived from wastes and the whole careless "chuck-it-in-the-river" phase skipped by the new town planners. One could therefore envisage as the essential external input into basic needs—food, water, sanitation, skills, health, and employment—a sum of the order of $20 billion a year over and above present flows of concessionary aid. (They run at about $15 billion.)

And, once again, this figure largely leaves out at least two further essential requirements—energy and investment in new sources of raw materials. In view of energy's importance in any development program and the crushing effects of oil price rises on poor countries, it might be assumed that the development of energy sources, especially indigenous energy sources, would be a concern of the highest priority within the United Nations and the various aid-giving bodies. But the only energy agency in the United Nations system—the International Atomic Energy Agency (IAEA)—is almost exclusively concerned with nuclear power and finds itself in the dual role of promoter and regulator of this technology. Both the IAEA and the multilateral agencies have concentrated their support on large electricity-generating units and have virtually ignored decentralized energy production to meet local needs. The IAEA forecast of the investment needed for energy technologies—of the order of $11 billion per year over the next twenty years—is thus likely to be too big both in terms of real need and in its overconcentration on large-scale technology. At the same time, it may well be playing down a vital component—the renewable energy technologies, especially decentralized energy technologies that meet local needs, such as solar-energy techniques, tree plantations for firewood, biogas plants, and small hydro units. Scaling down the proposed investment figure while putting greater emphasis on renewable energy technologies and rural energy needs might give an estimate of $6 billion to $7 billion per year.

In view of the relative poverty of many non-OPEC countries—including the whole of the Indian subcontinent where some very extensive hydropower development is still feasible—perhaps a $5 billion external commitment would be in order. This could include the $500 million per year the World Bank proposes to invest in developing oil resources in more than fifty Third World nations as part of its wider investment in primary materials. Recent estimates suggest that much of the still-undiscovered oil of the planet may be found in developing countries. Yet recently, private investment there—as a result of recession but also through fear of political instability and inadequate prospective profits for multinational interests—has fallen to a small fraction of all expenditure on oil exploration. The Bank clearly hopes to provide an element of catalytic example and a promise of security in order to encourage the renewal of exploration. There could then be a number of Third World countries enjoying Mexico's happy chance—of having undergone a slump in the oil industry during the twenty years of rockbottom oil prices and now perhaps sitting on a reserve of a Saudi Arabian scale with oil at eighteen or more dollars a barrel.

When we add together potential investments in the whole program for meeting basic needs, the net figure is still rendered uncertain by two questions whether the transfer would cover present Third World payments on licenses and patents (several billion dollars per year), and how the inordinate present debt of the non-OPEC Third World should be handled. Since 1974, private and public sources have provided over $200 billion, largely of recycled OPEC funds. No one knows for certain whether a figure of 20 percent of foreign earnings earmarked for interest is compatible with Third World expansion, or whether the biggest borrowers—Brazil, Mexico, Indonesia, Pakistan, India—can maintain reasonable dynamism without some significant rescheduling of debt. But in spite of these uncertainties, it is perhaps not too ambitious to suggest that basic needs and the new resources to undergird them, particularly in the critical area of renewable resources, might usefully and effectively absorb an extra $30 billion per year in the transfer of resources from rich to poor, with an increasing share of this figure provided by an automatic process equivalent to a world tax system. To put the scale of the proposed transfer into context, one should recall that it is roughly equal to 1 percent of the developed nations' GNP and less than 10 percent of the world's annual $400 billion spent on arms.

24 HOW NEW AN ORDER?

THERE IS MUCH TO commend the theory of a global compact based upon the application to the planetary community of certain of the basic principles which govern and harmonize domestic society. For the rich themselves, as they struggle with prolonged stagflation, with fifteen million unemployed and at least $200 billion in spare savings and capacity awaiting creative use, it has become a matter of dogma, at summit conference after summit conference, to suggest that one or other of the leading developed economies should launch itself into renewed growth and provide the stimulus for expansion in weaker economies. The difficulty is that, given the high degree of development, consumer saturation, trade union power, and business concentration in all of these states, a really sizable stimulus risks setting in motion a new cycle of inflation. It follows that once more, at summit after summit, the task is tacitly declined and passed on to yet another unwilling key economy.

But the negative arguments need not apply to an ambitious and sustained economic stimulus directed toward the poor nations. They are not sated. They are not overprovided. They are not competing one another into the earth with steel and motorcars and shipbuilding capacity. They are not organized for instant wage increases. At least a third of their citizens have barely entered the market at all, and the development among them of skills, health, education, and local resources will not instantly send up the demands of already well provided pressure groups, It will generate genuinely *new* resources and by doing so exercise the counterinflationary pressure of providing rising supplies of goods to match rising purchasing power.

This is not a hypothetical supposition. It is straight historical experience. In the economic breakdown of 1929, it was above all the sharp spreading decline of demand among primary producers (including

America's farmers) after the boom of the 1920s that produced Wall Street's first signal of collapsing confidence. It was then met, not by restoring markets and investments, but by a fatal retreat into protectionism. Then came the culminating collapse of 1931 and the road to ruin and war. But in 1947, when Europe and all its world dependencies were at a comparable degree of economic dislocation after the five-year struggle, the Americans, with unparalleled generosity, gave away for five years about 2 percent of a GNP less than half its present size, and their Marshall Plan restored the productivity and hence the consuming power of their allies and potential trading partners all round the world. It is perfectly possible to argue today that a comparable gesture—2 percent of GNP from the rich and the OPEC nations transferred to the developing nations in order to revolutionize the productivity of the poor world—would, cumulatively, have the same result. The time required would be longer. In 1947, it was in the main already developed economies that were being restored. Today it is again and again a question of primary development. A "Marshall Plan" lasting for two decades would probably be required. In the longer run, the introduction of automatic transfers would in any case cut out uncertain questions about time limits. Need, debt, world liquidity, harvests, particular disasters would, as in domestic society, determine year by year the necessary scale of transfer. The critical fact today is that there are vast undeveloped resources and needs in the poorer lands, large unused capacity among the rich, unsecured liquidity—from the OPEC surpluses and private bank lending—on a scale to threaten continued monetary instability, and so far barely a trace of the Marshall type of vision and statesmanship required to bring needs and opportunities together in a new global initiative.

While the central political will is lacking, there is little use in suggesting all the ways in which the possibly inflationary effects of such a program could be mitigated. A 10 percent cut in the world's lunatic arms spending would release more than the whole proposed sum and do so from the most inflationary of current uses. An appeal to earlier and perhaps not forgotten instincts of solidarity among the poor might persuade the rich nations' trade unions to undertake some restraint in demanding pay increases during the early "start-up" phase of the program, before the new materials and goods and skills began to come on stream and provide counterinflationary balance. One could even envisage a period when, as in the last war, some of the payment to the more fully re-employed work forces of the industrial world might take the form of indexed tax credits, which would be recovered with interest at the time of the worker's retirement and thus underpin future demand while taking the strain off the early stages of redeployment. But it is not the tactics of the approach that create the problem. It is the large central lack of strategy, and this in turn is rooted in a planet still without the principles, institutions, and interests of genuine community.

Rich-nation philosophy has still, in the main, to get past 1840. The market will provide. Economic life will generate energy and direction. The growth of the rich will pull up the poor in its wake. Political, social, and moral principles of solidarity are irrelevant. And if the result turns out to be not progress, but misery for the many and well-being for the few, that is simply the way in which the laws of economics work. For a century or more we have been modifying this stupid, unworkable, and dangerous philosophy *within* our economies. At the planetary level the effort is still hardly even engaged. Our revolutionary 1848s, our 1905s, our 1917s, our 1949s, could all lie ahead. So, too, in mindless conflicts of fear, aggression, and aggrandizement could our 1914s and our 1939s. Above all, within a single living generation we have experienced a way that has failed—that of the 1931 collapse—and one that has triumphantly succeeded—the Marshall approach of political vision and unprecedented generosity. History is rarely so obliging as to write up its lessons in indelible characters within sight of each other. But it is at times increasingly difficult to suppress doubt as to whether some of the leaders of the seventies can actually read.

We also do not know what the reaction might be in the Third World if much larger transfers of funds from rich to poor and some principles of automaticity were introduced into a possible planetary compact. As we have seen, the programs of the Group of 77 have very understandably been developed to a considerable degree on what one might call an adversary basis—on the need to change the world's whole bias of privilege and wealth. The particular proposals of the Group—for assured and possibly indexed commodity prices, communally financed buffer stocks, a larger absolute share of industry, freer access to developed markets, some rescheduling of debt, more equal and balanced methods of decision-making, the right to develop local resources under national control—all tend to reflect resentful responses to the long colonial years and the predominance gained from those years by the Northern states.

Given this background of profoundly experienced and prolonged inequality, it is perhaps not surprising that suggestions, however well meaning, from the North that the primary aim of any new international order should be aid for the poorest, the satisfaction of basic needs, and the development of resources for that purpose do not have the self-evidence and general acceptability their proponents appear to expect. Northerners are surprised, sometimes even shocked, if the citizens of developing countries argue that the needs and welfare of their people are the direct responsibility of their own governments: Why should external donors and authorities expect to fix national priorities for domestic leadership? Are you Northerners not, once again, trying to tell us Southerners how to run our own affairs? Shall we wake up one morning and find that, say, agreement to an internationally financed buffer stock for copper is conditional upon acceptance of further ''sites-and-services'' programs in Lusaka? Will various degrees of access to developed markets be made conditional upon our reserving agreed percentages of our local budgets for health and education? Are you in fact telling us to develop our own economies under all manner of social and environmental constraints you never practiced yourselves? Is there still not a strong smack in all this of patronage and privilege? Your job is to make it more possible for us to earn a fair share of the world's income and the world's influence. It is *not* to tell us what to do with them.

Another range of suspicions is aroused by the new emphasis on appropriate technology in many Northern programs. Could this not mean a denial of the use of really modern scientific methods and a condemning of the local economy to more primitive and less powerful means of production? An insistence upon biogas plants, mini-tractors, small-scale irrigation, to the exclusion of other methods, can become a way of limiting the growing political and economic muscle of the poorer nations and ensuring a continued state of dependency. At the other extreme, critics attack transnational corporations for bringing in capital-intensive technology inappropriate to local labor surpluses and reinforcing a sort of vicious dualism between a traditional sector which is forced below subsistence and the new world of shining offices, computer banks, and petrochemical complexes where everything is available except jobs. Bringing in outsiders for exploration and mineral development could, in particular, mean even less control over a nation's own resources. Colonialism would continue in its new transnational garb.

Yet there may be hope that the resentful and wholly unconstructive moods bred on both sides by years of deadlocked negotiation *can* be broken, if only for the simple, straightforward reason of self-interest. Throughout the colonial period, only metropolitan powers were allowed to have explicit economic interests. Then, in the changing political, postimperial world of the 1950s and 1960s, the underlying assumption of what little economic dialogue there was had its root—like Victorian charity again—in the idea that something had to be done for the poor continents but that *no* vital Northern interests were at stake. The developed states had mastered the secret of forging ahead. They certainly needed no Southern help in their breakneck advance. This continuous display of complacency and self-congratulatory behavior on the part of the rich was certainly one of the threads weaving its way through poor-world resentment.

The first break in the mood was clearly triggered by the oil embargo. But we will soon be nearly a decade further along in the world's great debate. What is slowly but perhaps irreversibly dawning on the rich nations is that they—who thought they were conferring all the favors from their 80 percent monopoly of wealth—are also in need of changed relationships, wider markets, new opportunities, a better global management of resources and, above all, some end to the almost claustrophobic reproduction of one another's industrial capacities and industrial rigidities with which they have now all but competed one another to a standstill. In fact, in 1977, the United States sold the developing countries manufactures for a total of $29.5 billion, and bought back goods for $18 billion. The figures for 1972 were $9.5 billion for exports, $6 billion for imports. The surplus has trebled, and created jobs all over America. Figures for Europe tell the same story. In 1977, the European Economic Community sold manufactures to the Third World for a total of $60 billion, and bought back goods for $14 billion. Again, the surplus has tripled since 1972. In addition, Europe and North America profit enormously from the immigration of thousands of trained doctors and scientists from the Third World. The rich communities receive the benefit of their skills, the poor nations bear all the costs of their preparation. Their total contribution to the West's GNP is probably higher that the West's aid budget. There are thus already concrete facts to support the argument that if the nations of the developed world can come to see in three-quarters of humanity the potential for new human skills, new resources, renewable materials, and hence new purchasing power, they will find that they are beginning to help not only the Third World's destitute and underprivileged poor but their own selves, their own interests, and their own citizens. This could be the psychological basis of a genuinely new "new international economic order"—the basis that it serves *all* the global community and cannot in any way be taken as distasteful, condescending charity on the part of the few.

True, the recognition involves some changes in industrial patterns—the developing world moving forward in textiles and footwear, the developed world in high technology and services. No one pretends these are propitious times for proposals which appear to put more developed-world jobs at risk, and it is an unhappy fact that the degree to which expanding trade with the Third World is already creating more employment than competition has not been made in any way clear by developed governments. In fact, only the Dutch authorities are effectively linking their longer-term industrial policy with their support for the "new international economic order" and are putting at the center of this strategy specific and appropriate help to enable traditional domestic industries to move to new types of production and not to persist in activities which compete with Third World types of production.

It is also true that only the rich nations can physically underpin the new concept of a global compact. They alone have the resources, the capacity, and the range of needed skills, and they have yet to demonstrate anything like a sufficient degree of enlightened self-interest to see the Third World as their "new frontier." There is also the danger that even if they did and simply announced, say, a thirty billion dollar annual addition to concessional flows of aid, the result might be a whole new tide of angry suspicions that what was offered as a compact was in fact once more an instrument of control. However, this danger is not insuperable. There is an answer—to introduce at the planetary level a principle essential to understanding and good will *within* domestic society. Call it participation. Call it co-determination. Call it the application of democratic principles. The essence is that those who are to be concerned with any enterprise and whose lives will be strongly affected by it have the right to play a full part in the consultations and decisions which lead up to the shaping of the final strategy.

It was one of the many acts of imagination in the preparations for the Marshall Plan that the Europeans themselves were invited to help to frame the policies from which they were so greatly to benefit. Big brother did not move in from Washington and tell them what to do. In the Franks Report, they were asked for their recommendations. It was, in short, a genuinely co-operative venture. If today, with a comparable combination of vision and common sense, the rich nations coupled their firm offer of doubled resource transfers with a complete readiness to discuss the terms, the aims, the institutions, the audit, and the staffing of a sustained plan of world development and world conservation—a plan of equal interest and importance to *all* the parties to the venture—it is surely not inconceivable that the hesitations and resentments and suspicions of the beneficiaries would be at least sufficiently lessened for a genuine dialogue of equals to be engaged.

Within such a new psychological framework, problems of jurisdiction and sovereignty which seem insoluble now could be accommodated by reasonable discussion and compromise. The institutions needed to direct the flow of the new resources and the future automatic transfers would no doubt lie somewhere between the free voting patterns of the General Assembly and the overweighing toward the rich nations, of, say, the International Monetary Fund. An increasing proportion of the actual resources would, no doubt, be distributed through international agencies, to underline the completely unpaternalistic and co-operative nature of the whole approach. A delicate issue—the actual supervision of the *use* of aid to ensure that it reached its true developmental and environmental goals—could probably be best undertaken by international and regional institutions (the development banks, for instance) suitably strengthened and staffed for the purpose. Even the troubled debate over the role of multinational enterprises could be settled by some agreed-upon code of practice acceptable both to the incoming corporations and the host governments and guaranteed to provide the flexibility, the renegotiability, the ''transparency,'' and the equity such arrangements require if they are to be acceptable after the Third World's first burst of industrializing enthusiasm.

But all these institutional developments depend upon equal bargaining, equal interest, and a dialogue of true confidence and respect. And just possibly in the course of the dialogue, the participants would discover that their genuine equality—of possible survival, of potential

disaster—is at a far more profound and inevitable level than their
acknowledged economic interdependence. The planet we are creating is
one in which no nation, no race, no culture, can escape a truly global
destiny. There is no choice about this fact. The only choice available is
to recognize it—and to do so in time.

25 THE FINAL CONSTRAINTS

IF WE WERE to depend solely upon the record of our political history, we could well doubt whether any widening of understanding and solidarity to a planetary level was even conceivable. Wars and rumors of wars, fierce tribal, communal, and national loyalties, fear and hatred of the stranger, pillage and destruction—are these not to an overwhelming extent the tragic determinants of human destiny? Why should we hope for anything different today? Surely we should need some quite new concept of reality, some revolutionary upheaval in past habits of thought, even to suppose that we could escape from the old "melancholy wheel" of ever repeated conquest, decline, defeat, and conquest again.

But it is at least just possible that such a concept is beginning to gather strength in our imagination. Still perhaps no more self-evident than human rights at the time of Magna Carta, or anticolonialism in 1775, yet it has begun to make its first impact on human thinking, with results which may over time prove to be as unpredictably radical and hopeful. This is the concept, made increasingly explicit by new methods and tools of scientific research, of the entirely inescapable physical interconnectedness of the planet which the human race must share if it is to survive.

Precisely those areas where immensity and distance have seemed to reign—climates, oceans, atmosphere—are beginning to be seen as profoundly interdependent systems in which the cumulative behavior of the inhabitants of the planet, the various activities of each seemingly separate community, can become the common destiny of all. This is not to say that earlier philosophers and sages have not sensed this underlying unity and spoken, with virtual unanimity, of a universal moral order—of human respect, of modesty and restraint, of Lao-tzu's "frugality" and "compassion." But these were dreams and visions. The radical change of the last century is the discovery that in literal, unchangeable scientific fact, interdependence is a reality and—what is an even more vital insight—that the connections which underlie it do not depend upon vast forces and changes alone. Rather, so delicate is much of the environment, so precarious are its balances, that human actions and interactions (especially now that they are armed with the forces of modern science) can have vast, potentially catastrophic and even irreversible effects. The whole picture is not yet clear. Systematic monitoring is only just beginning. Moreover, only a third of humanity has so far plunged into the full-scale technological organization of society which, in its first century or so, has been based upon a totally blind and exploitative reaction to the planet's own life-support systems. We are thus, in the most fundamental sense, at a hinge of history. If we can learn from the growing evidence of destructive risk in our present practices to determine that the next phase of development shall respect and sustain and even enhance the environment, we can look to a human future. If on the contrary we have learned so little that every present trend toward pollution, disruption, decay, and collapse is merely to be enhanced by its spread all round the planet, then the planet's own capacity to sustain such insults will be ineluctably exceeded. This fact cannot be too sharply underlined. All of the policies, all of the strategies outlined in the preceding chapters, have been designed to lessen environmental strain, to increase reliance on safe and renewable sources of energy, to maintain a planet that is in balance between its needs, its demands, and its numbers. Taken separately, they may not appear to strike at the central issue of human survival. Cumulatively they do.

Our global atmosphere and regional climates are maintained by forces which would seem to be on a scale virtually to exclude human influence or intervention. The planet's mean temperature is maintained by the balance between incoming solar radiation that is absorbed and eventually reradiated back into space and that which is reflected. Within the general balance, the poles absorb less solar radiation than the tropics. The uneven absorption of solar radiation by the earth's surface causes the winds to develop, and this vast continuous interchange, complicated by the effects of the earth's spinning on its axis, gives us the specific climates of particular regions, all entirely integrated into the total system and thus, one might guess, on too vast a scale to be affected save very locally by the pygmy acts of man.

But the balance is not, over geological time, at all stable. Evolution went forward together with a changing atmosphere and changing temperatures. For much of its existence, the planet had no ice caps at all and an atmosphere lacking free oxygen. For the last two million years, there has been a succession of prolonged glacial epochs, or ice ages. We are recovering from the last ice age, eight to ten thousand years ago, which at its peak brought glaciers to Missouri. The whole climatic system may be vast, but it is influenced by many physical factors—among them, the carbon dioxide and dust concentration in the atmosphere, the cloud cover, and the earth's reflectivity, or "albedo." The largest, stablest seesaw in the world can be budged by shifting weight a few inches at one of its edges. Similarly, human intervention within a complex climatic system, if it takes place, as it were, at the edge of the planetary balance, might have catastrophic effects—a cooling down to another ice age, a heating up which could partially melt the ice caps and swamp lower-lying lands as the sea level rises. Some meteorologists put the potentially catastrophic average annual temperature change at no more than 3 degrees centigrade either way.

The difficulty at present is that although we know that changes *are* being brought about by human activities—for instance, the explosive growth in our use of energy in the last two centuries—it is much more difficult to be certain of the effects. Burning fossil fuels and cutting down forests for firewood has the effect of putting more carbon dioxide into the atmosphere, since these processes release the carbon locked up within the fossil fuel and within the wood. The concentration of carbon dioxide in the atmosphere has gone up by 12 percent since 1860, and of that, 5 percent was added in the last two decades. This trend will continue as more forests are cleared and fossil-fuel consumption goes on growing. And what is the effect? Here the debate begins. The increased carbon dioxide concentration helps a general warming-up process, since it absorbs some of the heat given off by sun-warmed lands and oceans which would otherwise be lost into space. To this indirect warming effect should be added thermal pollution, the heat produced by burning fossil fuels and uranium, since all the fuels we consume end up as waste heat in the atmosphere.

But this warming up is partially offset by the effect of other human activities—for instance, particle pollution by such substances as the sulphates massively released in the burning of fossil fuels. However, since these substances are linked to cancer and respiratory disease, most efforts at conservation are now designed to prevent them from escaping from their source—the power plant, factory, or automobile engine—and no one is likely to advocate their release in order to offset possible warming up of the planet, especially when one remembers that some particle pollution can itself contribute to the warming-up process instead of compensating for it. In short, the effect of particulate matter on the temperature of the atmosphere is variable and unpredictable, and it must be offset by placement of the maximum emphasis on conservation and on a steady shift to the renewable energy resources—sun, wind, falling water—which involve no thermal, carbon dioxide, or particulate pollution. Massive reafforestation to provide fuel for the poor and to protect fragile soils will also help to reabsorb some of the carbon lost through deforestation. Fuel conservation reduces both carbon dioxide and thermal pollution in that less fuel is used to do the same task. And tapping renewable energy sources leaves nature's own climatic system to operate without destabilizing human encroachment.

The argument is only reinforced by the degree to which, in spite of our massive increases in scientific understanding of atmospheric phenomena, we still do not understand fully the incredible complexities and interactions within all the biosphere's natural systems. Only recently have we learned of the role of the ocean's phytoplankton and the plant's processes of photosynthesis in building up the atmospheric concentration of oxygen. The release of oxygen allowed the build-up of the ozone layer (ozone being a form of oxygen), which alone protects organic life from the sun's potentially lethal ultraviolet radiation. Recently, two classes of man-made pollutants have been found to react with the ozone layer, decreasing its protective effect—nitrogen oxides, coming mainly from fleets of supersonic aircraft, massive increases in the use of nitrogen fertilizer, and the combustion of fossil fuels; and chlorofluorocarbons, used as refrigerants and as propellants for aerosol sprays. Both have the capacity to float up through the various layers of the atmosphere and attack the ozone. Yet even a 10 percent reduction in ozone content could increase the incidence of skin cancer by anything from 7 to 50 percent. Thus at the global level we rediscover the effects of ignorances, the chemical risks, which we have already seen at work within domestic societies.

Action at the national level has begun. The Swedish government has banned the manufacture and import of virtually all aerosols containing chlorofluorocarbons. The United States federal government has severely restricted their use. Several major manufacturers of aerosol prays have voluntarily switched to alternative propellants. But the daunting question is whether anything like a global agreement on non-use can be achieved before dangerous ozone reduction has occurred.

As with the atmosphere, so with the oceans—on the face of it, they are so vast, so all-embracing, so seemingly independent of minute human interventions, that it is difficult for the imagination to see them as a single, interconnected natural system, vulnerable enough in its essential function of supporting life to be tampered with and even put at risk. Organic life evolved under the protection of the oceans; plants and animals moved from sea to rock to carry the evolution of organic life to the whole globe. The 70 percent of the earth's surface that remains the water's share, receives all the earth's detritus, breaks it down so its components are recycled, operates with the sun the giant purifying cycle of water desalination which returns the runoff of springs, lakes, and rivers in the form of rain for the whole world's harvests. And all the while it is moderating extreme temperatures—cooling the tropics, bringing warmer currents to chilly regions, and thus ensuring the habitability of a large part of the earth's surface. How could any system on such a scale be influenced by what must surely seem to be, in comparison, the all but marginal activities of human beings?

But once again, the growing insights of scientific research give us far more than visions of majesty and power. Vast the oceans may be, but like the atmosphere and climates, they contain critical points of vulnerability and fragility. The areas under greatest pressure from our activities are precisely those where such pressure can do most damage. Traditional fishing grounds no longer provide fish for all who want it. The world's fish catch tripled between 1950 and 1970, reaching an annual total of seventy million tons. It then fell sharply in the early seventies, and in 1974 and 1975 could not exceed the 1970 figure despite expanded fleets and greatly intensified efforts to catch the fish. Depleted fish stocks have led to international conflicts such as the British-Icelandic "cod wars" and to governmental restrictions on both domestic and foreign fishing fleets in newly defined territorial waters. This does not mean that the oceans' full capacity to produce food has been reached or even approached. Indeed, we fish only for certain choice species, with very considerable wastage in getting even these from the boat to the customer. But it does mean that traditional attitudes toward unrestricted fishing are having to be completely rethought. Take another example. At the beginning of the 1970s, less than 20 percent of the world's oil

drilling was done out at sea. By the 1980s, the figure may have in
creased to over 50 percent, with some of the drilling in polar regions
where oil spills could have lasting, unpredictable, and almost certainl
risky consequences. And while oil drilling increases, the scale of car
riers used round the world to transport the oil goes up comparably. A
late as 1948, no oil tanker was larger than 29,000 tons. Now we fin
monsters of over half a million tons, and even, on some demented draw
ing board, an 800,000-ton dinosaur. Yet by all but universal agreement
the training of crews and the handling equipment are inadequate. Th
arrangements for insurance and salvage are on a ludicrously meage
scale. A single disaster like that of the *Amoco Cadiz*—due, it seems, t
poor navigation, inadequate countermeasures, and even mid-disaste
squabbling over salvage—can let loose 200,000 tons of oil on an unof
fending coast. Yet on some of the busiest tanker lanes in the world th
vessels' masters ignore lane regulations and sail perilously close t
rocky shores—as with the *Amoco Cadiz*. Even the regulations that hav
been adopted by the relevant world body—the Inter-governmental Mar
itime Consultative Organization—are usually evaded by delays in sign
ing conventions. In addition, ship operators can register their vessel
under "flags of convenience," such as those of Panama and Liberia
and thus gain from cheaper labor rates, lower construction and repai
standards, and a far slacker imposition of fines and penalties for non
compliance with regulations.

And oil tankers present only one of the major risks in sea-born
trade. Add ships with nuclear wastes, add the new effluents of a plane
industrialized not by a third of its people but by all of them, add the new
prospects of deep-sea mining with (a dream still no doubt, but creepin
into the blueprints) nuclear power stations *in situ*, processing mineral
in mid-ocean, add in short the incorporation of the ocean systems int
full technological activity of every kind, and is it really irrational to fea
that even the oceans' productivity might suffer? The most productiv
ocean areas are the continental shelves adjoining the land masses. Mos
of the marine catch comes from these. And because of their shallownes
and their close proximity to land they receive the worst of technologica
society's water-borne wastes. Nor can any state, with Canute-like pre
tensions of sovereignty, bid other people's pollutions keep away. As th
"moving waters" go to their work around the planet, here at least unit
is incontestable. We have no choice but to share.

But how can we do so? Do not the sheer scale and immensity of at mosphere and ocean make it all but inconceivable that human beings should keep any sort of check upon the consequences of their own innumerable activities? It is one thing to give voice to the rhetoric of interdependence. But what hope is there of providing the concept with force and content sufficient for it to begin its fundamental task—that of changing the climate of our imagination, of clarifying our perception of the interconnections and interactions in our single planetary home?

But here all need not be darkness and discouragement. In the last two decades, the conquest of space and the infinite elaboration of instruments for tracing terrestrial and extraterrestrial movements—of air, of water, of heat, of changing tree cover, of areas of increasing desiccation (not to speak of the precise location of possible oil-bearing strata deep in the oceans or of surreptitious tankers emptying their bilges in contravention of agreed conventions)—all these new satellites and monitors have come just in time to give mankind a new and accurate picture of planetary events and changes which even thirty years ago were wholly beyond human assessment and comprehension. Whatever the would-be secrecy of certain societies and systems, the physical behavior of human beings is becoming increasingly open to view. So are the physical underpinnings of all their activities. People are now less likely to create, say, irreversible pollutions or desiccations or erosions by pure inadvertence. They have a clearer picture of how human activity affects the biosphere, even if there remain particular uncertainties, as with, for instance, the effect of inadequately tested chemicals still brought onto the market every year.

And however slowly and unwillingly, people do seem to be leaning away from some of the old arrogant sovereign habits of the past and realizing, marginally and cautiously, that the old ways no longer work. In all this effort to create what one can perhaps call a planetary awareness, the United Nations Environment Programme (UNEP), working closely with other organizations of the United Nations—the World Meteorological Office (WMO), the Food and Agriculture Organization, the World Health Organization, the regional commissions—is taking the lead in what must be, of very necessity, the first stage in some sort of world control of conservation, antipollution activities, and sane resource management. Its Global Environmental Monitoring System (GEMS) covers many of the relevant fields. On land, it co-ordinates and links research and monitoring, usually in collaboration with local research stations, on such critical matters as soil cover, inroads on tropical forests, the spread of deserts. In the oceans, it co-ordinates the monitoring of the entry of effluents and poisons into the marine environment, with special emphasis on the steadily growing emissions of petroleum hydrocarbons from ships, from land-based installations, from the exhausts of the world's rising fleet of motor vehicles. In the air, data on chemical content, turbidity, and the amount of carbon dioxide are being collected, in collaboration with WMO, and regularly published. In addition, the movements of pollution in the air—including such rising dangers as acid rain—are being studied in GEMS on a regional basis (where the gravest impacts are most likely to occur). The Economic Commission for Europe has become an early partner in this extension of UNEP's work with WMO, and research centers in Norway and the Soviet Union are also partners in the venture.

Acquiring the information is the first step. The next is to ensure that governments and other organizations are fully informed. An International Referral System for sources of environmental information has been set up by UNEP, and with it works an International Registry of Potentially Toxic Chemicals. Since a great majority of the developing countries still lack their own monitoring and information services, these UNEP systems have special significance for the Third World, and their establishment is perhaps one more hopeful signal that not all the errors of the early industrializing powers need be repeated by those who are coming after them.

Accurate information, widespread dissemination—neither would have been conceivable even two decades ago. But the biggest hurdle remains—the problem of obtaining action, a readiness by means of internationally shared sovereignty, expressed in formal conventions, to eliminate the dangers and undertake the positive activity, the ''spring cleaning'' of so much that is damaged and toxic in our small and vulnerable world. One should not for a moment underestimate the importance of monitoring and knowledge. They are essential for the formulation of effective policies. Equally important are the mechanisms for ensuring that the policies are followed. It is simply because satellites and other surveillance systems can be developed to trace delinquent tankers that controls over illegal oil spills can now be envisaged. It is because aerial reconnaissance and the various forms of radar already exist that it can make sense to suggest that in narrow waters, ships, like aircraft approaching airports, should be strictly kept to lanes established for them by a local authority. Yet although the new scientific instruments make effective co-operation possible, they do not ensure it. For that, there must be a new commitment to the whole concept of joint constructive work at the planetary level.

And here just possibly we may find that we have reached the last and most fateful of all barriers to survival. We know—although we cannot imaginatively grasp the fact—that each year we spend $400 billion on the means of of destroying one another. Our planet—and we ourselves—can be blasted back to little more than the bare and crumbling rock from which, over evolutionary aeons, we emerged. Indeed, so ludicrous is the scale of our "overkill" that we have at our disposal the equivalent of several tons of TNT for every person on the planet. But we have hardly the barest counterimage of working together to build up our capacities for co-existence, to create that community of feeling which can spring from common goals and common efforts, that dedication that can grow from working together with care and patience, that experience at every level of shared effort—building the village, the town, the shrine, the temple, the city, creating the common symbols and places and vistas of order and dignity—in which all can take pride and all can love.

If one looks about, almost with despair, at the poised missiles and bomber fleets, one wonders where in all the ludicrous apparatus of fear and hatred one unifying counter-aim of wisdom and loyalty can be found. Yet perhaps that wisdom, beginning in fear, can precisely be the realization that in a shared biosphere, no one will escape nuclear destruction, and that loyalty can be built, from however small a beginning, from a shared effort to keep that biosphere in a life-creating, life-enhancing, and life-preserving state. A fragile hope? The first microorganism must have seemed minute enough in the vast wash of the primitive oceans. Yet it had within it the seed of life. Let us at least be bold enough to hope and, where we can, begin to act.

And there is one further reason for moving our angle of vision from the sheer immensity of our environmental interdependence on to specific instances of particular acts and functions in particular places. Again and again in human history, it is the concrete example, the flash of individual insight, the last stroke of the brush on the masterpiece, that has brought life, new light, and new understanding into existence. Are there anywhere in our present experience of our geophysical interdependence those single instances of risk and opportunity which may suddenly have the power to precipitate human imagination into a new level of awareness, bringing with it entirely new reserves of courage and readiness to act? The oceans are, we know, all finally enclosed seas, all without exits for man's wastes and pollutions. They are therefore a complete paradigm of an interdependence we cannot evade or deny. But the whole system is on too large a scale for the flash of vision and insight we need to experience. Can we work to a smaller but still relevant scale? Are there more exact, more comprehensive parables among our actions waiting to be interpreted? Have we anywhere a picture vivid and compelling enough to make us, not in cliché but in reality, see with new eyes?

Once again it is perhaps in one part of the work of UNEP that such an instance can be found. From its earliest days of preparation, its directors have been aware that some of the world's most abused natural systems are to be found among the regional seas and enclosed waters of the planet. The Mediterranean, the Caribbean, the Gulf of Guinea, the Caspian, Lake Baikal, the Great Lakes—all are under pressure, and the kinds of pressure are once again just the sort of encroachments which world-wide industrialization for all the planet's peoples might inflict on the ultimate enclosed water—the whole oceanic system. We are, as it were, seeing through the wrong end of the telescope the vision of disorder and breakdown that might become global in scale if technological society at the same time tripled its numbers, its industrialization, its chemical and power installations, and multiplied by as much again the effluents discarded into rivers, lakes, and oceans—and left everything else unchanged. Of the various seas for which UNEP is now preparing action plans for monitoring and control, we can take the Mediterranean, because the processes of degeneration have gone far, because it in almost perfect geographical fashion illustrates the planet's North/South split, and because—in March 1978—a setback occurred to these plans of absolutely critical importance to our whole understanding of the world's dilemmas in conservation and development.

First, then, the degree of actual and potential pressure—population on the coast, already at 100 million, is likely to double in the next twenty years. But in addition, 100 million tourists crowd in every year, and their number will rise, bringing with it, on present showing, even more wall-to-wall hotels rounding every bay, with totally inadequate sanitary arrangements. And 120 coastal cities already empty their sewage into the sea, virtually without treatment. On the Northern side, industrialization has come like an inundation in the last two decades, with thousands of factories drawn to the shores to take advantage of no-cost dumping of waste products. Oil pollution as the tankers ply their way from Suez is reckoned to be about 300,000 tons a year, and land-based installations are adding at least 130,000 tons of hydrocarbon wastes annually. Add all this together—municipal sewage, industrial effluents, oil pollution—and it is not surprising to learn that the small bacteria whose task it is to decompose all the filth and put it harmlessly back into the food chains are already being threatened in some areas by lack of enough oxygen for the tasks of decomposition (i.e., enough oxygen to satisfy the so-called biochemical oxygen demand, or B.O.D.). This danger signal is already flashing at a time when the Southern states have comparatively few settlements and industries on their shores. Without radical redirection of policy, the Mediterranean could be no more than a few years away from being a place from which a fishing industry worth $700 million per year will have vanished, as well as tourists who will no longer tolerate oily beaches and the risks of hepatitis or even cholera along with their Greek temples and bathing resorts.

The response of UNEP has been rapid. By 1975, it had persuaded most of the coastal nations (even those in a state of some degree of hostility toward one another) to come together and to agree that their common problems required common action—systematic monitoring (to take place in what soon grew to be eighty research centers in fifteen different countries) and plans to share information about developmental and environmental policies at the national level. At a conference the following year, two protocols were agreed upon—one to restrict dumping of toxic pollutants from ships, the other to make joint action possible in emergencies. The essential preliminaries—accurate knowledge, its dissemination—were under way.

But in 1978 came the highly significant setback, when the coastal nations failed to agree on limiting land-based pollution. Three-quarters of the pollution in the Mediterranean is land-based, and the bulk of it comes from Italy, France, and Spain. The Southern states found themselves being asked to accept stringent and expensive pollution controls when they were not responsible for most of the existing pollution and their part of the Mediterranean was relatively clean. The attempt to secure agreed-upon uniform standards broke down. Monitoring would continue. The states would meet in eighteen months. But the most important part of the action plan had proved unacceptable.

And here surely in straightforward down-to-earth reality we have

the basic dilemma of any joint effort to see in the threatened world environment a cause of shared concern and a reason for acting together in
time to enjoy now and to leave to future generations a beautiful and
inhabitable planet. The dilemma is that three-quarters of mankind, having had little or nothing to do with the various threats and degradations,
can now see no reason for helping to pay to clean up a natural environment they did not themselves do much to pollute. Yet the rich on the
whole have as little sense that the bill is really theirs. But let us suppose
that at the Mediterranean consultations, the funds for development proposed in an earlier chapter had been easily and obviously available for
installing treatment plants and effluent controls. Would there have been
much deadlock about safe treatment and common standards? It is surely
significant that in the more co-operative atmosphere of the Persian-
Arabian Gulf, a six million dollar fund has already been set up not only
for joint monitoring of the effects of coastal installations but for more
rational management of development, with, for example, the optimum
siting of settlements and industry and the introduction of modern sewage and effluent-treatment systems. The very nations for whom the expenditure of $400 billion a year on arms is a matter of course apparently
cannot agree to a joint Mediterranean fund financed mainly by the developed nations. We can apparently envisage subsidized weapons systems for the poorer nations—indeed, we compete to supply them. But
sewage-treatment plants, effluent-control technology, ensuring marine
integrity—these apparently lie beyond our mental grasp. The contrast is
all the more devastating in that UNEP's estimate for the total cost of
controlling land-based pollution—the major expense in cleaning up the
Mediterranean—is $10 billion, little more than a week's expenditure on
world armaments.

But the final irony is that accepted responsibility, common consultation, and joint work are the only sure routes away from ultimate conflict. Each constructive joint scheme that is made to function is a step
away from catastrophe. Cleansing the Mediterranean and the other
regional seas, accepting a regime for the oceans with common environmental laws in the new exclusive economic zones and a joint authority
for the remaining seabed, a worldwatch for the forests and a reversal of
the world's trend to deforestation, UNEP's already articulated plan to
hold back the encroachment of the deserts, the development of Asia's
vast water resources, a world tax system for providing capital for investment in basic human needs, the siting and building of communities on a

human scale—how vast the prospects of peaceful construction could become, from farm to federation, from village to metropolis, if human faith and loyalty could grow to match the irreversible geophysical unity of our shared and single planet. We cannot change its nature. It envelops us, provides for us, sustains us. Our only choice is to preserve it in co-operative ventures or to end it and ourselves in a common ruin.

These are not the clichés of any kind of political rhetoric. If we turn back for a moment to the dilemmas outlined in the Prologue, we can surely in the light of the intervening chapters see that there is really only one central factor of doubt in our present debates. We are not irretrievably threatened by what are usually thought of as the most implacable constraints. Any lack of resources can be countered by conservation and care, while a sane use of science's immeasurable virtuosity can vastly increase useful materials and maintain the renewable resources that already exist. Energy is not a problem, given the breathing space for invention provided by the careful use of the still remaining reserves of fossil fuels and the promise of steady availability of energy derived directly or indirectly from the sun. Even the most widely canvassed risk—excessive population—has already been shown to be manageable, provided health, literacy, jobs, and hope are open to all the world's peoples.

No, the only fundamentally unsolved problem in this unsteady interregnum between imperial ages which may be dying and a planetary society which struggles to be born is whether the rich and fortunate are imaginative enough and the resentful and underprivileged poor patient enough to begin to establish a true foundation of better sharing, fuller co-operation, and joint planetary work. The significance of the Mediterranean setback is quite simply that it underlines how little those nations with the genuine power to act—for conservation, against pollution, for the shared commons—are yet ready to confront the cost, minimal though it is compared with the gargantuan wastes of war. In short, no problem is insoluble in the creation of a balanced and conserving planet save humanity itself. Can it reach in time the vision of joint survival? Can its inescapable physical interdependence—the chief new insight of our century—induce that vision? We do not know. We have the duty to hope.

Appendices

A. GLOSSARY

ACTINIDES: The group of the heaviest elements, all of which are radioactive. They include uranium, thorium, and plutonium.

ANAEROBIC DIGESTION: The process by which anaerobic bacteria (bacteria that work in the absence of oxygen) break down plants and organic wastes, such as animal and human excrement, to produce biogas and a residue which is a valuable, concentrated, organic fertilizer. See *Biogas*.

AQUIFER: An underground rock layer containing water, which often feeds springs and wells.

BARREL: A unit of volume used to measure crude oil; 1 barrel equals 42 U.S. gallons or 35 imperial gallons.

BIOCHEMICAL OXYGEN DEMAND (B.O.D.): A measure of the amount of oxygen removed from the water by all processes (mainly biological)—hence, a measure of the amount of oxygen required for the decomposition of organic solids in the water.

BIOCIDE: Any agent that kills living organisms; among the biocides are pesticides, fungicides, herbicides, and the like.

BIODEGRADABLE: Capable of being broken down or decomposed by natural biological processes.

BIOGAS: A mixture of methane and carbon dioxide, with traces of other gases. See *Anaerobic Digestion*.

BIOLOGICAL CONTROL: The use of living organisms—natural predators, parasites, diseases—to control pest animals and plants.

BIOMASS: The total weight, or mass, of all living matter in a particular area.

BIOSPHERE: The "zone of life" on the earth, encompassing all living organisms.

BREEDER REACTOR: A nuclear reactor that produces more fissile material than it consumes.

CANDU: Canadian Deuterium Uranium reactor.

CARCINOGEN: A substance capable of producing cancer.

COGENERATION: The generation of electricity accompanied by the direct use of residual (or "waste") heat for industrial processes or for space heating.

COMPOST: Decomposed plant and animal matter (for example garden and vegetable wastes) that is usually used as a fertilizer/soil conditioner.

ECOSYSTEM: A self-sustaining and self-regulating community of organisms within a given area, from the smallest microorganisms up to the largest plants and animals taken in relation to one another and to their environment.

FISSILE MATERIAL: A substance that will fission readily upon the absorption of neutrons into the nuclei of its atoms. Uranium 233, uranium 235, and plutonium 239 are termed fissile.

FISSION: The rupture of an atomic nucleus into (generally) two smaller nuclei (the fission products), with the release of neutrons and a very considerable release of energy.

FOOD CHAIN: The sequence of energy transfers from organism to organism in the form of food. For instance, a plant capturing solar energy through photosynthesis is eaten by a grazing animal which in turn is consumed by a carnivore.

FOSSIL FUEL: The remains of animals or plants in the earth's crust, from which energy may be obtained. Crude oil, coal, and natural gas are fossil fuels, derived from plants and aquatic animals that lived millions of years ago.

FUSION: The combining of light atomic nuclei to form heavier, more stable nuclei, in a process accompanied by the release of energy. One example is the combining of hydrogen nuclei to form helium nuclei in the core of the sun.

GEOTHERMAL ENERGY: Energy derived from the heat of the earth's interior.

GNP: The gross national product—the total value of goods and services produced in a defined area (usually a nation) in a defined time (usually a year).

GREENHOUSE EFFECT: The trapping of heat inside the atmosphere when such gases or substances as carbon dioxide, water vapor, and particulate matter inhibit the reradiation of the sun's heat from the earth's surface back into space.

GREEN REVOLUTION: Popularly, the change in agriculture involving the use of new, specially bred, or selected food crop seeds which, with the appropriate inputs of fertilizer, water, and so on, give greatly increased yields per hectare.

HEAVY METALS: A group of metallic elements with relatively high atomic weights. They include mercury, cadmium, and lead. Both in pure form and in many compounds, these three are highly toxic.

HUMUS: Nonliving organic matter in the soil, derived from the microbial decomposition of plant and animal substances. Humus serves as a major reservoir of plant nutrients and increases the soil's capacity to absorb water.

HYDROCARBONS: The class of organic compounds composed only of carbon and hydrogen. They are the principle constituents of petroleum and natural gas and serve as raw materials for the production of petrochemicals.

HYDROPONICS: The technique of growing plants without soil. For instance, plants may be grown in a bed of gravel through which is pumped a solution containing all the needed nutrients.

INTEGRATED PEST CONTROL: A method characterized by the combination of natural, biological, chemical, and cultural modes of control designed specifically for the particular pest in question.

KEROGEN: The source of petroleum in oil shales—a complex mixture of compounds containing mainly hydrogen and carbon.

LEACHING: The downward movement of dissolved nutrients and solids from the top layer of soil, caused by rainfall percolating through the soil.

MELTDOWN: The consequence of overheating in a nuclear reactor's core which allows part or all of the solid fuel in the reactor to reach the temperature at which components there will melt and collapse.

NUCLEAR FUEL REPROCESSING: The mechanical and chemical separation of spent fuel rods from a nuclear reactor into the unused uranium 235, plutonium, and radioactive wastes (mainly products of the fission reaction).

OIL SHALE: Finely grained shale rock containing hydrocarbons from which oil-like substances may be extracted.

ORGANOHALOGEN: A compound in which one or more atoms of a halogen—fluorine, chlorine, bromine, or iodine—are attached to carbon atoms.

OZONE: A form of oxygen with three atoms per molecule, instead of two. The ozone layer high in the atmosphere filters out harmful ultraviolet radiation from the sun.

PATHOGEN: An organism which causes disease.

PCBs: Polychlorinated biphenyls, a group of compounds, widely used in industry, which are toxic and are only very slowly broken down by natural systems.

PYROLYSIS: Chemical change brought about by heat alone, as in the process of heating organic wastes in the absence of oxygen to produce various liquids and gases, rich in hydrocarbons, that are usable as fuel or chemical feedstock.

RADIATION: The process of emitting electromagnetic energy (such as light or gamma rays) or subatomic particles (such as neutrons, protons, electrons). Also, the energy/particles which are thus emitted.

RADIOACTIVITY: The property exhibited by certain types of matter which spontaneously emit energy and subatomic particles.

SINGLE-CELL PROTEIN: Protein made from a food supply (usually oil) by the action of single-celled microorganisms.

B. AID AND DEVELOPMENT STATISTICS

TABLE I LISTS the 125 nations of the world with populations exceeding one million in 1976, and specifies for each the population, crude birth rate, GNP per capita, percentage of population in urban areas, per capita energy consumption, life expectancy, adult literacy rate, and percentage of population with access to safe water.

Table II lists the nations belonging to the Development Assistance Committee of the OECD, with the official development assistance these nations have given, expressed as a percentage of their GNP, for selected years. The table also includes estimates for 1977, 1978, and 1980, and estimates of the flow of overseas development assistance from members of the OPEC donor group—Algeria, Iran, Iraq, Kuwait, Libya, Nigeria, Qatar, Saudi Arabia, United Arab Emirates, and Venezuela.

All statistics in this appendix are drawn from the World Bank's publication *World Development Indicators* (1978), which of course supplies many more statistics than are given here. In addition, it lists the sources of the statistics, and indicates how they were calculated. Readers should be careful in interpreting the figures in these tables, particularly in comparing indicators across countries, since statistical practices, definitions, methodology, and coverage differ widely among the various countries.

TABLE I
NATIONS WITH POPULATIONS EXCEEDING ONE MILLION

	POPULATION, MID-1976 (MILLIONS)	CRUDE BIRTH RATE, 1975 (PER 1,000 POPULATION)	GNP PER CAPITA, 1976 (U.S. DOLLARS)	PERCENT OF POPULATION IN URBAN AREAS, 1975	ENERGY CONSUMPTION PER CAPITA, 1975 (KG. COAL EQUIV.)	LIFE EXPECTANCY AT BIRTH, 1975 (YEARS)	ADULT LITERACY RATE, 1974 (PERCENT)	POPULATION WITH ACCESS TO SAFE WATER, 1975 (PERCENT)
Low-Income Countries		47	150	13	52	44	23	25
Bhutan	1.2	43	70	3	—	44	—	—
Cambodia	8.1	47	—	23	16	45	—	—
Lao P.D.R.	3.3	42	90	11	63	40	—	—
Ethiopia	28.7	49	100	11	29	38	7	8
Mali	5.8	50	100	14	25	38	10	—
Bangladesh	80.4	46	110	9	28	42	23	56
Rwanda	4.2	51	110	4	14	41	23	68
Somalia	3.3	48	110	28	36	41	50	38
Upper Volta	6.2	49	110	8	20	38	—	25
Burma	30.8	34	120	22	51	50	67	17

TABLE I (*continued*)

	POPULATION, MID-1976 (MILLIONS)	CRUDE BIRTH RATE, 1975 (PER 1,000 POPULATION)	GNP PER CAPITA, 1976 (U.S. DOLLARS)	PERCENT OF POPULATION IN URBAN AREAS, 1975	ENERGY CONSUMPTION PER CAPITA, 1975 (KG. COAL EQUIV.)	LIFE EXPECTANCY AT BIRTH, 1975 (YEARS)	ADULT LITERACY RATE, 1974 (PERCENT)	POPULATION WITH ACCESS TO SAFE WATER, 1975 (PERCENT)
Burundi	3.8	48	120	4	13	39	10	—
Chad	4.1	44	120	14	39	39	15	26
Nepal	12.9	46	120	5	10	44	19	8
Benin	3.2	49	130	18	52	41	10	34
Malawi	5.2	54	140	6	56	41	25	—
Zaire	25.4	44	140	26	78	44	15	19
Guinea	5.7	46	150	20	92	41	—	14
India	620.4	36	150	22	221	50	36	31
Viet Nam	47.6	41	—	17	—	45	14	—
Afghanistan	14.0	51	160	12	52	35	14	9
Niger	4.7	52	160	9	35	39	—	27
Lesotho	1.2	40	170	3	—	46	40	17
Mozambique	9.5	43	170	6	186	44	—	—

Pakistan	71.3	47	170	27	183	51	21	25
Tanzania	15.1	47	180	7	70	45	63	39
Haiti	4.7	45	200	21	30	50	20	12
Madagascar	9.1	50	200	18	71	44	40	25
Sierra Leone	3.1	45	200	15	116	44	15	—
Sri Lanka	13.8	27	200	24	127	68	78	19
Central African Empire	1.8	43	230	36	34	41	—	—
Indonesia	135.2	40	240	19	178	48	62	11
Kenya	13.8	50	240	11	174	50	40	17
Uganda	11.9	47	240	8	55	50	25	35
Yemen Arab Republic	6.0	50	250	9	49	45	10	—
Middle-Income Countries		40	750	43	524	58	63	52
Togo	2.3	50	260	14	65	41	12	16
Egypt	38.1	35	280	48	405	52	40	—
Yemen P.D.R.	1.7	49	280	29	328	45	10	—
Cameroon	7.6	41	290	24	104	41	12	—
Sudan	15.9	49	290	13	140	49	15	—
Angola	5.5	47	330	18	174	39	—	—
Mauritania	1.4	45	340	11	108	39	10	—
Nigeria	77.1	49	380	29	90	41	—	—

TABLE I (continued)

	POPULATION, MID-1976 (MILLIONS)	CRUDE BIRTH RATE, 1975 (PER 1,000 POPULATION)	GNP PER CAPITA, 1976 (U.S. DOLLARS)	PERCENT OF POPULATION IN URBAN AREAS, 1975	ENERGY CONSUMPTION PER CAPITA, 1975 (KG. COAL EQUIV.)	LIFE EXPECTANCY AT BIRTH, 1975 (YEARS)	ADULT LITERACY RATE, 1974 (PERCENT)	POPULATION WITH ACCESS TO SAFE WATER, 1975 (PERCENT)
Thailand	43.0	34	380	17	284	58	82	25
Bolivia	5.8	44	390	37	303	47	40	34
Honduras	3.0	48	390	28	232	54	61	41
Senegal	5.1	47	390	28	195	40	10	—
Philippines	43.3	36	410	36	326	58	87	40
Zambia	5.1	51	440	37	504	45	43	42
Liberia	1.6	50	450	28	404	44	15	—
El Salvador	4.1	40	490	40	248	58	63	53
Papua New Guinea	2.8	41	490	13	278	48	32	20
Congo, People's Republic	1.4	45	520	40	209	44	50	38
Morocco	17.2	48	540	38	274	53	26	—

Country								
Zimbabwe-Rhodesia	6.5	47	550	20	764	52	—	35
Ghana	10.1	49	580	32	182	44	25	—
Ivory Coast	7.0	45	610	20	366	44	20	—
Jordan	2.8	47	610	56	408	53	62	62
Colombia	24.2	33	630	62	671	61	74	64
Guatemala	6.5	43	630	35	237	53	47	39
Ecuador	7.3	45	640	42	442	60	69	36
Paraguay	2.6	39	640	37	153	62	81	13
Korea, South	36.0	24	670	47	1,038	61	92	66
Nicaragua	2.3	46	750	48	479	53	57	46
Dominican Republic	4.8	38	780	44	458	58	51	55
Syrian Arab Republic	7.7	46	780	46	477	54	53	
Peru	15.8	42	800	57	682	56	72	47
Tunisia	5.7	34	840	47	447	54	55	—
Malaysia	12.7	31	860	30	560	59	60	34
Algeria	16.2	48	990	50	754	53	35	77
Turkey	41.2	34	990	43	630	57	55	68
Costa Rica	2.0	29	1,040	40	544	68	89	72
Chile	10.5	23	1,050	83	765	63	90	70
Taiwan	16.3	23	1,070	64	1,427	71	82	
Jamaica	2.1	30	1,070	45	1,427	70	86	86
Lebanon	3.2	40	—	60	928	63	68	—

TABLE I (continued)

	POPULATION, MID-1976 (MILLIONS)	CRUDE BIRTH RATE, 1975 (PER 1,000 POPULATION)	GNP PER CAPITA, 1976 (U.S. DOLLARS)	PERCENT OF POPULATION IN URBAN AREAS, 1975	ENERGY CONSUMPTION PER CAPITA, 1975 (KG. COAL EQUIV.)	LIFE EXPECTANCY AT BIRTH, 1975 (YEARS)	ADULT LITERACY RATE, 1974 (PERCENT)	POPULATION WITH ACCESS TO SAFE WATER, 1975 (PERCENT)
Mexico	62.0	40	1,090	63	1,221	63	76	62
Brazil	110.0	38	1,140	60	670	61	64	—
Panama	1.7	31	1,310	51	865	67	82	77
Iraq	11.5	48	1,390	62	713	53	26	66
Uruguay	2.8	20	1,390	81	942	70	91	98
Romania	21.4	19	1,450	45	3,803	69	98	—
Argentina	25.7	21	1,550	80	1,754	68	93	66
Yugoslavia	21.5	18	1,680	39	1,930	68	85	—
Portugal	9.7	20	1,690	29	983	68	70	—
Iran	34.3	45	1,930	44	1,353	51	50	51
Hong Kong	4.5	18	2,110	95	1,119	70	90	—
Trinidad and								

Venezuela	12.4	37	2,570	82	2,639	65	82	—
Greece	9.1	16	2,590	65	2,090	72	82	—
Singapore	2.3	18	2,700	90	2,151	70	75	—
Spain	35.7	19	2,920	70	2,147	72	94	100
Israel	3.6	26	3,920	84	2,806	71	84	—
Industrialized Countries		16	6,200	76	5,016	72	99	—
South Africa	26.0	42	1,340	50	—	52	—	—
Ireland	3.2	22	2,560	55	3,097	72	98	—
Italy	56.2	16	3,050	67	3,012	72	98	—
United Kingdom	56.1	15	4,020	78	5,265	72	98	—
New Zealand	3.1	21	4,250	83	3,111	72	99	—
Japan	112.8	18	4,910	75	3,622	73	99	—
Austria	7.5	14	5,330	53	3,700	71	99	—
Finland	4.7	14	5,620	55	4,766	70	100	—
Australia	13.7	19	6,100	86	6,485	72	100	—
Netherlands	13.8	15	6,200	79	5,784	74	99	—
France	52.9	16	6,550	76	3,944	73	99	—
Belgium	9.8	14	6,780	72	5,584	73	99	—
German Federal Republic	62.0	12	7,380	83	5,345	71	99	—
Norway	4.0	16	7,420	46	4,607	75	99	—
Denmark	5.1	15	7,450	82	5,268	74	99	—

TABLE I (continued)

	POPULATION, MID-1976 (MILLIONS)	CRUDE BIRTH RATE, 1975 (PER 1,000 POPULATION)	GNP PER CAPITA, 1976 (U.S. DOLLARS)	PERCENT OF POPULATION IN URBAN AREAS, 1975	ENERGY CONSUMPTION PER CAPITA, 1975 (KG. COAL EQUIV.)	LIFE EXPECTANCY AT BIRTH, 1975 (YEARS)	ADULT LITERACY RATE, 1974 (PERCENT)	POPULATION WITH ACCESS TO SAFE WATER, 1975 (PERCENT)
Canada	23.2	17	7,510	78	9,880	72	98	—
United States	215.1	16	7,890	76	10,999	71	99	—
Sweden	8.2	13	8,670	84	6,178	73	99	—
Switzerland	6.4	14	8,880	57	3,642	72	99	—
Capital-Surplus Oil Exporters		46	6,310	31	1,398	53	—	87
Saudi Arabia	8.6	48	4,480	21	1,398	45	15	64
Libya	2.5	44	6,310	31	1,299	53	—	87
Kuwait	1.1	46	15,480	89	8,718	67	55	89

Centrally Planned Economies							
		18	2,280	57	3,624	70	—
China, People's Republic	835.8	26	410	24	693	62	—
Korea, North	16.3	37	470	43	2,808	61	—
Albania	2.5	32	540	38	741	69	—
Cuba	9.5	21	860	62	1,157	70	—
Mongolia	1.5	38	860	51	1,091	61	—
Hungary	10.6	16	2,280	48	3,624	70	98
Bulgaria	8.8	16	2,310	58	4,781	72	—
U.S.S.R.	256.7	18	2,760	61	5,546	70	99
Poland	34.3	18	2,860	57	5,007	70	98
Czechoslovakia	14.9	17	3,840	58	7,151	70	—
German Democratic Republic	16.8	12	4,220	75	6,835	73	—

TABLE II
OFFICIAL DEVELOPMENT ASSISTANCE
(As a percentage of GNP)

	1960	1970	1973	1974	1975	1976	1977*	1978*	1980*
Italy	0.22	0.16	0.14	0.14	0.11	0.13	0.12	0.11	0.10
United Kingdom	0.56	0.37	0.34	0.37	0.37	0.38	0.37	0.37	0.38
New Zealand	—	0.23	0.27	0.31	0.52	0.43	0.37	0.45	0.49
Japan	0.24	0.23	0.25	0.25	0.23	0.20	0.21	0.27	0.30
Austria	—	0.07	0.15	0.18	0.17	0.12	0.24	0.18	0.19
Finland	—	0.07	0.16	0.17	0.18	0.18	0.17	0.17	0.20
Australia	0.38	0.59	0.44	0.55	0.60	0.42	0.45	0.47	0.49
Netherlands	0.31	0.61	0.54	0.63	0.75	0.82	0.85	1.00	1.03
France	1.38	0.66	0.57	0.59	0.62	0.62	0.63	0.62	0.63
Belgium	0.88	0.46	0.51	0.51	0.59	0.51	0.46	0.64	0.67
West Germany	0.31	0.32	0.32	0.37	0.40	0.31	0.27	0.32	0.31
Norway	0.11	0.32	0.43	0.57	0.66	0.71	0.82	0.96	0.98
Denmark	0.09	0.38	0.48	0.55	0.58	0.56	0.60	0.67	0.70
Canada	0.19	0.42	0.43	0.50	0.54	0.46	0.51	0.61	0.66
United States	0.53	0.31	0.23	0.24	0.26	0.25	0.22	0.26	0.26
Sweden	0.05	0.38	0.56	0.72	0.82	0.82	1.00	0.97	1.00
Switzerland	0.04	0.15	0.16	0.14	0.19	0.19	0.15	0.16	0.17
Total, DAC Countries	0.52	0.34	0.30	0.33	0.36	0.33	0.32	0.35	0.37
OPEC Donor Countries*			1.4	2.0	2.7	2.1			

*Figures for 1977, 1978, and 1980 are estimates. So too are the figures for the OPEC donor countries.

C. SUGGESTED FURTHER READING

(For titles appearing in the United States and in the United Kingdom, both publishers are listed.)

Energy

The Energy Question, Gerald Foley (Penguin, U.S. and U.K., 1976).

Rays of Hope: The Transition to a Post-Petroleum World, Denis Hayes (Norton, U.S., 1977).

A Low Energy Strategy for the United Kingdom, Gerald Leach et al. (Science Reviews, U.K., 1979).

Soft Energy Paths, Amory Lovins (Ballinger, U.S.; Penguin, U.K.; 1977).

Energy: Global Prospects 1985–2000, Workshop on Alternative Energy Strategies (McGraw-Hill, U.S., 1977).

Nuclear Power, Walter Patterson (Penguin, U.S. and U.K., 1976).

Nuclear Power and the Environment, Royal Commission on Environmental Pollution, Sixth Report (H.M.S.O., U.K., 1976).

Whose Power to Choose? International Institutions and the Control of Nuclear Energy, Brian Johnson (International Institute for Environment and Development, 1977). Available from IIED, 10 Percy St., London WIP ODR, U.K.

Energy Policy for the Rural Third World, Arjun Makhijani (IIED, 1976). Available from IIED, 10 Percy St., London WIP ODR, U.K.

Energy for Rural Development (National Academy of Sciences, U.S., 1976).

Environment and Conservation

Only One Earth, Barbara Ward and René Dubos (Norton, U.S.; Penguin, U.K., 1972).

The Conservation Alternative, Raymond Dasmann (Wiley, U.S. and U.K., 1975).

Material Gains: Reclamation, Recycling and Re-use, Christine Thomas (Friends of the Earth, London).

Repairs, Re-use, Recycling, Denis Hayes (Worldwatch Paper, U.S. and U.K., 1978).

Environmental Quality, Annual Report of the U.S. Council on Environmental Quality (U.S.).

Recycling, Resources, Refuse, Andrew Porteous (Longman, U.K., 1977).

Food and Agriculture

World Food Resources, Actual and Potential, Michael Allaby (International Ideas, U.S., 1978; Applied Science Publishers, U.K., 1977).

"Food and Agriculture," *Scientific American* (September 1976).

Food First: Beyond the Myth of Scarcity, Francis M. Lappé and Joseph Collins (Houghton Mifflin, U.S., 1977).

Radical Agriculture, edited by Richard Merrill (New York University Press, U.S., 1976).

Energy and Food Production, Gerald Leach (IPC Science and Technology Press, U.K., 1976).

Losing Ground: Environmental Stress and World Food Prospects, Erik Eckholm (Norton, U.S., 1976).

Forest Farming, Sholto Douglas and Robert Hart (Robinson and Watkins, U.K., 1976).

Settlements

The Home of Man, Barbara Ward (Norton, U.S.; Penguin, U.K.; 1976).

Housing by People, John Turner (Pantheon, U.S., 1977; Marion Boyars, 1976, U.K.).

Global Review of Settlements 1976 (United Nations).

Housing, Sector Policy Paper (World Bank, 1976).

Urban Land Policies and Land Use Control Measures: Global Review (United Nations, 1976).

Third World Studies

Land Reform: A World Survey, Russell King (Westview, U.S., 1978; Bell, U.K., 1977).

Appropriate Technology: Problems and Promises, Nicolas Jequier (OECD, U.S. and U.K., 1976).

World Development Report (World Bank, 1978).

The Poverty Curtain, Mahbub ul Haq (Columbia University Press, U.S., 1976).

Development Reconsidered, Edgar Owens and Robert Shaw (Heath, U.S., 1972).

The Economic Development of the Third World since 1900, Paul Bairoch (U. of California Press, U.S.; Methuen, U.K.; 1975).

Employment

Employment, Growth and Basic Needs: A One World Problem (International Labour Office, 1976).

Jobs and Energy (Environmentalists for Full Employment, U.S.; 1976).

Size, Efficiency and Community Enterprise, Barry Stein (Center for Community Economic Development, U.S., 1974).

Worker-Owners: The Mondragon Achievement (Anglo German Foundation, U.K., 1977).

The Lucas Aerospace Workers' Campaign, David Elliott (Fabian Society Pamphlet, U.K., 1977).

The Potential for Substituting Manpower for Energy (Battelle Geneva Research Center, 1977).

Rural Enterprise and Nonfarm Employment (World Bank, 1978).

Employment and Development of Small Enterprises (World Bank, 1978).

The Urban Informal Sector (World Bank, 1975).

China

Rural Development: Learning from China, Sartaj Aziz (Holmes and Meier, U.S.; Macmillan, U.K.; 1978).

China's Economic Revolution, Alexander Eckstein (Cambridge University Press, U.S., 1977).

General

Small Is Beautiful: Economics As If People Mattered, E. F. Schumacher (Harper and Row, U.S.; Abacus, U.K., 1973).

The New International Economic Order, Jyoti Singh (Praeger, U.S., 1977).

Rich World Poor World, Geoffrey Lean (Allen and Unwin, U.K., 1978).

Statistical Sources

World Development Indicators (World Bank, 1978).

The World in Figures (The Economist, U.K., 1976).

The U.S. and World Development: Agenda for Action (Praeger, U.S.). A yearly report of the Overseas Development Council, with a comprehensive statistical annex.

INDEX